In Praise of *Delusions of Power*

"*Delusions of Power* is an important book for our time on the nature of political power. Robert Higgs describes the government's use of wars and real and fabricated crises to expand its power. It is history well-told and should be thought-provoking to all, whatever their political preferences."

> —**Stanley L. Engerman**, John H. Munro Professor of Economics and
> Professor of History, University of Rochester

"There is no economist today who has thought more seriously than Robert Higgs about the relationship between the state and the economy. His examinations of the state are grounded in historical scholarship, rigorous analytics, and in a lively and blunt style. In the process the reader will see many historical myths exploded and sacred cows skewered. *Delusions of Power* is a must read for anyone who wants to understand the permanent-war economies that have been created in the 20th and 21st centuries. War, as Randolph Bourne argued many years ago, is 'the health of the state'. Robert Higgs more than any other contemporary economist explains what that means for economics as a discipline and for the economy as a consequence of the growth of the state in scale and scope."

> —**Peter J. Boettke**, University Professor of Economics,
> George Mason University

"Even James Madison asked throughout his lifetime 'In a free society, what is the proper relationship between individuals and the state?' Few scholars in American history have contributed more to the freedom side of that inquiry than Robert Higgs. For years, his magisterial *Crisis and Leviathan* was the bible for all who wished intellectual ammunition to address Madison's quandary. Now, Bob has done what once seemed impossible: He has written another book equally as vital to the issue. In *Delusions of Power*, Professor Higgs has assembled a lifetime of wisdom and analysis about this continually-asked question; and future generations will look here for the courageous intellectual fire-power with which to challenge the federal beast that consumes our freedoms every day."

> —**Judge Andrew P. Napolitano**, Senior Judicial Analyst,
> Fox News Channel

"Towering thinkers of the past have identified the risks of submitting to the authority of a state. In this impressive book, Robert Higgs shows that in modern times these risks have grown immensely because of new technologies of communication, the erosion of constitutional protections, the empowerment of coalitions dependent on the state, and, most important, ideological currents that have blinded us to the inefficiencies of expanding the scope of government. Lively throughout and based on deep historical knowledge, *Delusions of Power* can be read profitably by anyone interested in the fundamental controversies of economics and politics."

—**Timur Kuran**, Professor of Economics and Political Science, and Gorter Family Professor of Islamic Studies, Duke University

"No scholar has done more than Robert Higgs to demonstrate that a principled and powerful advocate of free markets can also be—should also be—a principled and powerful opponent of many of the most cherished notions by both liberals and conservatives regarding government power. And no notion is more cherished than the belief that the military is immune to the many problems that cause other government agencies to squander resources while failing in their alleged missions. Higgs's careful scholarship in *Delusions of Power* exposes this notion as being a dangerous delusion."

—**Donald J. Boudreaux**, Professor of Economics, George Mason University

"*Delusions of Power*, a new book on an old, ever-important theme by an excellent economic historian acting as prosecutor, invites thought beyond the indictment. The author Robert Higgs tersely describes the state as 'the most destructive institution human beings have ever devised.' The charge is supported by a massive array of data and a narrative of the process by which the U.S. government has preempted an ever-increasing portion of its citizens' resources and rolled back their liberty. It is striking that the charge of destructiveness is substantiated by analyzing the government's deeds and misdeeds in the United States alone—a country widely regarded as having the most admired constitution and proud of its democratic roots. The reader cannot but think of most of Africa and much of the Middle East, Asia, and Latin America, where the state has always wrought destruction that passes belief and whose peoples dream of America as a haven of prosperity and liberty. Government by the people is credited with powers to protect them; Higgs shows that this credit is undeserved even in the country where it is believed to be the strongest. God save the rest of the world, where such protective power is not even imagined to prevail."

—**Anthony de Jasay**, author of *The State* and *Against Politics*

DELUSIONS
OF POWER

The INDEPENDENT INSTITUTE

THE INDEPENDENT INSTITUTE is a non-profit, non-partisan, scholarly research and educational organization that sponsors comprehensive studies in political economy. Our mission is to boldly advance peaceful, prosperous, and free societies, grounded in a commitment to human worth and dignity.

Politicized decision-making in society has confined public debate to a narrow reconsideration of existing policies. Given the prevailing influence of partisan interests, little social innovation has occurred. In order to understand both the nature of and possible solutions to major public issues, the Independent Institute adheres to the highest standards of independent inquiry, regardless of political or social biases and conventions. The resulting studies are widely distributed as books and other publications, and are debated in numerous conference and media programs. Through this uncommon depth and clarity, the Independent Institute is redefining public debate and fostering new and effective directions for government reform.

DELUSIONS
OF POWER

New Explorations of the
State, War, and Economy

ROBERT
HIGGS

The INDEPENDENT
INSTITUTE

Oakland, California

The Independent Institute
100 Swan Way, Oakland, CA 94621-1428
Telephone: 510-632-1366
Fax: 510-568-6040
Email: info@independent.org
Website: www.independent.org

Cover Design: Christopher Buenaventura
Cover Image: © Frederic Cirou / Getty
Interior Design and Composition by Leigh McLellan Design

Library of Congress Cataloging-in-Publication Data

Higgs, Robert.
  Delusions of power : new explorations of the state, war, and economy / Robert Higgs.
    p. cm.
  ISBN 978-1-59813-045-4 (pbk.) ISBN 978-1-59813-052-2 (hardcover)
  1. Power (Social sciences)--United States. 2. United States--Military policy. 3. United States--Economic policy--20th century. 4. United States--History, Military--20th century. 5. United States--Politics and government--20th century. 6. Politics and war--United States--History--20th century. 7. War--Economic aspects--United States--History--20th century. I. Title.
  JK271.H57 2012
  355'.033573--dc23
                    2011027480

16 15 14 13 12   5 4 3 2 1

For David and Mary Theroux

amicus certus in re incerta cernitur

Acknowledgments

The following articles were first published on LewRockwell.com and are Reprinted with Permission by LewRockwell.com: "War Is Horrible, but . . . ," (September 16, 2006); "Blame the People Who Elected Them?" (November 26, 2007); "Truncating the Antecedents: How Americans Have Been Misled about World War II," (March 18, 2008).

The following articles were first published by *The Freeman* and are Reprinted with Permission: "How U.S. Economic Warfare Provoked Japan's Attack on Pearl Harbor," (May 2006); "What Did FDR Know? Robert Higgs replies [to a letter from Bettina Bien Greaves]," (July/August 2006); "Wartime Origins of Modern Income-Tax Withholding," (November 2007); "Nixon's New Economic Plan," (January/February 2009); Review of *The Pearl Harbor Myth: Rethinking the Unthinkable*, by George Victor, (May 2008); Review of *Churchill, Hitler, and the Unnecessary War: How Britain Lost Its Empire and the West Lost the World*, by Patrick J. Buchanan, (July/August, 2009); Review of *New Deal or Raw Deal? How FDR's Economic Legacy Has Damaged America*, by Burton Folsom, Jr., (September 2009).

The following articles were first published by The Independent Institute in *The Independent Review*, The Newsroom, or *The Beacon* and are Reprinted with Permission: "Who Was Edward M. House?," (Winter 2009); " Benefits and Costs of the U.S. Government's War Making," (Spring 2005); "Military-Economic Fascism: How Business Corrupts Government and Vice Versa," (Fall 2007); "Caging the Dogs of War: How Major U.S. Neo-imperialistic Wars End," (Fall 2008); "Recession and Recovery: Six Fundamental Errors of the Current Orthodoxy," (March 5, 2009); "To Fight or Not to Fight? War's Payoffs to U.S. Leaders and to the American People," (Summer 2011); "Derek Leebaert's *Magic and Mayhem*," [a review essay on] *Magic and Mayhem: The Delusions of American Foreign Policy from Korea to Afghanistan*, by Derek Leebaert," (March 6, 2011).

The following articles were first published by the Ludwig von Mises Institute and are Reprinted with Permission under a Creative Commons license: "Democracy and Faits Accomplis," in *Property, Freedom, and Society: Essays in Honor of Hans-Hermann Hoppe*, (2009); "A Revealing Window on the U.S. Economy in Depression and War: Hours Worked, 1929–1950," *Libertarian Papers* (2009); "If Men Were Angels: The Basic Analytics of the State versus Self-Government," *Journal of Libertarian Studies* 21 (Winter 2007).

Reprinted with Permission of the Mercatus Center at George Mason University: "A Dozen Dangerous Presumptions of Crisis Policy Making," *Mercatus on Policy*, (April 2009); "The Political Economy of Crisis Opportunism," *Mercatus Policy Series* (October 2009).

Reprinted with Permission: "Cumulating Policy Consequences, Frightened Overreactions, and the Current Surge of Government's Size, Scope, and Power," *Harvard Journal of Law and Public Policy* 33, no. 2 (Spring 2010).

Reprinted with Permission: Review of *Is War Necessary for Economic Growth? Military Procurement and Technology Development*, by Vernon W. Ruttan, Economic History Services, Copyright © 2006 by EH.NET.

Reprinted with Permission of Springer Science Publishers: "An Economic Analysis of National Reconstruction at Gunpoint: Review essay on *After War: The Political Economy of Exporting Democracy*, by Christopher J. Coyne," *Review of Austrian Economics* 21, no. 4 (2008). Copyright © Springer Science.

Reprinted with Permission: "Sheldon Pollacks's Interpretation of War, Taxation, and the U.S. State," Review essay on *War, Revenue, and State Building: Financing the Development of the American State*, by Sheldon D. Pollack," *Journal of Policy History* 23 (2011). Copyright © Cambridge University Press.

Review of *Unwarranted Influence: Dwight D. Eisenhower and the Military-Industrial Complex*, by James Ledbetter, *Journal of Cold War Studies*. © 2012 by the President and Fellows of Harvard College and the Massachusetts Institute of Technology, *Journal of Cold War Studies* Vol. 14, No. 2, Spring 2012.

Reprinted with Permission, unpublished speeches and papers by Robert Higgs: "The Song that Is Irresistible: How the State Leads People to Their Own Destruction," (2007); "The Economics of the Great Society: Theory, Policies, and Consequences," (2011); "Do Arguments for Slavery and Arguments for Government (as We Know It) Appeal to the Same Rationalizations?"

Contents

Introduction

JAMES MADISON, in *The Federalist No. 51*, expresses one of the most memorable opinions in political philosophy in general and in the constitutional history of the United States in particular: "[W]hat is government itself, but the greatest of all reflections on human nature? If men were angels, no government would be necessary. If angels were to govern men, neither external nor internal controls on government would be necessary. In framing a government which is to be administered by men over men, the great difficulty lies in this: you must first enable the government to control the governed; and in the next place oblige it to control itself."[1] Readers have generally understood this passage as a rationale for Madison's argument in favor of building checks and balances into the government's constitutional structure so that ambition would counteract ambition, and thus government abuses would be curbed.

In a more profound sense, however, Madison's famous passage constitutes an enormously seductive instance of question begging. In *The Federalist*, Madison, Alexander Hamilton, and John Jay were arguing in favor of the new constitution drafted in Philadelphia in the summer of 1787 by delegates who had set in motion a coup against the national government under the Articles of Confederation. Sent to Philadelphia to amend the Articles, the delegates instead had tossed out the Articles and written an entirely new overarching constitution for the thirteen newly independent states, giving the central government immensely greater powers, most significantly the powers to lay and collect taxes and to maintain a standing national army and navy. In these critical regards,

---

1. James Madison, *The Federalist No. 51*, 1788, in *The Federalist* (New York: Modern Library, n.d.), 337.

the proposed form of government resembled that of other strong states, such as the British Empire, from which the colonists had recently seceded. In the exercise of its stipulated powers, the proposed state would claim a monopoly of coercive force over everyone in the national territory, even if some of the individuals residing there objected to its operation. The new government was not offering to provide services, such as protection of civil and property rights, in exchange for a mutually agreeable fee. It was going to operate as its officers might decide from time to time, and it was going to force everybody subject to the taxes it levied either to pay as ordered or to suffer the violent consequences.

The new government's operation in this manner is part and parcel of what Madison means when he refers to "government": a coercive organization that supports its activities at the expense of all those living in its territory, including those—perhaps a multitude—who have not given explicit, individual, voluntary consent to the government's activities or even to its existence and may well object to the new state and everything it undertakes to do. (Subsequent developments, such as the formation of the ephemeral Free Republic of Franklin and the vigorously suppressed Whiskey Rebellion, among many others, demonstrated that such objections to the new government were scarcely imaginary.) In the key sentence, Madison states: "If men were angels, no government would be necessary." Because no reasonable person will maintain that men are angels, the implication embedded in Madison's construction is that therefore "government"—which is to say, a government in precisely this coercively imposed form—is desirable and, indeed, indispensable.

Without firing a shot, Madison thus dispatches every alternative conception of how people might govern themselves, perhaps by forms requiring the explicit, individual, voluntary consent of every responsible adult subject to the government's authority. Hence, he begs the greatest question in political philosophy: Under what conditions may some persons legitimately exert or threaten to exert violent force against others who have not violated anyone's just rights? Madison's artful construction shoves this question off the table by implicitly assuming that so long as men are not angels, government *as we know it* constitutes our only effective means for the protection of our rights to life, liberty, and property. Although he seems sincerely concerned about the abuse of government power by those who will exercise it, at no point does he consider the possibility that by constructing a government as we know it, one has created, however inadvertently, a Frankenstein's monster that awaits only a sufficiently powerful bolt of lightning to send it lumbering forth to wreak mayhem on the very citizens for whose protection it was supposedly created.

Madison and almost all of the respectable commentators and scholars who have followed his powerful and influential reasoning in political science have—to use the fashionable, if ungrammatical language—*privileged the state*. The extent to which their resulting implicit premises about the state's establishment, functions, and actions have transformed these analysts into de facto apologists for despotism is too vast to comprehend. Suffice it to say that if this Madisonian foundation stone were removed, a great many edifices of political argument would collapse.

One of my purposes in this book is to challenge the habitual use of this foundation stone—to call into question the intellectual and moral acceptability of privileging the state as we know it. My efforts in this regard therefore qualify as radical, a characterization that I have no desire to deny. When I was young, I accepted as natural and right the ruling institutions of the world into which I was born. It did not occur to me to ask, for example: Should the U.S. government in its present form exist? Should the government fight all of the wars it was fighting, one after another in quick succession? Should people have to hand over their money to the Internal Revenue Service (IRS) as instructed or go to prison? Should Congress enact statutes empowering the Department of Agriculture to make rules for how much cotton a farmer may plant or how many lemons he may send to market? These and countless similar questions did not arise in my mind until I had progressed far enough in my learning to see beyond the familiar, taken-for-granted institutions and powers and to hone my ability to distinguish the government's ostensible purposes from its actual purposes. So my radicalism did not take root in the thin soil of youth, but only in the greater knowledge and intellectual independence I gained over the years.

The essays and reviews gathered (in revised form) in this book, all of which were written in the past few years, reflect the radical position at which I arrived. Several of them question the very existence of the state as we know it. I am accustomed to having my arguments in this regard dismissed as utopian. My reply is that the true utopians are those who continue to look to government as we know it for the protection of people's just rights to life, liberty, and property. The experiment in avowedly "limited" government, it now seems to me, was destined to fail and has indubitably done so.

One need only open one's eyes to the clear historical trend. The United States verges ever closer to totalitarianism, yet at every moment the bulk of America's people and most of its intellectuals insist that we live in a free country; some even insist that it is becoming steadily freer! Although one may point to events such as the abolition of slavery, the overthrow of the Jim Crow system, and the abandonment of the military draft as evidence for such an argument, these undeniably important pieces of counterevidence stand out as clear exceptions to the dominant trends. With every passing day, the police, the numerous surveillance agencies, the so-called security apparatus centered in the Department of Homeland Security, the military forces, and the rest of the Praetorian Guard tighten the chains with which all of us outside the walls of the state are bound in the United States. In 2010 alone, federal regulatory agencies issued 3,573 final rules—a fairly typical number in recent years—and the Federal Register reached an all-time high of 81,405 pages. Each year state and local governments add countless rules, regulations, and ordinances of their own. Very few such rules are ever repealed, so the total number of them grows steadily greater. A standard compilation of federal tax rules, regulations, and IRS rulings, for example, contains 72,536 pages, most of which only a tax lawyer or tax accountant has any chance of understanding, although every taxpayer bears a risk of penalties, fines, and imprisonment for violating them. Whistling past this graveyard avails us nothing. The United States is a dreadfully unfree country, all things being considered, and it is becoming less free all the time. The little patches of freedom that remain, scattered here and there, are too few and too insignificant to refute this generalization.

If Americans are ever to reverse the changes that have brought them to this pathetic condition, they must begin to ask and to answer honestly the kinds of radical questions I am raising in this book. For a very long time, they have rested content with the Myth of the Land of the Free; they have accepted creature comforts, lavish entertainments, and the illusion of security as good substitutes for living in a free country. Such disregard of reality allows them to drift steadily toward a whirlpool of tyranny from which they will be unable to escape.

In questioning the received wisdom with regard to the indispensability and justice of the state as we know it and in delving into the question of whether various U.S. wars contributed anything positive to the people at large, as opposed to the state itself and its allied special-interest groups, I seek to bring to the forefront the difference between "them" (the persons who constitute the state and its supporting coalition, especially its large financial backers) and "us" (the great mass of the population subject to state power but without any effective means of controlling how it is used). Under democracy, the rulers constantly urge the subjects to identify themselves with the state, to forget that "they" (the rulers) are not "we" (the ruled) and even to believe that the two groups are one and the same. In this country, the powers that be have unfortunately achieved considerable success in indoctrinating the public with this myth, which helps to explain why so many people have handed over themselves and their children to serve as cannon fodder in the rulers' endless, unnecessary wars.

It is said, of course, that democracy serves as a check on the rulers, but owing to a variety of practical difficulties, including the problem of faits accomplis that I discuss in this volume, this check is a feeble one, indeed. On careful inspection, the two-party system turns out to be a fraud because whenever the powers and privileges of the political elite as a whole are challenged, the parties coalesce rather than compete. It is more accurate to say that in effect the United States has a one-party state with two factions that compete to a limited extent, but only with regard to secondary matters. By constantly emphasizing the parties' differences and their political conflicts, the politicians and the news media divert the public's attention from the parties' solidarity in regard to everything fundamental to their shared hold on state power.

My challenges in this book pertain not only to democracy and the state itself, but also to a variety of sacred cows, many of which have to do with the state's crisis management. The growth of government in U.S. history has lurched into high gear whenever a national emergency has arisen or has appeared to have arisen. Especially from the Progressive Era onward, people have demanded that the government "do something" in a crisis to allay the perceived threat. In voicing this demand, they have allowed their fears to overcome their good judgment, which ought to have instructed them that in all likelihood the rulers know neither what to do nor how to do it effectively, and even if they did know, they would have little incentive to act accordingly rather than in the service of augmenting their own powers.

In various ways, my reassessments take up the world wars, the Great Depression and the New Deal, the political and economic crises from 1964 to 1974, the Great Society, the faux-conservative Nixon administration, and the financial debacle and recession that began in 2008, as well as the central figures in these episodes. These "great men"—Woodrow Wilson, Franklin D. Roosevelt, Lyndon B. Johnson, Richard M. Nixon, George W. Bush, Barack Obama, and their right-hand men—have come down to us in many cases as larger than life, whereas in reality they were not only of quite human dimensions, but, indeed, of diminutive moral stature. As Lord Acton aptly taught us, so-called great men are, at least in the political and governmental realm, usually bad men.

While knocking from their pedestals some of the "great men" of the past century, I also devote attention to debunking a variety of ideas and related programs that flourished along with these leaders, such as business–government cooperation, pump priming via government deficit spending, Johnson's War on Poverty, Nixon's New Economic Plan, and the antirecession "stimulus" and bailouts carried out recently by the Bush and Obama administrations. Such ideas cloak a frenzy of opportunism in which politicians snatch new powers and special interests enrich themselves at public expense, all in the guise of saving the day—more often than not, a day that needs saving only because of destructive actions the government has taken previously. Thus, for example, no matter how often the government's mismanagement of its fiscal, monetary, and regulatory powers brings on economic crisis, the response invariably elicited during the past sixty years—a rapid increase of government spending and money creation—only makes matters worse, eventually if not immediately. Yet the general public, bewitched by what I call "vulgar Keynesianism," accepts such counterproductive measures as responsible and blames only the politicians (if any) and others who have the temerity to question such crackpot economic remedies.

Alas, while Americans have been losing the struggle to retain their liberties, they have also been losing the struggle to hold on to sound ideas about economics. Even after vulgar Keynesianism seemed to have been completely discredited by its manifest failures in the 1970s, it came roaring back in the wake of the financial debacle of 2008. Even many well-credentialed mainstream economists, drowning in a sea of their own incomprehension, immediately grabbed hold of this lead life preserver. Small wonder that the general public never seems to make any intellectual headway with regard to public affairs, whether these affairs pertain to the economy or to foreign relations: many of those in power or shouting in power's amen corner have a vested interest in keeping foolish but useful (to them) ideas in circulation.

My main purpose in this book is to make a small contribution to dissipating the prevailing intellectual fog. Having wrestled with the issues discussed here for forty years or more, I believe that I have cleared away at least some of the fog pumped into my own mind early on by teachers, politicians, the news media, and the special interests who strive relentlessly to sway the climate of opinion. In any event, I hope that readers will find the arguments and information presented here helpful as they strive to clear their own minds.

PART I

The Nature of the State, Democracy, and Crisis Policymaking

1

If Men Were Angels

The Basic Analytics of the State versus Self-Government

IN THE FEDERALIST NO. 51, arguably the most important *Federalist* of all, James Madison wrote in defense of a proposed national constitution that would establish a structure of "checks and balances between the different departments" of the government and, as a result, constrain the government's oppression of the public. In making his argument, Madison penned the following paragraph, which comes close to being a short course in political science:

> [T]he great security against a gradual concentration of the several powers in the same department, consists in giving to those who administer each department the necessary constitutional means and personal motives to resist encroachments of the others. The provision for defence must in this, as in all other cases, be made commensurate to the danger of attack. Ambition must be made to counteract ambition. The interest of the man must be connected with the constitutional rights of the place. It may be a reflection on human nature, that such devices should be necessary to control the abuses of government. But what is government itself, but the greatest of all reflections on human nature? If men were angels, no government would be necessary. If angels were to govern men, neither external nor internal controls on government would be necessary. In framing a government which is to be administered by men over men, the great difficulty lies in this: you must first enable the government to control the governed; and in the next place oblige it to control itself. A dependence on the people is, no doubt, the primary control on the government; but experience has taught mankind the necessity of auxiliary precautions.[1]

---

1. James Madison, *The Federalist No. 51*, 1788, in *The Federalist* (New York: Modern Library, n.d.), 337.

Table 1.1 Madison's Model

	No State	State
Men are angels.	OK	OK
Men are not angels.	Not conceivable	Best conceivable

The passage that refers to the angels is a rhetorical masterpiece, so memorable that it has become almost a cliché. In Madison's argument, however, it does more than emphasize that human nature is somewhat less than angelic. It also serves as a springboard that propels Madison directly into a consideration of "framing a government which is to be administered by men over men," which is "but the greatest of all reflections on human nature." In short, it moves Madison directly to a consideration of government as we have known it for the past several thousand years—a monopoly operating ultimately by threat or actual use of violence, making rules for and extracting tribute from the residents of the territory it controls. Henceforth, for clarity, I refer to this all-too-familiar type of organization as "the state."

Perhaps everyone will agree that if we all were angels, no state would be necessary, and if angels were the governors, they would require neither internal nor external constraints to ensure that they governed justly. In terms of table 1.1, we would be indifferent regarding the choice between the two cells in the first row.

In Madison's mind, the no-state option was inconceivable, for reasons he expressed obliquely when he wrote: "In a society under the forms of which the stronger faction can readily unite and oppress the weaker, anarchy may as truly be said to reign as in a state of nature, where the weaker individual is not secured against the violence of the stronger; and as, in the latter state, even the stronger individuals are prompted, by the uncertainty of their condition, to submit to a government which may protect the weak as well as themselves; so, in the former state, will the more powerful factions or parties be gradually induced, by a like motive, to wish for a government which will protect all parties, the weaker as well as the more powerful."[2] Thus, Madison, apparently following John Locke, believed that individuals would not choose to remain in a stateless condition and would submit to the authority of a state in order to attain greater security

---

2. Madison, *The Federalist No. 51*, 340.

of person and property. Countless other thinkers over the years have reasoned likewise, as Mancur Olson did in his final book when he concluded, "If a population acts to serve its common interest, it will never choose anarchy."[3]

Disorder, Liberty, and the State

Nothing is more common than the assumption that without a state, a society will fall necessarily and immediately into violent disorder; indeed, anarchy and chaos are often used as synonyms. The *Random House Dictionary* gives the following four definitions for anarchy:

1. A state of society without government or law.
2. Political and social disorder due to absence of governmental control.
3. A theory that regards the absence of all direct or coercive government as a political ideal and that proposes the cooperative and voluntary association of individuals and groups as the principal mode of organized society.
4. Confusion; chaos; disorder.

Suppose, however, that the situation described by the third definition were not merely an ideal, but a genuine possibility, perhaps even a historically instantiated condition.

Locke, Madison, Olson, and nearly everybody else, of course, have concluded from their theoretical deliberations that the stateless option cannot exist—at least, not for long—because its deficiencies make it so manifestly inferior to life in a society under a state. The alleged absence of significant historical examples of large, stateless societies during the past several thousand years buttresses these theory-based conclusions: just as "the poor we have always with us," so, except among primitive peoples, society and the state are taken to have always coexisted.

One need not spend much time, however, to find theoretical arguments— some of them worked out in great detail and at considerable length—about why and how a stateless society can work successfully.[4] Moreover, researchers have

3. Mancur Olson, *Power and Prosperity: Outgrowing Communist and Capitalist Dictatorships* (New York: Basic Books, 2000), 65.

4. For examples of particularly detailed and thoughtful conceptions, see Murray Rothbard, *For a New Liberty: The Libertarian Manifesto,* rev. ed. (New York: Collier Books, 1978), and David Friedman, *The Machinery of Freedom: Guide to a Radical Capitalism,* 2nd ed. (La Salle, Ill.: Open Court, 1989).

Table 1.2 More Realistic Model

	No State	State
Men are angels.	OK	OK
Men are not angels.	Bad situation	Worse situation

adduced historical examples of large stateless societies, ranging from the ancient Harappan civilization of the Indus Valley[5] to Somalia during the greater part of the past decade and a half.[6] Given the enormous literature that has accumulated on stateless societies in theory and in actual operation, we may conclude that, if nothing else, such societies are conceivable.[7]

In this light, both cells in the second row of Madison's model must be seen as live options, whose most likely outcomes are, I suggest, as indicated in table 1.2, the "More Realistic Model."

Although I admit that the outcome in a stateless society will be bad because not only are people not angels, but many of them are irredeemably vicious in the extreme, I conjecture that the outcome in a society under a state will be worse, indeed much worse: first, because the most vicious people in society will tend to gain control of the state;[8] and, second, because by virtue of this control over the state's powerful engines of death and destruction, they will wreak vastly more harm than they ever could have caused outside the state.[9] It is unfortunate that some individuals commit crimes, but it is stunningly worse when such criminally inclined individuals wield state powers.

Lest anyone protest that the state's true "function" or "duty" or "end" is, as Locke, Madison, and countless others have argued, to protect individuals' rights

---

5. Thomas J. Thompson, "An Ancient Stateless Civilization: Bronze Age India and the State in History," *The Independent Review* 10, no. 3 (Winter 2006), 365–84.

6. Robert Higgs, *Against Leviathan: Government Power and a Free Society* (Oakland, Calif.: The Independent Institute, 2004), 374, 376, and Yumi Kim, "Stateless in Somalia and Loving It," *Mises.org*, February 21, 2006, at http://www.mises.org/story/2066.

7. For a far-reaching compendium on the entire subject, see Edward P. Stringham, ed., *Anarchy and the Law: The Political Economy of Choice* (Oakland, Calif.: The Independent Institute, 2007).

8. See Friedrich A. Hayek, *The Road to Serfdom* (Chicago: University of Chicago Press, 1944), 134–52; F. G. Bailey, *Humbuggery and Manipulation: The Art of Leadership* (Ithaca, N.Y.: Cornell University Press, 1988); and Higgs, *Against Leviathan*, 33–56.

9. Higgs, *Against Leviathan*, 101–5.

to life, liberty, and property, the evidence of history clearly shows that, as a rule, real states do not behave accordingly. The idea that states actually function along such lines or that they strive to carry out such a duty or to achieve such an end resides in the realm of wishful thinking. Although *some* states in their own self-interest may *some*times protect *some* residents of their territories (other than the state's own functionaries), such protection is at best highly unreliable and all too often nothing but a solemn farce. Moreover, it is invariably mixed with crimes against the very people the state purports to protect because the state cannot exist at all without committing the crimes of extortion and robbery, which states call taxation, and, as a rule, this existential state crime is but the merest beginning of its assaults on the lives, liberties, and property of its resident population.[10]

In the United States, for example, the state at one time or another during recent decades has confined millions of persons in dreadful steel cages because they had the temerity to engage in the wholly voluntary buying and selling or the mere possession of officially disapproved products. Compounding these state crimes (of kidnapping and unjust confinement) with impudence, state officials brazenly claim credit for their assaults on the victims of their so-called war on drugs. State functionaries have yet to explain how their rampant un-provoked crimes comport with the archetype described and justified in Locke's *Second Treatise of Government.* In vain do many of us yearn for relief from the state's duplicitous cruelty: Where is the state of nature when we really need it?

An Application of the Precautionary Principle

In pondering the suitability of the More Realistic Model, we might well apply the *precautionary principle,* which has been much discussed (and nearly always misapplied) in recent years in relation to environmental policy. This principle holds that if an action or policy might cause great irreparable harm, then, notwithstanding a lack of scientific consensus, those who support the action or policy should shoulder the burden of proof. In applying this prin-ciple to the state's establishment and operation, the state's supporters would appear to stagger under a burden of proof they cannot support with either logic

---

10. Albert Nock, "The Criminality of the State," *American Mercury* (March 1939), at http://www.lewrockwell.com/nock/nock6.html.

or evidence. Everyone can see the immense harm the state causes day in and day out, not to mention its periodic orgies of mass death and destruction. In the past century alone, states caused hundreds of millions of deaths, not to the combatants on both sides of the many wars they launched, whose casualties loom large enough, but to "their own" populations, whom they chose to shoot, bomb, shell, hack, stab, beat, gas, starve, work to death, and otherwise obliterate in ways too grotesque to contemplate calmly.[11]

Yet in an almost incomprehensible fashion, people fear that without the state's supposedly all-important protection, society will lapse into disorder, and people will suffer grave harm. Even an analyst so astute as Olson, who speaks frankly of "governments and all the good *and* bad things they do," proceeds immediately to contrast "the horrible anarchies that emerge in their absence," although he gives no examples or citations to support his characterization of anarchy.[12] But the state's harms—"the bad things they do"—are here and now, undeniable, immense, and horrifying, whereas the harms allegedly to be suffered without the state are specters of the mind and almost entirely conjectural.

This debate would not appear to be evenly matched. Defending the continued existence of the state, despite having absolute certainty of a corresponding continuation of its intrinsic engagement in robbery, destruction, murder, and countless other crimes, requires that one imagine nonstate chaos, disorder, and death on a scale that nonstate actors seem incapable of causing. Nor, to my knowledge, does any historical example attest to such large-scale nonstate mayhem. With regard to large-scale death and destruction, no person, group, or private organization can even begin to compare to the state, which is easily the greatest instrument of destruction known to man. All nonstate threats to life, liberty, and property appear to be relatively petty and therefore can be dealt with. Only states can pose truly massive threats, and the horrors with which they menace mankind come invariably to pass sooner or later.

The lesson of the precautionary principle is plain: because people are vile and corruptible, the state, which holds by far the greatest potential for harm and tends to be captured by the worst of the worst, is much too risky for anyone to justify

---

11. R. J. Rummel's latest estimate of twentieth-century democide stands at 262 million persons; for the details, see R. J. Rummel, "20th Century Democide," n.d., at http://www.hawaii.edu/powerkills/20TH.HTM.

12. Olson, *Power and Prosperity,* 66, emphasis added.

its continuation. To tolerate it is not simply to play with fire, but to chance the total destruction of the human race.

Dynamic Considerations

In thinking about the social disorder that so many people have been led to fear if the state is not present, we can organize our thoughts with reference to table 1.3, which shows the degree of disorder and the scope for liberties with and without the state over time. The notation in the table indexes the degree of social disorder (D) and the scope of liberties (L) in a society with no state (NS) and in a society with a state (S) at successive points in time 0, 1, 2, and so on.

Classic discussions of state versus nonstate societal outcomes usually involve static comparisons; they ignore the changes that occur systematically with the passage of time. Thus, for example, a Hobbesian or Lockean account stipulates that in a "state of nature," which has no governing state, a great deal of disorder prevails, and adoption of a state brings about a more orderly condition: in terms of my notation, $D\text{-}NS(0) > D\text{-}S(0)$. Analysts recognize that the people sacrifice some of their liberties when they adopt a state; Hobbes goes so far as to suppose that the people sacrifice *all* their liberties to an omnipotent sovereign in exchange for his protection of their lives. Even if the trade-off is less severe, however, the inequality will be $L\text{-}NS(0) > L\text{-}S(0)$ upon the establishment of a

Table 1.3 Disorder, Liberties, and the State

	No State	State
Degree of Disorder	$D\text{-}NS(0)$	$D\text{-}S(0)$
	$D\text{-}NS(1)$	$D\text{-}S(1)$
	$D\text{-}NS(2)$	$D\text{-}S(2)$
	etc.	etc.
Scope of Liberties	$L\text{-}NS(0)$	$L\text{-}S(0)$
	$L\text{-}NS(1)$	$L\text{-}S(1)$
	$L\text{-}NS(2)$	$L\text{-}S(2)$
	etc.	etc.

Note: D = social disorder; L = scope of liberties; NS = society with no state; and S = society with a state.

state. A ruler always assures his victims that their loss of liberties is the price they must pay for the additional security (order) he purports to establish.

Well might we question whether the ruler has either the intention or the capability to reduce the degree of social disorder. Plenty of evidence exhibits state-ridden societies boiling with disorder. In the United States, for example, a country brimming with official "protectors" of every imaginable stripe, the populace suffered in 2004, according to figures the government itself endorses, approximately 16,000 murders, 95,000 forcible rapes, 401,000 robberies, 855,000 aggravated assaults, 2,143,000 burglaries, 6,948,000 larcenies and thefts, and 1,237,000 motor vehicle thefts.[13] The governments of the United States have taken the people's liberties—if you don't think so, you need to spend more time reading *U.S. Statutes at Large* and the *Code of Federal Regulations*, not to mention your state and local laws and ordinances—but where's the protective quid pro quo? They broke the egg of our liberties, without a doubt, but where's the bloody omelet of personal protection and social order?

Suppose, if only for purposes of discussion, we concede that the initial establishment of the state reduces the degree of social disorder. The obvious question, however seldom philosophers may have asked it, then becomes, What happens next? Does the degree of social disorder remain constant at D-S(o)? Everything we have discovered in theory and by observation flies in the face of such constancy. In fact, the likely progression over time is: D-S(o) < D-S(1) < D-S(2), and so forth. Under state domination, social disorder tends to increase.

This tendency exists because the state attempts in countless ways to compel people to act against their perceived self-interest, and the people respond by resorting to all sorts of evasions, black markets, and crimes. Consider, for example, what happened when the state ordered people not to make, sell, possess, or consume alcoholic beverages or certain narcotics—black markets and crime galore, including countless assaults and murders. Of course, the state's orders to pay stipulated taxes or fees have given rise to manifold evasive measures, some of them carrying violence against persons or the destruction of property in their train. Perhaps equally important, the state's concentration of its police forces on tax collection, enforcement of victimless crimes, and other measures at odds

---

13. U.S. Census Bureau, *Statistical Abstract of the United States: 2007* (Washington, D.C.: U.S. Government Printing Office, 2007), 191.

with the people's perceived self-interest diverts those forces from making any more than a token attempt to prevent such everyday crimes as murder, rape, robbery, and fraud, whose prevention the people actually value. Over time, the social misallocation of the state's "protective" resources grows as the state itself shifts more and more resources toward the enforcement of laws adverse to the people's genuine interests and as the people make "moving targets" of themselves in ways that augment the degree of social disorder.[14]

If the degree of social disorder in a society under the state tends to increase, then even if the initial establishment of the state did reduce disorder, a time (t) will come when the degree of social disorder will exceed the disorder of the society with no state: that is, in my notation, D-S(t) > D-NS(o). If so, then—with the myth of a social contract momentarily taken for granted—the initial bargain the people struck will come to be seen as a pact with the devil, a bargain that held, at best, advantages in the short term but proved to be a disappointing deal all around in the longer term.

Moreover, for compelling reason, the inequality stated in the preceding can be generalized as follows: D-S(t) > D-NS(t), for t sufficiently large. This more general condition will exist not only because social disorder tends systematically to increase with the state, but also because social disorder tends systematically to decrease without the state. The latter tendency reflects the progressive, mutually advantageous solution of social problems characteristic of a spontaneous order. We have had three centuries of instruction in the workings of the spontaneous order of a free society, stretching from Bernard de Mandeville, Adam Ferguson, and Adam Smith in the eighteenth century to Carl Menger in the nineteenth century to F. A. Hayek and Murray Rothbard in the twentieth century to their numerous followers in the early twenty-first century.[15] Unlike the forced exchanges and coerced arrangements enforced by the state, the protective and productive innovations of a spontaneous nonstate order can achieve acceptance only voluntarily, which is to say only when all who participate in them expect them to produce net benefits. Consider, for example, the householder who keeps

---

14. On the "moving targets" of government economic policies, see George P. Shultz and Kenneth W. Dam, *Economic Policy Beyond the Headlines* (New York: W. W. Norton, 1977), 8–10.

15. Steven Horwitz, "From Smith to Menger to Hayek: Liberalism in the Spontaneous Order Tradition," *The Independent Review* 6, no. 1 (Summer 2001): 81–97.

a watchful eye on his neighbor's property when the owner is away, just as the neighbor will watch the householder's property when he is away, and contrast this simple, effective cooperative form of protection with the faux protection of the state's police officer, who occupies himself at great public expense driving about aimlessly, harassing citizens pointlessly, or loitering in the doughnut shop. Neighborliness spreads naturally and beneficially, whereas state "protection" spreads cancerously and harmfully. The one preserves liberties; the other destroys them.

Thus, reverting to the notation of table 1.3, we have ample grounds for statement of the following inequalities:

$$D\text{-}NS(0) > D\text{-}NS(1) > D\text{-}NS(2), \text{ and so forth,}$$
$$\text{and}$$
$$L\text{-}S(0) > L\text{-}S(1) > L\text{-}S(2), \text{ and so forth.}$$

The latter inequalities, of course, merely state in abstract symbols what Thomas Jefferson stated more eloquently in words when he wrote, "The natural progress of things [in society under a state] is for liberty to yield and government to gain ground." Thus, although the (mythical) people entering into a social contract might have considered their sacrifice of liberties to the state a price they were willing to pay *at that time*, they could scarcely have suspected that with the passage of time, they would also have to pay their remaining liberties, one after another, notwithstanding the outcome that the social order they initially received from the state in return would systematically diminish.

Does Anarchy Entail Poverty?

Arguments have been advanced, of course, that a society without a state must necessarily remain very poor—that, however gloriously free the people's life might be without the state, the opportunity cost of anarchy is unacceptably high. Thus, Olson advances the following propositions:

1. Some of the labor in an anarchic society will be devoted to taking or stealing rather than producing.
2. The output forgone when less productive but theft-resistance forms of production are used is, of course, an implicit cost of anarchy.

3. Anarchy not only involves loss of life but also increases the incentives to steal and to defend against theft and thereby reduces the incentive to produce.

   [Therefore]

4. If a population acts to serve its common interest, it will never choose anarchy.[16]

The character of these arguments is reminiscent of the character of those advanced by the "market-failure" school of neoclassical welfare economics: having identified flaws in the freely chosen arrangement, the analyst leaps immediately to the conclusion that a state-dominated arrangement must necessarily be superior. As Harold Demsetz famously characterized this sort of argumentation, it falls victim to the Nirvana Fallacy. It finds the free arrangement worse than an unattainable blackboard ideal that it assumes the government can implement perfectly and costlessly, but it does not compare the actual free arrangement with the actual government "solution."

Returning to Olson's list of anarchy's flaws, one has only to ask: Does substitution of the state for anarchy avoid these flaws? The answer in every case is that not only does it not avoid them, but it actually exacerbates them and adds new problems on top of the old ones it purports to be solving.

So, considering Olson's first proposition, we may readily admit that without a state "some of the labor . . . will be devoted to taking or stealing rather than producing." Yet, one might argue, with a state almost *all* of the labor expended by state functionaries and *much* of the labor of other people will also be "devoted to taking or stealing rather than producing." Although the state may produce some goods and services of genuine value—absent an expression of voluntary individual choice, such as freely made purchases, we have no persuasive evidence of such value or of its magnitude—it seems perfectly obvious that a great deal of state "production" creates either nothing valuable at all or, worse, outputs that many taxpayers despise and would gladly pay to avoid. These obnoxious outputs are produced nonetheless because state functionaries and their cronies in the so-called private sector with whom they contract are in effect "taking or stealing rather than producing" due to their exercise of the state's

---

16. Olson, *Power and Prosperity*, 63–65.

coercive power. Moreover, as Gordon Tullock and other public-choice analysts have demonstrated repeatedly, the state encourages enormous social waste as real resources are committed to a competition for state privileges of all sorts: social waste incurred in the process of seeking what is itself wasteful for those from whom resources are extracted to prop up the state and all its schemes.[17] In sum, Olson's first proposition about anarchy versus society under the state is almost ludicrously backward.

His second proposition fares no better. Yes, without a state, output is "forgone when less productive but theft-resistance forms of production are used," but in truth we may say the same thing about a society with a state. It is obvious that people constantly adjust the form of their production to avoid taxes and regulations—that is, to avoid the state's robbery, oppression, and violation of their natural rights. Neoclassical economists have produced countless articles and books about how the state can "reshape behavior" by the appropriate design and enforcement of its taxes, subsidies, laws, and regulations. When people abandon their otherwise most-valued forms of production in reaction to these state sanctions, socially valued outputs are lost. When the state comes to be engaged in the economy as pervasively as it is now in all of the economically advanced countries, we can scarcely avoid the conclusion that the scale of these losses must be immense because people are being diverted from the socially most-valued forms of production at nearly every turn. In sum, Olson's second proposition about anarchy versus society under the state is almost ludicrously backward.

We can readily agree with Olson's third proposition, though: "Anarchy not only involves loss of life but also increases [relative to the nirvana level] the incentives to steal and to defend against theft, and thereby reduces the incentive to produce." But is the situation in these regards any better under the state? Certainly, as I have argued already, the loss of life is immensely greater with the state than without it. Since its maturation in the fifteenth and sixteenth centuries, the modern nation-state has functioned as a veritable killing machine. It defies reason to suppose that people left to their own individual devices would have killed hundreds of millions of people as states did in the twentieth century

---

17. Gordon Tullock's article "The Welfare Cost of Tariffs, Monopolies, and Theft," *Western Economic Journal* 5 (June 1967): 224–32, launched a thousand papers about rent seeking.

alone. Following public-choice analysis, we can make a similar statement about stealing and defending against theft. Because the state is a standing invitation to (legal) theft for all who can gain a grip on any of its many levers of power, it constitutes a constant menace against which one and all must devote time, energy, and resources in defense lest they be subjected to utter spoliation. Unfortunately, once the stampede for control of state power gets under way widely in society, almost everybody comes to view his own attempt to engage in legal plunder as essentially defensive: "The state is going to tax and regulate me no matter what I do; unless I get something back via state action, I will be a chump, a sucker, a net loser." The wonder is that people produce anything at all under a state. Their production will eventually diminish, however, as state power continues its seemingly inexorable expansion—indeed, if the state is going to strip you naked, why produce at all? Any ship, even a magnificent economy, can be sunk if enough people continue to poke holes in it, small as each individual hole might be. In sum, Olson's third proposition about anarchy versus society under the state is almost ludicrously backward.

Concluding Thoughts

In view of the foregoing arguments, we might well restate Olson's ultimate economic conclusion on anarchy as follows: If a population acts to serve its common interest, it will never choose the state. In reaching this conclusion, we need not deny the countless problems that will plague the people living in a society without the state; any anarchical society, being peopled in normal proportion by vile and corruptible individuals, will have crimes and miseries aplenty. But everything that makes life without a state undesirable makes life with a state even more undesirable. The idea that the antisocial tendencies that afflict people in every society can be cured or even ameliorated by giving a few persons great discretionary power over all the others is seen, upon serious reflection, to be a wildly mistaken notion. Perhaps it is needless to add that the structural checks and balances on which Madison relied to restrain the government's abuses have proven to be increasingly unavailing and, with the expansive claims and actions under the present U.S. regime borne in mind, are now almost wholly superseded by a form of executive caesarism in which the departments of government that were designed to check and balance each other have instead coalesced in a mutually supportive design to plunder the people and reduce them to absolute domination by the state.

My arguments in support of self-government as opposed to society under a state may have little point, of course: if people do not choose the state, but rather, as I think, simply have it imposed on them, then it makes no practical difference that the state is unnecessary to solve any particular kind of problem and that life without the state would be superior.[18] Life without cancer would be superior, too, but so far we have not found a way to get rid of it, and we have no guarantee that we ever will find a way, so we can only strive to make the best of a bad situation. We need also to consider the likely outcome if our society has no state, but another society does, and that state has the capacity to harm us greatly and, for whatever reason, seeks to do so. I am not convinced that this particular problem is insoluble, and, indeed, I believe that the state's defenders may have blown it out of proportion, but I do not dismiss it entirely. The Irish monks of the sixteenth century may have had the better argument, but it availed them little when Henry VIII decided to rip the roof off the monastery.

Here, however, I have tried only to show how we may think more clearly about the choice between a society under the state and a society composed of self-governing individuals. Assuming that we really had such a choice, the better option seems to me fairly obvious. If the reader takes anything away from my arguments here, I hope that it will be an appreciation of how highly warranted is an application of the precautionary principle in choosing between self-governance and the state. Fire has proven to be a magnificent aid to human beings, but a fire that cannot be contained portends our utter destruction, and the state is precisely such a fire.

---

18. Randall G. Holcombe, "Government: Unnecessary but Inevitable," *The Independent Review* 8, no. 3 (Winter 2004): 325–42.

2

Do Slavery and Government Rest on the Same Rationalizations?

You may say I'm a dreamer
But I'm not the only one.
I hope someday you will join us
And the world will live as one.
    —*John Lennon, "Imagine"*

SLAVERY EXISTED FOR thousands of years in all sorts of societies and all parts of the world. To imagine human social life without it required an extraordinary effort. Yet from time to time eccentrics emerged to oppose this institution, most of them arguing that slavery is a moral monstrosity and advocating that people should get rid of it. Such advocates were generally met with reactions that ranged from gentle amusement to harsh scorn and violent assault.

When people bothered to give reasons for opposing the abolitionists' proposal, they advanced many different ideas. Although some people no doubt presented these views sincerely, others appear to have offered them more as rationalizations than as genuine reasons. Here are ten such ideas I have encountered in my reading:

1. Slavery is natural. People differ, and we must expect that those who are superior in a certain way—for example, in intelligence, morality, knowledge, technological prowess, or capacity for fighting—will make themselves the masters of those who are inferior in this regard. Abraham Lincoln gave classic expression to this idea in one of his famous 1858 debates with Senator Stephen Douglas: "[T]here is a physical difference between the white and black races which I believe will forever forbid the two races living together on terms of social and political equality. And inasmuch as they cannot so live, while they do remain together there must be the position of superior and inferior, and I as much as any other man am in favor of having the superior position assigned to the white race."[1]

2. Slavery has always existed. This reason exemplifies the logical fallacy *argumentum ad antiquitatem* (appeal to tradition). Although it lacks logically compelling content, it often persuades people, especially those of conservative bent. Even those who are not inclined toward a conservative outlook may give it some weight on the quasi-Hayekian ground that although we do not understand why a social institution persists, its persistence may nevertheless be well grounded in a logic we have yet to understand.

3. Every society on earth has slavery. The unspoken corollary is that every society *must have* (or, at least, must once have had) slavery. The pervasiveness of an institution seems to many people to constitute compelling proof of its necessity, just as its longevity seems to constitute compelling proof that it is somehow integral to the workings of social life. Perhaps, as one variant has it, every society has slavery because certain kinds of work are so difficult or degrading that no free person will do them, and therefore unless we have slaves to do these jobs, they will not get done. Someone, as the saying went in the Old South, has to be the mud sill, and free people will not tolerate serving in this capacity.

4. The slaves are not capable of taking care of themselves. This idea was popular in the United States in the late eighteenth and early nineteenth centuries among people, such as George Washington and Thomas Jefferson, who regarded slavery as morally reprehensible yet who continued to hold slaves and to obtain personal services from them and income from the products that these "servants" (as they preferred to call them) were compelled to produce. It would be cruel, they said, to set free people who would then, at best, fall into destitution and suffering.

5. Without masters, the slaves will die off. This idea is the preceding one pushed to its extreme. Even after slavery was abolished in the United States in 1865, many people continued to voice this idea. Northern journalists traveling in the South immediately after the war reported that, indeed, the blacks were in the process of becoming extinct because of the high death rate and the low birth

---

1. "Lincoln–Douglas Debates of 1858," Wikipedia, at http://en.wikipedia.org/wiki/Lincoln-Douglas_debates_of_1858.

rate among the emancipated people.[2] Sad but true, some of them declared, the freed people really were too incompetent, lazy, or immoral to act in a manner consistent with their own group survival.

6. Where the common people are free, they are even worse off than slaves. This argument became popular in the South in the decades before the War Between the States. Its leading exponent was the pro-slavery writer George Fitzhugh, whose book titles speak for themselves: *Sociology for the South, or, the Failure of Free Society* (1854) and *Cannibals All!, or, Slaves Without Masters* (1857).[3] Fitzhugh seems to have taken many of his ideas from the reactionary, rabidly racist Scottish writer Thomas Carlyle.[4] The still-heard expression "wage slave" echoes this antebellum outlook. True to his sociological theories, Fitzhugh wanted to extend slavery in the United States to working-class white people for their own good!

7. Getting rid of slavery would occasion great bloodshed and other evils. Many people assumed that the slaveholders would never permit the termination of the slave system without an all-out fight to preserve it. Sure enough, when the Confederacy and the Union went to war—set aside that the immediate issue was not the abolition of slavery, but the secession of eleven Southern states— great bloodshed and other evils did ensue. These tragic events seemed in many people's minds to validate the reason they had given for opposing abolition. (They evidently overlooked that, except in Haiti, slavery was abolished everywhere in the Western Hemisphere without large-scale violence.)

8. Without slavery, the former slaves would run amuck, stealing, raping, killing, and generally causing mayhem. The preservation of social order therefore forbids the abolition of slavery. Southerners lived in dread of slave uprisings. Northerners in the mid–nineteenth century found the situation in their own region already sufficiently intolerable owing to the massive influx of drunken, brawling Irishmen into the country in the 1840s and 1850s. Throwing Negroes, whom the Irish generally disliked, into the bloody mix would well nigh guarantee social chaos.

---

2. Robert Higgs, *Competition and Coercion: Blacks in the American Economy 1865–1914* (New York: Cambridge University Press, [1977] 2008), 14–15.

3. See "George Fitzhugh," *Wikipedia,* at http://www.wikipedia.org/wiki/George _Fitzhugh.

4. See "Thomas Carlyle," *Wikipedia*, at http://www.wikipedia.org/wiki/Thomas_Carlyle.

9. Trying to get rid of slavery is foolishly utopian and impractical; only a fuzzy-headed dreamer would advance such a cockamamie proposal. Serious people cannot afford to waste their time in considering such far-fetched ideas.

10. Forget abolition. A far better plan is to keep the slaves sufficiently well fed, clothed, housed, and occasionally entertained and to take their minds off their exploitation by encouraging them to focus on the better life that awaits them in the hereafter—to focus, that is, on what the Wobbly troubadour Joe Hill mocked in song as "pie in the sky bye and bye."[5] We cannot expect fairness or justice in this life, but all of us, including the slaves, can aspire to a life of ease and joy in paradise.

. . .

At one time, countless people found one or more of the foregoing reasons an adequate ground on which to oppose the abolition of slavery. Yet, in retrospect, these reasons seem shabby—more rationalizations than reasons. They now appear to nearly everyone to be, if not utterly specious, then shaky or at best unpersuasive, notwithstanding an occasional grain of truth. No one dredges up these ideas or their corollaries to support a proposal for reestablishing slavery. Although vestiges of slavery exist in northern Africa and a few other places, the idea that slavery is a defensible social institution is defunct. What once, not so long ago, seemed to be compelling reasons for opposing the abolition of slavery now packs no intellectual punch.

Strange to say, however, the same ideas once trotted out to justify opposition to the abolition of slavery are now routinely trotted out to justify opposition to the abolition of government (as we know it). Libertarian anarchists bold enough to have publicly advanced their proposal for abolishing the state will have encountered many, if not all, of the arguments used for centuries to prop up slavery. Thus, we may make a parallel list along the following lines:

1. Government (as we know it) is natural. Without government, everybody would do as he pleased, and, hence, total disorder would prevail. To preclude this chaos, some men must impose rules on the rest and enforce those rules violently, if need be. Every society does so. A society that did not do so would

---

5. See "Joe Hill," *Wikipedia*, at http://www.wikipedia.org/wiki/Joe_Hill.

destroy itself. People differ, and we must expect that those who are superior in a certain way—for example, in intelligence, morality, knowledge, technological prowess, capacity for fighting, or ability to attract favorable votes in a democratic election—will make themselves the rulers of those who are inferior in this regard.

2. Government (as we know it) has always existed. This reason exemplifies the logical fallacy *argumentum ad antiquitatem.* Although it lacks logically compelling content, it often persuades people, especially those of conservative bent. Even those who are not inclined toward a conservative outlook may give it some weight on the quasi-Hayekian ground that although we do not understand why a social institution persists, its persistence may nevertheless be well grounded in a logic we have yet to understand. (When all else fails, some characteristically obscurantist lines from the writings of Edmund Burke may be adduced to settle the issue.)

3. Virtually every society on earth has government (as we know it). The unspoken corollary is that every society *must have* such a government. The pervasiveness of an institution seems to many people to constitute compelling proof of its necessity, just as its longevity seems to constitute compelling proof that it is somehow integral to the workings of social life.

4. The subjects of government (as we know it) are not capable of taking care of themselves. It would be cruel to remove the government's protective umbrella from people who then at best would fall into destitution and suffering. Society contains many groups—the destitute, the sick, the abused wives and children, the elderly, the "minorities" of all sorts—who would have nowhere to turn if the government were not there to assist and protect them in a world that, absent government, would immediately revert to the law of the jungle.

5. Without government (as we know it), the subjects will die off. This idea is the preceding one pushed to its extreme. Just imagine, we are exhorted, how horrible conditions would be if we had no government to maintain a public-health system; to bring us potable water and carry away our sewage; to protect us from poisoned food and drugs; to prevent capitalist exploiters from reducing us to the subsistence level of wages or something worse; to regulate the swindlers (with the nerve to call themselves entrepreneurs) who offer to sell us goods and services; to keep the employers from dragging young children into the coal mines, textile mills, and sweat shops to work fourteen-hour days for ten cents a day; and so forth—not to mention no government to engage heroically in staving off the certain doom that global warming otherwise would cause before long.

6. Where the common people have no government (as we know it), they are much worse off. You libertarian anarchists want to get rid of government? So you want to live like the people of Somalia, right? No thanks, pal. I'm sticking with the good old USA. Our politicians may be crooks, but at least here everybody's got a big-screen TV and plenty of beer in the refrigerator. And, on top of that, pretty soon the government is going to give everybody free health care. You can have your dirt-eating anarchy.

7. Getting rid of government (as we know it) would occasion great bloodshed and other evils. Many people assume that the rulers and their privileged supporters will never permit the termination of their system without an all-out fight to preserve it. As if the government weren't already sufficiently huge, powerful, and overbearing, it has recently created the U.S. Army Northern Command[6] and assigned it the mission of maintaining "homeland security," which, in case you missed the announcement, includes killing or otherwise disabling any subjects who get so uppity that they take the defense of their rights to life, liberty, and property into their own hands, as the so-called Founding Fathers did in 1776. Uh-uh, my friend: not here, not now. The rivers would flow red with blood in short order.

8. Without government (as we know it), the former subjects would run amuck, stealing, raping, killing, and generally causing mayhem. Preservation of social order therefore forbids the abolition of the government. It's bad enough when the Los Angeles Lakers win the NBA championship. Just imagine how terrifying the mayhem would be without the government's cops there to smash those who get too far out of line.

9. Trying to get rid of government (as we know it) is foolishly utopian and impractical; only a fuzzy-headed dreamer would advance such a cockamamie proposal. Serious people cannot afford to waste their time in considering such far-fetched ideas.

---

6. "United States Northern Command," *Wikipedia*, at http://www.wikipedia.org/wiki /United_States_Northern_Command.

10. Forget anarchy. A far better plan is to keep the subjects sufficiently well fed, clothed, housed, and entertained and to take their minds off their exploitation by encouraging them to focus on the better life that awaits them in the hereafter—to focus, that is, on what the Wobbly troubadour Joe Hill mocked in song as "pie in the sky bye and bye." We cannot expect fairness or justice in this life, but all of us, including those outside the government and its privileged elites, can aspire to a life of ease and joy in paradise.

• • •

I trust that readers will not have found the foregoing presentation unbearably tedious and that my main point is sufficiently clear. Some readers, I'm sure, were irritated by my repetition of the cumbersome expression "government (as we know it)," but I have chosen to tax readers' patience in this way for a reason. When the typical person encounters an advocate of anarchism, his immediate reaction is to identify a list of critical government functions—preservation of social order, maintenance of a legal system for resolving disputes and dealing with criminals, protection against foreign aggressors, enforcement of private-property rights, support of the weak and defenseless, production and maintenance of economic infrastructure, and so forth. This reaction, however, shoots at the wrong target.

Libertarian anarchists do not deny that such social functions must be carried out if a society is to function successfully. They do deny, however, that we must have government (as we know it) to carry them out. Anarchists prefer that they be carried out by private providers with whom the beneficiaries have agreed to deal. When I write about government "as we know it," I am referring to the *monopolistic, individually nonconsensual* government that now exists everywhere.

Readers may object that at least some existing governments *do have* the people's consent. But where's the evidence? Show me the properly signed and witnessed contracts. Unless *all* of the responsible adults subject to a government's claimed authority have *voluntarily* and *explicitly* accepted its governance on specific terms, the presumption must be that the rulers have imposed their rule. Propaganda statements, civics texts, opinion surveys, barroom allegations, political elections, and so forth are beside the point in this regard. No one would think of proffering such forms of evidence to show that I have a valid contract with, say, the local Hyundai dealership to pay specified amounts of cash at specified times in exchange for ownership of a particular automobile. I signed the contract to purchase the car. When will the governments of the United States, the state of Louisiana, and St. Tammany Parish send me the contracts wherein I may agree (or not) to purchase *their* "services" on mutually acceptable terms? I'm not holding my breath awaiting their arrival.

The parallels between the rationalizations of continued slavery and the rationalizations of continued government (as we know it) deserve serious consideration. Unless I have missed something important, the similarities between arguments against the abolition of slavery and arguments against the abolition of government as we know it (see table 2.1) should shake the faith of all Americans who still labor under the misconception that ours is a "government of the people, by the people, for the people." From where I stand, it looks distressingly like an institutional complex that rests on the same shaky intellectual foundations as slavery.

Table 2.1 Arguments against the Abolition of Slavery and
Arguments against the Abolition of Government as We Know It

Slavery	Government (As We Know It)
Slavery is natural.	Government (as we know it) is natural.
Slavery has always existed.	Government (as we know it) has always existed.
Every society on earth has slavery.	Every society on earth has government (as we know it).
The slaves are not capable of taking care of themselves.	The people are not capable of taking care of themselves.
Without masters, the slaves will die off.	Without government (as we know it), the people will die off.
Where the common people are free, they are even worse off than slaves.	Where the common people have no government (as we know it), they are much worse off.
Getting rid of slavery would occasion great bloodshed and other evils.	Getting rid of government (as we know it) would occasion great bloodshed and other evils.

Slavery	Government (As We Know It)
Without slavery, the former slaves would run amuck, stealing, raping, killing, and generally causing mayhem.	Without government (as we know it), the people would run amuck, stealing, raping, killing, and generally causing mayhem.
Trying to get rid of slavery is foolishly utopian and impractical; only a fuzzy-headed dreamer would advance such a cockamamie proposal.	Trying to get rid of government (as we know it) is foolishly utopian and impractical; only a fuzzy-headed dreamer would advance such a cockamamie proposal.
Forget abolition. A far better plan is to keep the slaves sufficiently well fed, clothed, housed, and occasionally entertained and to take their minds off their exploitation by encouraging them to focus on the better life that awaits them in the hereafter.	Forget anarchy. A far better plan is to keep the ordinary people sufficiently well fed, clothed, housed, and entertained and to take their minds off their exploitation by encouraging them to focus on the better life that awaits them in the hereafter.

3

Democracy and Faits Accomplis

NO INSTITUTION OF modern life commands as much veneration as democracy. It comes closer than anything else to being the supreme object of adoration in a global religion. Anyone who denies its righteousness and desirability soon finds himself a pariah. One may get away with denouncing motherhood and apple pie, but not with speaking ill of democracy, which is now the principal icon of political and social life throughout the world. Many people are atheists, but few are antidemocrats.

Worship of this particular political arrangement has emerged relatively recently, however, and in earlier ages political philosophers were more apt to condemn democracy than to praise it. Aristotle, whose views received great weight for millennia, did not recommend democracy. Along with many other criticisms of this type of government, he wrote in his *Politics:*

> The final form of democracy has characteristics of tyranny: women dominate in the household so that they can denounce their husbands, slaves lack discipline, and flatterers—demagogues—are held in honor. The people wish to be a monarch. (1313b:32–41)

> It is best for citizens in a city-state to possess a moderate amount of wealth because where some have a lot and some have none the result is the ultimate democracy or unmixed oligarchy. Tyranny can result from both these extremes. It is much less likely to spring from moderate systems of government. (1295b:39–1296a:5)

> Some democracies, like tyrannies, rest on force and are not directed toward the common advantage. (1276a:12–14)

Ultimate democracy, like unmixed and final oligarchy, is really a tyranny divided [among a multitude of persons]. (1312b:35–38)[1]

The founders of the United States of America had mixed views about democracy. Nearly all of them seem to have feared it more than they respected it. They recognized that concessions to fairly wide participation in politics might have to be made to placate the masses—who, after all, had served as cannon fodder in the recently concluded war of secession from the British Empire—but they designed a system in which voting would be hobbled and circumscribed so that the common people would be kept from giving direct vent to their passions by seizing control of the government and using it to plunder the rich. The founders conspicuously feared "mob rule" and associated it with untrammeled democracy. All of the newly independent states required property holding and other qualifications for voting, and in practice the franchise was limited in most places to a small minority of the population—a subset of the adult, white males. The Constitution of the United States does not contain the word *democracy,* although it stipulates certain protocols for the election of officials, and it relies instead on federalism and the separation of powers to preserve liberty.

Although democracy made giant ideological strides in the nineteenth century, a few writers still had the courage to condemn it even well into the twentieth century. Among the most astute of them was Joseph A. Schumpeter. In *Capitalism, Socialism and Democracy,* he posits as a point of departure for analysis the classical conception of democracy: "[T]he democratic method is that institutional arrangement for arriving at political decisions which realizes the common good by making the people itself decide issues through the election of individuals who are to assemble in order to carry out its will." He then proceeds to demolish the pretention that this conception makes sense. "If we are to argue that the will of the citizens *per se* is a political factor entitled to respect," he argues, "it must first exist. That is to say, it must be something more than an indeterminate bundle of vague impulses loosely playing about given slogans and mistaken impressions." Schumpeter calls attention to "the ordinary

---

1. Quoted in Thomas R. Martin, with Neel Smith and Jennifer F. Stuart, "Democracy in the Politics of Aristotle," in *Dēmos,* July 26, 2003, at http://www.stoa.org/projects/demos /article_aristotle_democracy?page=2&greekEncoding=.

citizen's ignorance and lack of judgment in matters of domestic and foreign policy" and adds, anticipating the *rational ignorance* concept of public-choice theory, that "without the initiative that comes from immediate responsibility, ignorance will persist in the face of masses of information however complete and correct."[2]

Moreover, Schumpeter says, "even if there were no political groups trying to influence him, the typical citizen would in political matters tend to yield to extrarational or irrational prejudice and impulse." Matters are even worse once we recognize the "opportunities for groups with an ax to grind," who "are able to fashion and, within very wide limits, even to create the will of the people," leaving political analysts to ponder "not a genuine but a manufactured will" that is "the product and not the motive power of the political process."[3]

Schumpeter conceded that in the long run the general public may come to hold a more perceptive view of the world and to reward or punish officeholders in its light when they cast their ballots, but this eventual adjustment itself has a fatal flaw because history "consists of a succession of short-run situations that *may alter the course of events for good*": "If all the people can in the short run be 'fooled' step by step into something they do not really want, and if this is not an exceptional case which we could afford to neglect, then no amount of retrospective common sense will alter the fact that in reality they neither raise nor decide issues but that the issues that shape their fate are normally raised and decided for them." Because "electorates normally do not control their political leaders in any way except by refusing to reelect them or the parliamentary majorities that support them,"[4] the distinct possibility—nay, the great likelihood—exists that the voters will find themselves time after time concerned about a horse that has already fled the barn, never to be retrieved.

This bleak view of the political process under representative democracy becomes even bleaker once we recognize that office seekers typically either speak

---

2. Joseph A. Schumpeter, *Capitalism, Socialism and Democracy,* 3rd ed. (New York: Harper and Brothers, 1950), 250, 253, 261, 262.

3. Schumpeter, *Capitalism,* 263. For a more recent study that grapples with this problem, see Robert Higgs and Anthony Kilduff, "Public Opinion: A Powerful Predictor of U.S. Defense Spending," in Robert Higgs, *Depression, War, and Cold War: Studies in Political Economy* (New York: Oxford University Press, 2006), 195–207.

4 Schumpeter, *Capitalism,* 264, 272, emphasis added.

in vague, emotion-laden generalities or simply lie about their intentions. After taking office, they may act in complete disregard of their campaign promises, trusting that when they run for reelection, they will be able to concoct a plausible excuse for their infidelity and betrayal of trust. Thus, the voters remain permanently immersed in a fog of disinformation, emotional manipulation, and bald-faced mendacity. No matter what a candidate promises, the voters have no means of holding him to those promises or of punishing his misbehavior until it may be too late to matter. In many cases, unfortunately, the officeholders' decisions give rise to irreversible consequences—outcomes that cannot possibly be undone ex post.

Garet Garrett had a similar vision of the uselessness of democracy as a means of making government accountable to the "will of the people" (or to anything else except the rulers' own desires). Writing at mid–twentieth century, shortly after Schumpeter's death, in an essay titled *Ex America,* Garrett posed the following hypothetical scenario: "Suppose a true image of the present world had been presented to them in 1900, the future as in a crystal ball, together with the question, 'Do you want it?' No one can imagine that they would have said yes— that they could have been tempted by the comforts, the gadgets, the automobiles and all the fabulous satisfactions of midcentury existence, to accept the coils of octopean government, the dim-out of the individual, the atomic bomb, a life of sickening fear, the nightmare of extinction. Their answer would have been no, terrifically." Having set the scene, he asked: "Then how do you account for the fact that everything that has happened to change their world from what it was to what it is has taken place with their consent?" To which he added: "More accurately, first it happened and then they consented."[5]

Garrett proceeded to list and discuss briefly a series of cataclysmic, course-altering political events in the United States, including getting into World War I, launching the New Deal, getting into World War II, and joining the United Nations, and he noted that in each instance the people did not vote for the government's action, yet "to all of this the people have consented, not beforehand but afterward."[6]

---

5. Garet Garrett, *Ex America: The 50th Anniversary of The People's Pottage* (Caldwell, Idaho: Caxton Press, 2004), 70.
6. Garrett, *Ex America,* 72.

One might object at this point by asking, What difference does it makes whether the people consent beforehand or afterward, so long as they consent? Indeed, Bruce Ackerman has written an entire book to argue precisely that the most profound constitutional changes in U.S. history occurred not when the people formally amended the Constitution, but when the government acted outside its constitutional authority in a crisis *and later received electoral and judicial validation of its actions*, and that these de facto constitutional revolutions deserve our approbation; indeed, they ought to serve as models for future constitutional revolutions.[7]

Ackerman's view may be challenged by noting the frequency with which constitutional revolutionaries engineer the alleged ex post validation of their actions. People in power have the greatest ability to gerrymander the voting districts, bias the electoral rules, buy votes with taxpayers' money, stuff the ballot boxes, and otherwise ensure that those in power—regardless of how they got there—remain in power. People in power similarly have the greatest ability to appoint new judges, alter judicial jurisdictions, and change the size or number of courts of appeal to ensure that those in power—regardless of how they got there—gain judicial vindication of their (heretofore unconstitutional) actions.[8]

Despite the force of the preceding objections, Ackerman might refuse to consider them a knockout blow to his thesis. The people, he might insist, will sooner or later be able to vote against policies they find offensive, and judges will sooner or later be able to overturn the constitutionality of laws that transcend the government's true constitutional authority. The political winners can't rig the game forever, so if the people and the judges never avail themselves of opportunities to express their aversion to the constitutional revolutionaries and their policies, we may presume that they actually approve of what has been done—or, as Garrett put it, "first it happened and then they consented."

In a sense, this interpretation may be correct, but I doubt that the sense I have in mind is one that Ackerman would welcome. If the people never avail

---

7. Bruce Ackerman, *We the People 2: Transformations* (Cambridge, Mass.: Belknap Press of Harvard University Press, 1998).

8. Robert Higgs, "On Ackerman's Justification of Irregular Constitutional Change: Is Any Vice You Get Away With a Virtue?" *Constitutional Political Economy* 10 (November 1999): 375–83.

themselves of the opportunity to overturn what was done initially without their consent, they may thereby reveal only that people who have been fed thin gruel for a long time get used to eating it and even come to consider it nutritious.[9] In less metaphorical terms, my claim is that ideological change is often path dependent: where a dominant ideology stands and where it is most likely to go in the future depend significantly on the preceding course of events.[10]

Bearing in mind this aspect of political, social, and economic dynamics, we may come to understand better how, for example, in each decisive episode in the great transformation of America's political economy between 1900 and 1950 "first it happened and then they consented," and the people looked back on these episodes afterward not so much with regret as with pride and a sense that the nation had overcome great challenges. Moreover, the people subsequently elevated to the pantheon of "greatness" the presidents who had taken it upon themselves to plunge the nation into these cauldrons and endowed them with sainthood in the Church of Democracy—thus, Woodrow Wilson, Franklin D. Roosevelt, and, in the same mold, Abraham Lincoln.[11]

• • •

After World War I erupted in Europe in August 1914, the overwhelming majority of Americans preferred that their government remain neutral and not become engaged in the fighting. "Aversion to joining in the carnage," writes Walter Karp, "was virtually unanimous."[12] President Wilson represented himself as striving above all to end the fighting and to resist the temptation to enter the war in reaction to various provocations by both warring sides. We may well doubt the sincerity of his avowals of neutrality, however. Thomas Fleming writes that "in an unguarded moment, Wilson confessed to a friend that he hoped for an Allied victory in the war but was not permitted by his public neutrality to say

---

9. For visual representation of this phenomenon, nothing can surpass the Spartan regimen depicted in early scenes of the splendid film *Babbette's Feast* (1987).
10. Robert Higgs, "The Complex Course of Ideological Change," *American Journal of Economics and Sociology* 67 (October 2008): 547–65.
11. Robert Higgs, "Great Presidents?" in *Against Leviathan: Government Power and a Free Society,* 53–56 (Oakland, Calif.: The Independent Institute, 2004).
12. Walter Karp, *The Politics of War: The Story of Two Wars Which Altered Forever the Political Life of the American Republic (1890–1920)* (New York: Harper and Row, 1979), 169.

so."[13] There is no doubt, however, that the president and his election managers perceived that the best way for him to gain reelection in 1916 was by continuing to represent himself as a man of peace—hence, the campaign slogan "He kept us out of war."

Yet, despite this slogan, less than a month after beginning his second term, Wilson asked Congress for a declaration of war, resting his request on the astonishing ground that Americans had an absolute right to travel unmolested on the high seas on ships carrying munitions to a warring power. "Even after Wilson broke off relations with Germany in February 1917," Karp writes, "an overwhelming majority of Americans still opposed entering the war. Even when the United States had already been at war for some months a majority of Americans remained a sullen, silenced opposition, more profoundly alienated from their own government than any American majority has ever been before or since." Karp concludes: "Representative government had failed them at every turn."[14] Democracy in action?

Probably no single event of the past century has been such a prodigious source of evils as the U.S. entry into World War I, because of the Versailles Treaty that U.S. entry made possible. The conquests of Bolshevism, Nazism, and fascism and the manifold catastrophes known collectively as World War II, not to mention endless troubles in the Middle East, may arguably be traced directly to this source.[15] In the United States, World War I prompted the government to embrace what contemporaries called "war socialism" (though it was, in more precise language, "war fascism" for the most part), which provided blueprints for an immense variety of government interventions in the economy and society, many of which continue to impoverish Americans and to crush

---

13. Thomas Fleming, *The Illusion of Victory: America in World War I* (New York: Basic Books, 2003), 75.

14. Karp, *The Politics of War,* 169, 324.

15. Among recent sources, see, for example, Jim Powell, *Wilson's War: How Woodrow Wilson's Great Blunder Led to Hitler, Lenin, Stalin, & World War II* (New York: Crown Forum, 2005); and Patrick J. Buchanan, *Churchill, Hitler, and the Unnecessary War: How Britain Lost Its Empire and the West Lost the World* (New York: Crown, 2008), the latter of which is reviewed in Chapter 24 in this volume.

their liberties more than ninety years later.[16] The war could have such extreme and enduring consequences because it also brought about abrupt ideological changes: many Americans became convinced by their perception of the wartime controls that the government was capable of successfully engaging in socio-economic engineering on a wide front. Thus, the war put the final nail into the coffin of nineteenth-century liberalism, at least in the eyes of the major political players. As Bernard Baruch, the wartime head of the War Industries Board, declared later, "We helped inter the extreme dogmas of laissez faire, which had for so long molded American economic and political thought."[17]

Democracy's next colossal failure in the United States occurred in 1932. By the time of the presidential election in November, the country had experienced more than three years of worsening economic performance: falling output, rising unemployment, increasing numbers of business failures, and the loss of growing numbers of homes and businesses to foreclosure or to seizure for failure to pay taxes. Not without plausible reasons, people blamed President Herbert Hoover for these dreadful developments and gave Franklin D. Roosevelt, the Democratic challenger, the benefit of the doubt.

Roosevelt campaigned on a platform that the old Grover Cleveland–style Democrats of the nineteenth century might have endorsed comfortably. As Jesse Walker summarizes this platform,

> The very first plank calls for "an immediate and drastic reduction of gov-
> ernmental expenditures by abolishing useless commissions and offices,
> consolidating departments and bureaus, and eliminating extravagance
> to accomplish a saving of not less than twenty-five per cent in the cost
> of the Federal Government." (It also asks "the states to make a zealous
> effort to achieve a proportionate result.") Subsequent planks demand a
> balanced budget, a low tariff, the repeal of Prohibition, "a sound currency
> to be preserved at all hazards," "no interference in the internal affairs of

---

16. Robert Higgs, *Crisis and Leviathan: Critical Episodes in the Growth of American Government* (New York: Oxford University Press, 1987).

17. Bernard M. Baruch, *Baruch: The Public Years* (New York: Holt, Rinehart and Winston, 1960), 74.

other nations," and "the removal of government from all fields of private enterprise except where necessary to develop public works and natural resources in the common interest." The document concludes with a quote from Andrew Jackson: "equal rights to all; special privilege to none."[18]

Having made these promises, Roosevelt swept to a lopsided victory at the polls.

Yet the merest child knows that Roosevelt's New Deal, a huge hodge-podge of domestic interventions, controls, subsidies, taxes, threats, seizures, and other troublemaking amounted to nearly the exact opposite of what he had promised the voters during the campaign.

"So what?" we may hear Professor Ackerman asking offstage. "Didn't the people endorse these actions by reelecting Roosevelt with an even greater margin of victory in 1936?" Yes, of course, they did. But by that time the president and his party had turned the federal government into a vast vote-buying apparatus that covered the entire country and penetrated every county, town, and village. As John T. Flynn described the situation, "Roosevelt's billions, adroitly used, had broken down every political machine in America. The patronage they once lived on and the local money they once had to disburse to help the poor was trivial compared to the vast floods of money Roosevelt controlled. And no political boss could compete with him in any county in America in the distribution of money and jobs."[19]

Nor was this garden-variety political corruption the worst of it. Far more significant in the long run were the loss of faith in the free market among the masses and the boost given to ideological support for economic fascism. Owing to the Great Depression and the New Deal, later generations would live in chronic fear of economic privation and rest their hopes for security in a fervent belief that if the economy turned down, the government could and should rescue them. The Employment Act of 1946 codified this public dependency. Rugged individualism, to the extent that it had ever really existed, died a cruel death at

---

18. Jesse Walker, "The New Franklin Roosevelts: Don't Count on a Candidate's Campaign Stances to Tell You How He'll Behave in Office," *Reasononline*, April 10, 2008, at http://www.reason.com/news/show/125921.html.

19. John T. Flynn, *The Roosevelt Myth* (Garden City, N.Y.: Garden City Books, 1949), 65.

the hands of the New Deal—precisely what Roosevelt had *not* promised when he first campaigned for the presidency. Democracy in action?

Roosevelt was still in office when in 1940 the next great travesty of democracy occurred. War between the great powers had resumed in Europe, as everyone had expected it eventually would after the Versailles Treaty was signed in 1919. Just as the great majority of Americans had wished to keep away from the fighting in 1914, so a great majority again wanted nothing to do with the European bloodletting occurring now. Roosevelt, as the leader of the small minority that favored going to war—to save the British and (dare we conjecture?) to permit him to achieve the "greatness" that only wartime leadership brings—had to play his cards carefully. For two years, mendacity would be his major political device as he sought to maneuver Germany and Japan into an "incident" so inflammatory that it would shock the public into supporting U.S. entry into the war.[20]

Roosevelt's vaulting ambition fed his quest for reelection to an unprecedented third term. Given the massive public opposition to war—opposition, that is, to the very objective whose attainment Roosevelt sought above all others—the president, who had already begun to involve the country in the war in discreet ways, lifted his dishonesty to a higher level as the election approached. In a campaign speech at Boston on October 30, 1940, he declared bluntly: "I have said this before, but I shall say it again and again: Your boys are not going to be sent into any foreign wars." As David M. Kennedy notes, "Conspicuously, Roosevelt omitted the qualifying phrase that he had used on previous occasions: 'except in case of attack.'"[21] Relying on this seemingly frank promise, the electorate returned Roosevelt to office for another term.

---

20. Among the many sources relevant to this maneuvering, see the recent works by Robert B. Stinnett, *Day of Deceit: The Truth About FDR and Pearl Harbor* (New York: Free Press, 2000); Thomas Fleming, *The New Dealers' War: F.D.R. and the War Within World War II* (New York: Basic Books, 2001); and George Victor, *The Pearl Harbor Myth: Rethinking the Unthinkable* (Dulles, Va.: Potomac Books, 2007). Victor's book is reviewed in Chapter 25 of this volume.

21. David M. Kennedy, *Freedom from Fear: The American People in Depression and War, 1929–1945* (New York: Oxford University Press, 1999), 463 (Roosevelt quote on this page also).

In return, of course, they found themselves being pushed farther and farther toward open U.S. belligerency, until finally the Japanese attack on Pearl Harbor gave the president what he, his chief subordinates, and his closest supporters had been seeking from the start: declared engagement in the greatest armed conflict of all time. Democracy in action?

By the time this conflict ended, Americans had suffered more than a million casualties, including more than 400,000 servicemen's deaths, and four years of economic fascism on the home front, with extensive controls and government takeovers that dwarfed those of any comparable episode in the United States before or since. Moreover, the entire world had been altered, as the Soviet Union, America's wartime ally, now stood astride all of eastern Europe and much of central Europe, too, as far west as Czechoslovakia, so that when the violence ended in 1945, only a tense pseudo-peace took its place, and the world was condemned to live in fear of nuclear annihilation from that time forward.

For this dismal result, we may credit the democratic system that put Franklin D. Roosevelt and his party in power and allowed them to make the United States the decisive factor in the war's outcome. Without America's active involvement in the war, the British might have been forced to sue for peace, and the Germans and the Soviets might have bled one another to death—a grisly outcome, to be sure, but would it have been any worse than what actually happened? We cannot know, of course; history is not ours to rerun like a controlled experiment with reset conditions. Yet we can scarcely deny that the devastated world of 1945—with 60 million dead, tens of millions left sick, wounded, or homeless, and a murderous Communist dictator in control of half of Europe—was scarcely what most Americans sought to bring about when they cast their votes for Roosevelt in 1940.

• • •

Democracy has always had its critics. No one claims that it is a perfect system for choosing political leaders or for putting in place the policies and laws the public prefers. Obviously, when individual preferences differ, no one political outcome can please everybody, and the "tyranny of the majority" stands as a constant menace to the lives, liberties, and property of unpopular minorities. Yet most people continue to insist that democracy, with all its faults, offers the best institutional arrangement for making rulers accountable to the people. So long as elections continue to be held, the possibility always remains of "throwing the rascals out."

What has not been widely recognized, however, is the problem of faits accomplis. Once elected rulers have taken office, the democratic system provides little or no effective means for the people to bring them to heel short of the next election. The great problem is that by that time, it may be impossible to reverse the outcomes the rulers have brought about. Wilson was not elected in 1916 to plunge the nation into the Great War. Roosevelt was not elected in 1932 to impose the New Deal on the country. Nor was he elected in 1940 to maneuver the United States into the greatest war of all time. Yet in each case the president did the opposite of what he had promised to do, and the people were left with no recourse. The world of 1919, the United States of 1936, and the world of 1945—each was so massively, so irrevocably altered from the preceding status quo that any genuine restoration of the previous conditions was unimaginable. Like it or not, people were to a great extent simply stuck with what the deceitful politicians had done.

Worse, owing to "ideological learning," many people who initially had not desired these changes *did* approve of them in the circumstances in which they later found themselves—circumstances that they had in no way chosen, not even indirectly, but into which they had been forcibly shoved by the ruling decision makers. Contemplating this situation, one readily recalls Goethe's dictum that "none are more hopelessly enslaved than those who falsely believe they are free."

Still worse, during the next round of democratic choice, unconstrained decisions by elected officials, and the resulting faits accomplis, an altered ideological context sets the stage from which a society may be propelled even farther from the course it initially preferred. If people believe that democracy is a means by which ordinary people may ensure that they exercise some control over their own societal fate, they are fooling themselves. If the persons elected to office have a free hand to act as they please, then the sense that they are truly accountable to the electorate is an illusion. It comes closer to the truth to say that the people are completely at the mercy of the officials they have elected.

"Democracy," wrote H. L. Mencken, "may be a self-limiting disease, as civilization itself seems to be. There are thumping paradoxes in its philosophy, and some of them have a suicidal smack."[22] Whether it will prove suicidal for its adherents only time will tell, but we might note that so far only the United States of America, whose leaders and people tout their country as the greatest of all democracies, has employed nuclear weapons in war. It is not inconceivable that Woodrow Wilson's war to make the world safe for democracy, owing to the train of consequences it set in motion, may ultimately make the world safe for democracy, to be sure, but not safe for mankind.

22. H. L. Mencken, *A Mencken Chrestomathy* (New York: Knopf, 1949), 157.

4

Blame the People Who Elected Them?

DISCUSSIONS OF CALAMITOUS government actions—engagements in pointless, costly, and bloody wars; counterproductive actions to avert or shorten economic recessions; botched relief and reconstruction efforts after natural disasters—often arrive at, if they do not begin with, condemnation of government leaders. Thus, in the United States, for example, people have blamed Harry Truman for ordering U.S. military forces into the Korean War, Herbert Hoover for worsening the economic bust of 1929–33, and George W. Bush for presiding over the Federal Emergency Management Agency fiasco associated with Hurricane Katrina in 2005.

As soon as such a denunciation has been made, however, critics invariably intervene to challenge its perspicacity and to propose a seemingly more discerning, if disquieting, alternative: Don't blame leader X; blame the people who elected him. Given that in accordance with the protocol of majority-rule democracy, leader X was in a position to make the bad decision only because he had received more votes than the other electoral contenders, the critics maintain that the devastating government blunder we have witnessed represents nothing but the blessings of democracy as H. L. Mencken described them: "Democracy is the theory that the common people know what they want, and deserve to get it good and hard."[1]

This seemingly incontestable objection to blaming democratic leaders themselves for their harmful decisions appears not only to let the scoundrels off the hook, but also to shift the blame to a huge, incorrigible group of citizens or—horror of horrors!—to the democratic system itself. Thus, one who has stoutly

---

1. H. L. Mencken, *A Mencken Chrestomathy* (New York: Knopf, 1949), 622.

maintained that Truman, Hoover, and Bush brought about the dire outcomes in question and should be held accountable, if only in the court of historical judgment, finds himself on the defensive. He cannot deny that millions of voters cast their ballots for Truman, Hoover, and Bush and therefore that, roughly speaking, they "chose" the persons who as heads of state proceeded to make a hash of things.

I maintain, however, that the critics themselves are the less-discerning parties in this debate. Closer to the mark is the wit who observed, "Our politicians know what they want, and they act as if *we* deserve to get it good and hard."[2]

The critics' mistake is to trace responsibility back only one step, when several more steps must be taken to expose where the ultimate responsibility for "choosing" leader X lies. Yes, the people had a choice between Democrat X and Republican Y, and they gave, say, X more votes than Y. But who did what to make X and Y the major-party candidates in the first place?

Ambrose Bierce did not doubt that representative democracy is a sham: "You can effect a change of robbers every four years," he wrote. "Inestimable privilege to pull off the glutted leech and attach the lean one! And you cannot even choose among the lean leeches, but must accept those designated by the programmers and showmen who have the reptiles on tap."[3] Many, including yours truly, agree with him.

Anyone who prefers the plodding analytics of modern political science to this vibrant and clear-eyed commentary will find that Thomas Ferguson's view of the electoral system bears striking similarities to Bierce's, and it is heavily documented, to boot. Ferguson maintains that in order to become a major-party candidate, a person must obtain the financial support of a substantial faction of wealthy people. In his words, "*[A]s long as basic property rights do not emerge as the dominating issue*," then "competition between blocs of major investors drives the system."[4]

---

2. Comment by Mimus Pauly, at http://snarkypenguin.blogspot.com/2007/05/should -we-get-government-we-deserve.html.

3. Quoted in Robert Higgs, "Etceteras…," *The Independent Review* I, no. 1 (Spring 1996), 151.

4. Thomas Ferguson, *Golden Rule: The Investment Theory of Party Competition and the Logic of Money-Driven Political Systems* (Chicago: University of Chicago Press, 1995), 10, emphasis in original.

Alternative sources of electoral financing, such as the many dispersed individuals who might prefer that the government compress itself into a nightwatchman configuration, cannot organize themselves effectively or raise sufficient funds to swing the selection process toward a candidate of their choice. Hence, the major parties that put forward the actual candidates never place this plank or others that might have great popular appeal in their platforms. Parties are essentially organizations whose purpose is to secure the greatest share of the government loot for themselves in general—and for their principal financial backers in particular—and therefore the last thing they want is to put a stop to the looting. (The Libertarian Party, therefore, is a self-contradictory organization, and we should scarcely be surprised that it attracts only negligible financial and electoral support.)

I hold no brief for Friedrich Engels, but no one ever spoke the unvarnished truth more plainly than he when he observed: "[W]e find here [in the United States] two great gangs of political speculators, who alternately take possession of the state power and exploit it by the most corrupt means and for the most corrupt ends—and the nation is powerless against these two great cartels of politicians, who are ostensibly its servants, but in reality exploit and plunder it."[5] Can anyone seriously deny that this state of affairs, which Engels was characterizing in 1891, still exists in exactly the same general form?

Thus, the people do choose their smarmy and transparently dishonest leaders, to be sure, but they choose only from "the reptiles on tap." Forming a new political party is futile. Dissident parties that seek to challenge the status quo cannot accumulate the wherewithal to place their candidates on the state ballots, familiarize the voters with their names, publicize their policy positions, and bring substantial news media attention to bear on them. Moreover, the major parties have rigged the electoral rules to favor—*quel surprise!*—the major parties, especially their incumbent candidates. In an irresolvably disputed election, the major parties can turn, as the Bush gang did in 2000, to the justices of the Supreme Court, each of whom had gained his position by virtue of making himself attractive to major-party officeholders and their investor-supporters.

---

5. Friedrich Engels, "1891 Introduction by Frederick Engels, on the 20th Anniversary of the Paris Commune [Postscript]," in *The Civil War in France*, at http://www.marxists .org/archive/marx/works/1871/civil-war-france/postscript.htm.

If the people at large are to be blamed, they must be blamed not for the way they cast their ballots, but for their toleration of the whole predatory political setup that shamelessly passes itself off as a regime "of the people, by the people, for the people"—surely one of the most successful Big Lies of all time. Yet the people have been so massively miseducated, propagandized, cowed, and treated with cynical disregard of their rights for so long that for the most part not only have they lost all capacity to stand on their own feet, but, worse, they have in most cases come to love the Big Brother whose boot is grinding their faces. Willingly and sometimes even eagerly they present themselves and their children to be sacrificed on the altar of their own exploiters, leaving the survivors to carry home the folded flag, persuaded that Johnny not only did his "duty" but acted "heroically" in devotion to the Greater Good. For making the state their god, they may indeed be rightly condemned, even as we also denounce the false prophets who led them down the statist path to their own destruction.

As for Truman, Hoover, Bush, and the rest of them, of course we may properly blame them for their bad decisions, regardless of who paved their roads to power. Leaders must always bear personal responsibility for how they turn the wheel, once they have occupied the driver's seat. It is one thing for us to understand the economic, social, and ideological milieu in which key players elevate certain persons to positions of political power; it is a separate—and altogether fitting—thing for us to declare those persons guilty of the harmful and wicked actions they take when they exercise the power.

5

The Song That Is Irresistible

*How the State Leads People
to Their Own Destruction*

MARGARET ATWOOD'S POEM "Siren Song" begins:

> This is the one song everyone
> would like to learn: the song
> that is irresistible:
> the song that forces men
> to leap overboard in squadrons
> even though they see the beached skulls.[1]

Our rulers know how to sing that song, and they sing it day and night. The "beached skulls" are those of our fathers and our sons, our friends and our neighbors, for whom the song proved not only irresistible, but fatal.

The state is the most destructive institution human beings have ever devised—a fire that at best can be controlled for only a short time before it o'erleaps its improvised confinements and spreads its flames far and wide. Whatever promotes the growth of the state also weakens the capacity of individuals in civil society to fend off the state's depredations and therefore augments the public's multifaceted victimization at the hands of state functionaries. Nothing promotes the growth of the state as much as national emergency—war and other crises comparable to war in the seriousness of the threats they are believed to pose.

• • •

---

1. Margaret Atwood, "Siren Song," available at http://www.poemhunter.com/poem/siren-song/.

51

States by their very nature are perpetually at war—not always against foreign foes, of course, but always against their own subjects. The state's most fundamental purpose, the activity without which it cannot even exist, is robbery. The state gains its very sustenance from robbery, which it pretties up ideologically by giving it a different name *(taxation)* and by striving to sanctify its intrinsic crime as permissible and socially necessary. State propaganda, statist ideologies, and long-established routine combine to convince many people that they have a legitimate obligation, even a moral duty, to pay taxes to the state that rules their society.

They fall into such erroneous moral reasoning because they are told incessantly that the tribute they fork over is actually a kind of price paid for essential services received and that in the case of certain services, such as protection from foreign and domestic aggressors against their rights to life, liberty, and property, only the government can provide the service effectively. They are not permitted to test this claim by resorting to competing suppliers of law, order, and security, however, because the government enforces a monopoly over the production and distribution of its alleged "services" and brings violence to bear against would-be competitors. In so doing, it reveals the fraud at the heart of its impudent claims and gives sufficient proof that it is not a genuine protector, but a mere protection racket.

All governments are, as they must be, oligarchies: only a relatively small number of people have substantial effective discretion to make critical decisions about how the state's power will be brought to bear. Beyond the oligarchy itself and the police and military forces that compose its Praetorian Guard, somewhat larger groups constitute a supporting coalition. These groups provide important financial and other backing to the oligarchs and look to them for compensating rewards—legal privileges, subsidies, jobs, exclusive franchises and licenses, transfers of financial income and wealth, goods and services in kind, and other booty—that are channeled to them at the expense of the mass of the people. Thus, the political class in general—that is, the oligarchs, the Praetorian Guard, and the supporting coalition—uses government power (which means ultimately the police and the armed forces) to exploit everyone outside this class by wielding or threatening to wield violence against all who fail to pay the tribute the oligarchs demand or to obey the rules they dictate.

Democratic political forms and rituals, such as elections and formal administrative proceedings, disguise this class exploitation and trick the masses into the false belief that the government's operation yields them net benefits. In the most extreme form of misapprehension, the people at large become convinced that, owing to democracy, they themselves "are the government." Individual passages back and forth across the boundary between the political class and the exploited class testify, however, to nothing more than the system's cunningly contrived flexibility and openness. Although the system is inherently exploitative and cannot exist in any other form, it allows some leeway at the margins in the determination of which specific individuals will be the victimizers and which the victims. At the top, a modest degree of "circulation of elites" within the oligarchy also serves to mask the political system's essential character.

It is a sound interpretive rule, however, that anything that cannot be accomplished except with the aid of threats or actual exercise of violence against unoffending persons cannot be beneficial to one and all. The mass belief in the general beneficence of democracy represents a kind of Stockholm syndrome writ large. Yet no matter how widely this syndrome may extend, it cannot alter the basic fact that owing to the operation of government as we know it—that is, government without genuine, express, individual consent—a minority lives on balance at the expense of the rest, and the rest therefore lose on balance in the process, while the oligarchs (elected or not, it scarcely matters) preside over the enormous web of criminal organizations we know as the state.

Notwithstanding the ideological enchantment with which official high priests and statist intellectuals have beguiled the plundered class, many members of this class retain a capacity to recognize at least some of their losses, and hence they sometimes resist further incursions on their rights by publicly expressing their grievances, by supporting political challengers who promise to lighten their burdens, by fleeing the country, and, most important, by evading or avoiding taxes and by violating legal prohibitions and regulatory restraints on their actions, as in the so-called underground economy or "black market." These various forms of resistance together compose a force that opposes the government's constant pressure to expand its domination. These two forces, working one against the other, establish a locus of "equilibrium," a boundary between the set of rights the government has overridden or seized and the set of rights the plundered class has somehow managed to retain, whether by formal constitutional constraints or by everyday tax evasion, black-market transactions, and other defensive violations of the government's oppressive rules. Politics in the largest sense may be viewed as the struggle to push this boundary one way or the other. For members of the political class, the crucial question is always: How can we push out the frontier, how can we augment the government's dominion and plunder, with net gain to ourselves, the exploiters who live not by honest production and voluntary exchange, but by fleecing those who do so?

• • •

National emergency—war or a similarly menacing crisis—answers the political class's crucial question more effectively than anything else because such a crisis has a uniquely effective capacity to dissipate the forces that otherwise would obstruct or oppose the government's expansion.

Virtually any war will serve, at least for a while, because in modern nation-states the outbreak of war invariably leads the masses to "rally 'round the flag," regardless of their previous ideological stance in relation to the government. Recall the situation in 1941, for example, when public-opinion polls and other evidence indicated that a great majority of the American people (approximately 80 percent as late as the autumn of that year) opposed outright U.S. engagement in the world war, but engagement was exactly what Franklin D. Roosevelt and his administration had been seeking relentlessly by hook and by crook from the very beginning. When news of the Japanese attack on Pearl Harbor reached the public, mass opposition to war dissolved overnight almost completely. No wonder the neocon intriguers expressed in a September 2000 report of the Project for the New American Century their yearning for "some catastrophic and catalyzing event—like a new Pearl Harbor."[2]

Although other kinds of great crises may not elicit the same immediate submission to the government's announced program for the people's salvation, they may prove equally effective if they are sufficiently menacing and persistent. Thus, the Great Depression, which pushed millions of Americans into eco-

---

2. Project for the New American Century, *Rebuilding America's Defenses: Strategy, Forces, and Resources for a New Century* (Washington, D.C.: Project for a New American Century, September 2000), 51.

nomic desperation in the early 1930s, was eventually viewed by almost everybody as, in Justice Louis Brandeis's words, "an emergency more serious than war."[3] Other pregnant crises have included nationwide strikes or widespread labor disturbances, so-called energy crises, such as those of the 1970s, perceived crime waves, great epidemics or health scares, and, recently, even a bogus scare about anthropogenic global warming.

In 2001, the attacks of September 11 (9/11) answered to perfection the neocon prayer for "a new Pearl Harbor." An administration that had been wallowing without a breeze in its sails was suddenly invested with overwhelming public support for aggressive military action abroad. In a Gallup poll taken during September 7–10, 2001, 51 percent of the respondents approved of "the way George W. Bush [was] handling his job as president," 39 percent disapproved, and 10 percent had no opinion—yielding an "opinion balance" of +12 percent (51 percent minus 39 percent).[4] A few days later, while the ruins of the World Trade Center's twin towers were still smoldering, 86 percent approved, 10 percent disapproved, and only 4 percent had no opinion—an opinion balance of +76 percent, or more than six times greater than it had been only a few days earlier. Although Bush had done absolutely nothing to demonstrate an abruptly improved performance of his job as president, nearly the entire population, many members of which roundly disliked the president, suddenly showered approbation on his performance in office. A week later, the opinion balance had risen even higher, to +84 percent, on the strength of a 90 percent approval response.

Bush's job-performance approval rating followed a long downward trend afterward, interrupted by only brief upticks, until it reached a very low range. In a Gallup poll of July 6–8, 2007, the opinion balance was negative 37 percent, and only 29 percent of the respondents rated the president's performance favorably. (In later polls, the balance stood a few points higher in the president's favor, but such small differences have little significance.) During the long downhill slide, Bush's performance approval rating held up amazingly well among Republicans but fell lower and lower among both Democrats and independents—

---

3. Justice Louis Brandeis, dissenting in *New State Ice Company v. Liebmann,* 285 U.S. 262 (1932), at 306.
4. Gallup polls are available at http://www.Gallup.com.

an expression of how normal political partisanship reasserted itself as the initial, unifying crisis slipped farther and farther into the background.

Similar movements may be seen in the Gallup polls that asked the respondents whether they viewed George W. Bush himself favorably or unfavorably: the opinion balance jumped from +25 percent in August 2001 to +76 percent in November 2001—a threefold increase—before beginning a long downward trend and becoming increasingly negative after mid-2005.

When the public's approval of the president's actions is broken down by specific issues, we see that his greatest 9/11-related jump occurred in the area of—mirabile dictu—foreign affairs. In the Gallup poll taken during July 10–11, 2001, the opinion balance in this area was +21 percent (54 percent favorable minus 33 percent unfavorable), but in the poll taken during October 5–6, 2001, the opinion balance had jumped to +67 percent, or more than three times higher (81 percent favorable minus 14 percent unfavorable).

The lesson is clear: if the president conducts foreign policy so as to antagonize foreigners and provoke them to launch massively destructive attacks on this country, the American public will respond with an enormous outpouring of approval of his actions, as if to prove that in our political system no failure goes unrewarded. Bertrand Russell long ago stated the underlying condition for this sort of perverse public reaction when he remarked that "neither a man nor a crowd nor a nation can be trusted to act humanely or to think sanely under the influence of a great fear."[5] Indeed, the fundamental condition of the entire process by which the government leads people to their own destruction is widespread public fear, which causes people to put aside their normal distrust of the state and to turn to it, especially to its chief, as a child turns to a parent, for security and reassurance that everything will be OK if only people do as they are told.

Not only did the events of September 11, 2001, cause the American public to look more favorably on the president as a person, as a president, and as the principal architect of U.S. foreign policy, but those events also apparently caused the public to express more trust in the federal government in general in its handling of *both* international and domestic matters. In the Gallup poll of

---

5. Bertrand Russell, "An Outline of Intellectual Rubbish," 1943, at http://www.scribd .com/doc/11387694/An-Outline-of-Intellectual-Rubbish-Bertrand-Russell.

September 7–10, 2001, 68 percent of the respondents expressed "a great deal" or a "fair amount" of trust and confidence in the government's handling of international problems, whereas 31 percent expressed "not very much" or "none at all," which implied an opinion balance of +37 percent (68 percent minus 31 percent). A month later, in the poll conducted during October 11–14, this opinion balance had risen to +67 percent (83 minus 16), almost doubling. The public's perversely increased trust in the government had also spilled inexplicably onto its handling of domestic problems, increasing this opinion balance from +21 percent (60 minus 39) in the early September poll to +56 percent (77 minus 21) in the October poll.

A final measure of public opinion, "trust in Washington to do what is right," which is normally a fairly stable indicator, also rose in an unusual way owing to 9/11. In the Gallup poll of July 6–9, 2000, 42 percent of the respondents expressed confidence that the government will do what is right "just about always" or "most of the time," whereas 58 percent responded "only some of the time" or "never," which implies an opinion balance of –16 percent. When the pollsters next asked this question, in October 5–6, 2001, however, the opinion balance had risen to +21 percent (60 minus 39), indicating a complete turnaround toward greater trust than distrust in government.

At the time of these events, as I considered everything that was going on, I was dismayed by what seemed to me to be a wholly unwarranted public stampede into the protective arms of the federal government—the same government that had been robbing and abusing most of the people in countless ways for as long as they could remember. Hardly anyone asked whether the government's actions abroad might actually have provoked the 9/11 attacks—of course, most were so ignorant of those actions that they had no inkling of how the government might have created such a provocation. Many people seemed consumed by a combination of fear and rage that manifested itself in a desire to "nuke" someone, anyone, who might have had something to do with the attacks. Standards of proof fell precipitously. People didn't want careful investigation; they didn't want to "get to the bottom" of what had happened. Instead, they wanted action, and in particular they wanted the government to "strike back" immediately at any and all plausible targets.

In searching for the cause of this tremendous, rationally unjustified "rallying 'round the flag," we do not have far to go. Such public reactions are always driven by a combination of fear, ignorance, and uncertainty against a background of intense jingoistic nationalism, a popular culture predisposed toward violence, and a general inability to distinguish between the state and the people at large. Because the government ceaselessly sings the siren song, relentlessly propagandizing the public to look upon it as their protector—such alleged protection being the principal excuse for its routinely robbing them and violating their natural rights—and because the mass media incessantly magnify and spread the government's propaganda, we can scarcely be surprised if that propaganda turns out to have entered deeply into many people's thinking, especially when they are in a state of near panic. Unable to think clearly in an informed way, most people fall back on a childlike us-against-them style of understanding the perceived threat and what should be done about it.

If any resistance should arise to the rulers' war making, the state has a time-tested means of disposing of the resisters. Perhaps the classic description of this tactic was given by the Nazi bigwig Hermann Göring when he was being held in prison during the trials at Nuremberg in 1946. This account comes to us from Gustave M. Gilbert, the German-speaking prison psychologist who had free access to all of the prisoners during the trials and talked to them frequently in private. On the evening of April 18, 1946, Gilbert visited Göring in his cell, and he later described their conversation as follows:

> We got around to the subject of war again and I said that, contrary to his attitude, I did not think that the common people are very thankful for leaders who bring them war and destruction.
>
> "Why, of course, the *people* don't want war," Goering shrugged. "Why would some poor slob on a farm want to risk his life in a war when the best that he can get out of it is to come back to his farm in one piece. Naturally, the common people don't want war; neither in Russia nor in England nor in America, nor for that matter in Germany. That is understood. But, after all, it is the *leaders* of the country who determine the policy and it is always a simple matter to drag the people along, whether it is a democracy or a fascist dictatorship or a Parliament or a Communist dictatorship."
>
> "There is one difference," I pointed out. "In a democracy the people have some say in the matter through their elected representatives, and in the United States only Congress can declare war."

"Oh, that is all well and good, but, voice or no voice, the people can always be brought to the bidding of the leaders. That is easy. All you have to do is tell them they are being attacked and denounce the pacifists for lack of patriotism and exposing the country to danger. It works the same way in any country."[6]

Göring was right, and matters have only become worse in this regard during the past sixty-five years. Under the postwar regime in the United States, of course, Congress never declares war—it has made no such declaration since June 5, 1942, when it declared war on Romania, Bulgaria, and Hungary—and the president now wages war solely at his own pleasure and caprice, as if he were Caesar.

"Dragging the people along," as Göring put it, remains as easy as ever because, as we have seen, an initial incident, even one the government itself has provoked or trumped up, invariably causes the masses to rally 'round the flag. We have also seen, however, that the ardent enthusiasm and mindless support for the government's war making begins to erode soon afterward. But when the people increasingly come to their senses, as casualties and other costs accumulate and as bits and pieces of the truth seep out, why does the system not revert to the status quo ante bellum?

• • •

The answer is that actions taken during the early days of the crisis, when the government responds practically without opposition to the public's fear and desire for retribution by vastly expanding its powers (Stage II of the ratchet phenomenon), take the form of political, legal, and institutional changes that set precedents or become so deeply embedded that not all of them are abandoned during the postcrisis stage of incomplete retrenchment (Stage IV of the ratchet phenomenon).

For example, soon after the Pearl Harbor attack, the government enacted the First War Powers Act (December 18, 1941) and the Second War Powers Act (March 27, 1942). These sweeping delegations empowered the president to rearrange the executive branch as he pleased, gave him a free hand to contract with

---

6. G. M. Gilbert, *Nuremberg Diary* (New York: Da Capo Press, [1947] 1995), 278–79.

munitions suppliers almost as he pleased, and gave him far-reaching control over international financial transactions and censorship power over all communications between the United States and *any* foreign country; they expanded the government's powers to seize private property for war purposes, empowered the president to set priorities for deliveries of designated goods and services, and gave the president effectively unrestrained power over resource allocation in the domestic economy, a power he delegated to the War Production Board under his direct oversight. Wielding all this authority, the president and his lieutenants became in effect central planners of a command economy for the duration of the war.[7]

Just six weeks after the 9/11 attacks, the government similarly enacted the USA PATRIOT Act, which greatly trenched on civil liberties and long-established rights, effectively demolished the Fourth Amendment, and gave a mighty boost to the U.S. police state. Other measures moving in the same direction followed soon afterward, including nationalization of the airline-security industry and creation of the bureaucratic monstrosity known as the Department of Homeland Security, an organization as menacing in its ideological underpinnings as it is feckless, insulting, and absurd in its day-to-day operations.[8]

Once the government has expanded greatly at the outset of a war or other crisis and then employed its new powers for an extended period, getting rid of all of the new weapons in the government's arsenal of power is virtually impossible even when the emergency ends and people clamor for a return to normal arrangements. Therefore, many of the crisis measures become permanent parts of the government's apparatus for dominating and robbing those outside the political class.

Wartime organizations may be retained to carry out new functions, as, for example, the War Finance Corporation of World War I was kept going for six years after the war, providing subsidized credit to exporters, agricultural cooperatives, and rural banks. After finally having been discontinued in 1925, it was revived in 1932 as the Reconstruction Finance Corporation (RFC), a huge

---

7. Robert Higgs, *Crisis and Leviathan: Critical Episodes in the Growth of American Government* (New York: Oxford University Press, 1987), 196–236.
8. Robert Higgs, *Resurgence of the Warfare State: The Crisis Since 9/11* (Oakland, Calif.: The Independent Institute, 2005).

lender to politically favored railroads, banks, and insurance companies during the Depression and later the government's chief agency for financing a variety of military-industrial undertakings during World War II. Retained after 1945, the RFC continued to make subsidized loans to privileged borrowers until it sank in a storm of scandal in 1953, only to be replaced—as a political quid pro quo— by a similarly egregious agency, the Small Business Administration, which has continued its politically driven misallocation of taxpayer money ever since.[9]

Cases such as that of the War Finance Corporation and its direct descendants exemplify how national emergency solidifies so-called iron triangles: alliances of government bureaucrats, congressional overseers, and privileged private-sector beneficiaries. These arrangements are called "iron" because they are so difficult to break. Their beneficiaries have great incentive to fight for the retention and even for the expansion of the triangle's activities, whereas the general public rarely has much incentive to fight against them, even when it is aware of them, because the public burden per capita is normally too small to justify anyone's expenditure of much time or effort in the requisite politicking.

Under modern conditions, high wartime taxes always stick to some extent, leaving the amount of the government's plunder much greater after the war than it was before the war. In the present so-called war on terror, the government has partially concealed this increased seizure of private property by running up the national debt rather than by jacking up ordinary tax rates or imposing new kinds of taxes, but this financial trick does not alter the raw fact that the government has been using more of the people's resources for its own purposes, as shown by the rapid run-up of its spending, leaving the public on the hook to pay the increased interest and eventually to repay the principal or to suffer the consequences if the government should attempt in effect to repudiate its obligations to creditors by inflating the money stock. During the George W. Bush administration, Treasury debt held by the public grew from $3.3 trillion (end of fiscal year 2001) to $7.5 trillion (end of fiscal year 2009), or by about 127 percent in only eight years.[10]

---

9. Robert Higgs, "From Wartime Expedient to Permanent Pork Barrel: WFC to RFC to SBA," *The Freeman* 54 (October 2004), 30–31.

10. *Budget of the United States Government: Historical Tables Fiscal Year 2011*, table 7.1, at http://www.gpoaccess.gov/usbudget/fy11/hist.html.

During the Great Depression, governments at every level greatly increased their tax revenues by increasing tax rates and by imposing new kinds of taxes—for example, state and local sales taxes, a federal undistributed-profits tax, and a Social Security tax on wages and salaries. In fiscal year 1940, with the Depression still lingering, the federal government collected 73 percent more total revenue than it had in the prosperous year 1927. Federal taxes relative to gross national product doubled between 1933 and 1940.[11]

Apart from the financial legacies that exacerbate the government's burden on the public, national emergencies leave institutional legacies of various kinds that enhance government power at the expense of the people's liberties. The rent controls of World War II, for example, never ended in New York City. For almost seventy years, they have denied landlords and tenants the liberty to contract on any mutually agreeable terms, and they have created incentives that foster the avoidance of maintenance for rented apartments and discourage the construction of the new structures that would be built if the housing market were free of these war-borne fetters. The institutional legacies of the New Deal, of course, are legion even now, more than seventy years after FDR's political momentum petered out: a vast system of agribusiness subsidies; intricate regulations of financial markets, union–management relations, and financial intermediaries; federal insurance of bank deposits, home mortgages, and other financial liabilities; direct federal involvement in electricity production and distribution—the list goes on and on.[12]

Perhaps most important, crisis has effects on the dominant ideology that work in favor of long-lasting government power and the permanent reduction of public liberties. During wartime or other crises, governments take many actions that would be more or less unthinkable in a reasonably free society during normal times because people would not tolerate them. Having tolerated them during a national emergency, however, people may come to regard them not only as permanently tolerable, but even as desirable. For example, nearly everything the U.S. government did during the Great Depression had an obvious wartime

11. *Budget of the United States Government,* table 1.2; U.S. Bureau of the Census, *Historical Statistics of the United States, Colonial Times to 1970* (Washington, D.C.: U.S. Government Printing Office, 1975), 1104–5.
12. Higgs, *Crisis and Leviathan,* 189–95.

precedent in the Great War. President Herbert Hoover declared, "We used such emergency powers to win the war; we can use them to fight the depression."[13] Everything from the Depression-era agricultural price controls to the industrial cartelization program, the public-housing program, the schemes to control oil and coal prices, the tax hikes, and the promotion of labor unionization had a precedent during 1917–18. Many of these war-inspired public policies then became permanent after their reinstitution in the 1930s. The military-industrial complex created from 1940 to 1945 similarly persisted after World War II ended. People can get used to almost anything, especially if it has a plausible justification. War and other great crises managed by government soften up formerly free people and habituate them to government controls and abuses that they would resist except for the controls' alleged emergency necessity. In this way, government emergency measures change the very character of once-free people by breaking down their will to be free and their determination to resist homegrown tyranny.

It is important to appreciate that all the effects on freedom that I have been discussing occur regardless of the rationale for the war or other crisis intervention itself. One may regard a war, for example, as ever so necessary and desirable or not, yet these effects will occur in any event. The logic of a government at war asserts itself in more or less the same fashion regardless of the war's provocation and purpose because every major war requires the government to take a much bigger bite out of the people's resources quickly, and it cannot do so successfully without suppressing many normal liberties and rights, especially those that might be exercised to obstruct the government's wartime programs and policies or to persuade people to resist the war or to demand its discontinuation or settlement. Hence, as Göring noted, the government and its supporters vigorously denounce all those who stand in the way of war as traitors, and the state encourages the masses to act as amateur G-men, identifying "disloyal" citizens, hounding them into buckling under, and reporting them to government officials. Great peacetime initiatives operate similarly. Many historians have noted the parallels between the U.S. government's intimidating public efforts to entice or browbeat

---

13. Quoted in Murray N. Rothbard, *America's Great Depression*, 5th ed. (Auburn, Ala.: Ludwig von Mises Institute, 2000), 323.

people into cooperation with the National Recovery Administration and the Nazi extravaganzas being staged in Germany at the same time.

Nowadays, for example, the government frequently encourages all of us to report any "suspicious" persons or actions to the police or the FBI, ostensibly to prevent terrorism. Needless to say, no free society can exist when everyone in effect has enlisted as a government informant, especially when the character of the threatening persons and actions is so vague that it is bound to give rise to abuses. People are not uncommonly now reported for nothing more than looking like an Arab or for speaking a "strange" language to "strange-looking" companions. This insidious enlistment of informants, so reminiscent of the atrocious American Protective League during World War I, is turning our once-open society into a sort of East Germany redux. Horror stories abound of perfectly innocent persons taken into custody for interrogation or worse.

While the government promotes mindless support of its war making and may induce a sort of patriotic hysteria in the most mentally fragile personalities, many citizens swing into action as faux patriots on strictly opportunistic grounds. War contractors, for example, position themselves to make a killing off of the actual killing; moreover, they parlay their wartime business as government suppliers into profitable postwar business that long outlives the war itself. The aircraft companies that suddenly profited so greatly during World War II, for example, became permanent, highly successful feeders at the government's trough, where some of them are feasting lavishly even now, the post-2001 military buildup having proved a godsend for them and a boon to their stockholders. Other people simply want a cushy job in the government's expanded wartime bureaucracy.

The so-called war on terror has given rise to a huge industry that has emerged almost from scratch during the past decade. According to a 2006 *Forbes* report, the Department of Homeland Security and its predecessor agencies paid private contractors at least $130 billion after 9/11, and other federal agencies spent a comparable amount. Thus, besides the *military*-industrial-congressional complex, we now have a parallel *security*-industrial-congressional complex. Between 1999 and 2006, the number of federal homeland-security contractors increased from 9 to 33,890 companies, and a multi-billion-dollar industry selling security-related goods and services emerged complete with specialized newsletters, magazines, Web sites, consultants, trade shows, job-placement services, and a veritable army of lobbyists working around the clock to widen the river of money that flows to these opportunists.[14] As Paul Harris writes, "America is in the grip of a business based on fear."[15] The last thing these vultures want, of course, is an abatement of the perceived terrorist threat, and we can count on them to hype any signs of an increase in such threats and, of course, to crowd the trough, happily slurping the taxpayers' money.

What chance does peace have when millions of well-heeled, politically connected opportunists of all stripes depend on the continuation of a state of war for their personal financial success? For members of Congress, the Department of Homeland Security quickly became the most magnificent dispenser of pork and patronage to come along in decades. Everyone is happy here, except for the beleaguered ordinary citizens, whose pockets are being picked and whose liberties are being overridden by politicians and private-sector predators with utter contempt for the people's intelligence and rights. Yet as long as the people continue to be consumed by fear and to fall for the age-old swindle that the government seeks only to protect them, these abuses will never end.

Along the U.S. Gulf Coast after September 2005, a legion of opportunists similarly rushed onto the scene to take advantage of the unprecedented sums of federal money pouring into the area in the guise of financing recovery from the damage wreaked by hurricanes Katrina and Rita. Bank accounts were stuffed with this loot, to be sure, but little in the way of genuine recovery and reconstruction came from it. Never mind: in the immortal words of President Bush, "Brownie, you're doin' a heck of a job." The ridiculous Brownie was subsequently sacked as the head of the Federal Emergency Management Agency, of course, but the "heck of a job" goes on as before, all at taxpayer expense and at great profit for the corporatist cronies, political favorites, and other privileged parties who are appropriating the people's money after it has been duly laundered through the federal treasury.

• • •

---

14. Robert Higgs, "The Security-Industrial-Congressional Complex (SICC)," LewRockwell.com, October 19, 2006, at http://www.lewrockwell.com/higgs/higgs50.html.
15. Paul Harris, "How US Merchants of Fear Sparked a $130 bn Bonanza," *The Observer*, September 10, 2006, at http://www.guardian.co.uk/world/2006/sep/10/september11.usa.

Recall Margaret Atwood's poem "Siren Song," with which I opened this essay. It begins:

> This is the one song everyone
> would like to learn: the song
> that is irresistible:
> the song that forces men
> to leap overboard in squadrons
> even though they see the beached skulls.

And the poem ends, "Alas / it is a boring song / but it works every time."

In the present regard, it works every time because the people falsely believe that those who sing it are their protectors rather than their exploiters. Until people learn to disregard the state's siren song of beneficence and protection, they will continue to suffer and die as victims of the state's wars, foreign and domestic. People yearn for security, and they look to the state to provide it, but they are calling on a wolf to guard the sheep. The state cannot refrain from crime because it is an inherently criminal enterprise, living by robbery (which it calls taxation) and retaining its turf by murder (which it calls law enforcement) or, if need be, by mass murder (which it calls war). Constantly singing the siren song, it seduces the people by giving back to them a portion of what it has previously extorted from them and by ceaselessly claiming to protect them from all manner of threats to their lives, liberties, property, and even self-esteem. If it protects them at all, however, it does so only as a shepherd protects his captive flock: not because he recognizes and respects the sheep's natural rights, but only to keep them unmolested in his sole possession and control until he finds it expedient to shear or slaughter them.

A peaceful state is an impossibility. Even a state that refrains from fighting foreigners goes on fighting its own subjects continuously to keep them under its control and to suppress competitors who might try to break into the domain of its protection racket. The people cry out for security, yet they will not take responsibility for their own protection, and, like the mariners of Greek mythology, they leap overboard immediately in response to the state's siren song.

According to the biblical account, after the Israelites had fled from their captivity in Egypt, they made do for centuries with only judges, yet they were not satisfied, and they eventually demanded a king, crying out: "We will have a king over us; That we also may be like all the nations; and that our king may judge us, and go out before us, and fight our battles" (1 Samuel 8:19–20). They got a king, all right, just as we Americans have embraced one of our own, though we call ours a president. As the prophet Samuel had warned, however, the Israelites were no better off for having a king: King Saul only led them from one slaughter to another (1 Samuel 14:47–48). Our rulers have likewise led us from one unnecessary slaughter to the next, and, to make matters worse, they have exploited each such occasion to fasten their chains around us more tightly. Like the ancient Israelites, we Americans shall never have real, lasting peace as long as we give our allegiance to a wicked and destructive king—that is, to the whole conglomeration of institutionalized exploiters and murderers we know as the state.

6

A Dozen Dangerous Presumptions
of Crisis Policymaking

CONGRESS AND THE PRESIDENT have adopted many critically important government policies in great haste during brief periods of perceived national emergency. During the first "hundred days" of the Franklin D. Roosevelt administration in the spring of 1933, for example, the government abandoned the gold standard, enacted a system of wide-ranging controls, taxes, and subsidies in agriculture, and set in motion a plan to cartelize the nation's manufacturing industries. In 2001, the USA PATRIOT Act was enacted in a rush even though no member of Congress had read it in its entirety. Since September 2008, the government and the Federal Reserve System have implemented a rapid-fire series of bailouts, loans, "stimulus" spending programs, and partial or complete takeovers of big banks and other large firms, acting at each step in great haste.

Any government policymaking on a large scale or in regard to a critical issue entails serious risks, but crisis policymaking stands apart from the more deliberate process through which new legislation is usually enacted or new regulatory measures are usually put into effect. Because formal institutional changes, however hastily adopted, have a strong tendency to become entrenched, continuing to operate for many years and in some cases for decades or longer, crisis policymaking has played an important part in fostering the long-term growth of government through a ratchet effect in which "temporary" actions permanently expand the government's size, scope, or power.

It therefore behooves us to understand better the typical presumptions that give crisis policymaking its potency. The twelve propositions given here express some of the ideas that are advanced again and again in connection with episodes of quick, fear-driven policymaking—events whose long-term consequences are often counterproductive.

1. Nothing like the present situation has ever happened before. If the existing crisis were seen as simply the latest incident in a series of similar crises, policymakers and the public would be more inclined to relax, appreciating that such rapids have been navigated successfully in the past and will be navigated successfully on this occasion, too. Fears would be relieved. Exaggerated doomsday scenarios would be dismissed as overwrought and implausible. Such relaxation, however, would ill serve the sponsors of extraordinary government measures, regardless of their motives for seeking adoption of these measures. Fear is a great motivator, so the proponents of expanded government action have an incentive to represent the current situation as unprecedented and therefore as uniquely menacing unless the government intervenes forcefully to save the day.

2. Unless the government intervenes, the situation will get worse and worse. Crisis always presents some sort of worsening of something: the economy's output has fallen; the price level has risen greatly; the country has been attacked by foreigners. If such untoward developments were seen as having occurred in a one-off manner, then people might be content to stick with the institutional status quo. If, however, people project the recent changes forward, imagining that adverse events will continue to occur and possibly to gather strength as they continue, then they will object to a "do nothing" response, reasoning that "something must be done" lest the course of events eventuate in an utterly ruinous situation.

To speed a huge, complex "antiterrorism" bill through Congress in 2001, George W. Bush invoked the specter of another terrorist attack. Barack Obama, invoking the specter of economic collapse, rushed through Congress early in 2009 the huge American Recovery and Reinvestment Act before any legislator had digested it. In a February 5 op-ed in the *Washington Post,* he wrote, "If nothing is done . . . our nation will sink deeper into a crisis that, at some point, we may not be able to reverse."[1] At a February 9 press conference, he

---

1. Barack Obama, "The Action Americans Need," *Washington Post,* February 5, 2009.

said, "[A] failure to act will only deepen this crisis" and "could turn a crisis into a catastrophe."[2]

3. Today is all important; we must act immediately. In his first inaugural address, Franklin D. Roosevelt declared, "This Nation asks for action, and action now." He then proceeded directly to speak of the most terrifying problem of the day, mass unemployment. "Our greatest primary task is to put people to work. . . . It can be accomplished in part by direct recruiting by the Government itself, *treating the task as we would treat the emergency of a war,* but at the same time, through this employment, accomplishing greatly needed projects to stimulate and reorganize the use of our natural resources." In any event, "The people . . . want direct, vigorous action."[3]

Barack Obama similarly declared not long after taking office, "The situation is getting worse. We have to act and act now to break the momentum of this recession."[4] "Doing nothing is not an option," he said in Elkhart, Indiana, on February 9. "The situation we face could not be more serious," and "we can't afford to wait."[5] In the February 5 op-ed, listing a series of objectives he claimed the pending legislation would achieve, he began four successive paragraphs with the words "now is the time to . . . ."[6]

4. Government officials know or can quickly discover how to remedy the problem. All government policies adopted to meet a crisis presume that the government knows how to effect the rescue it seeks. If the crisis arises from an attack by foreigners, the government purports to know how to mount military countermeasures that will defeat or disable the enemy. If the crisis consists of economic malfunctions, the government purports to know how to alter its spending, taxing, or regulation so that the economy will be restored to sound operation. These presumptions are in general counterfactual.

---

2. Quoted in Jacob Sullum, "Fear Is His Friend," *Reasononline,* February 11, 2009, at http://www.reason.com/news/.

3. "Franklin D. Roosevelt, First Inaugural Address, Saturday, March 4, 1933," at http://www.bartleby.com/124/pres49.html, emphasis added.

4. Quoted in Tom Baldwin, "Barack Obama Gets to Work on 'Very Sick' US Economy," *The Times Online,* January 6, 2009, at http://www.timesonline.co.uk/tol/news/world/us_and_americas/us_elections/article5454714.ece.

5. Quoted in Sullum, "Fear Is His Friend."

6. Obama, "The Action Americans Need."

The government may sometimes admit, as in the early New Deal, that it does not know exactly how to proceed, yet it maintains that "doing something" is better than doing nothing. Roosevelt maintained that the government ought to try something and, if that measure failed, then try something else. Thus, ignorant flailing about—on the assumption that "doing something" has no costs, adverse effects, or untoward long-term consequences—has been touted as a virtue, and, indeed, many members of the public, no more expert than the government itself, have agreed that the government ought to "try something."

5. **We may safely rely on the establishment and on its insiders for expertise in this crisis.** As a common first step in reacting to a crisis, the government often assembles a council of experts or some such group of wise men and women. These experts are invariably drawn from the government itself and from groups with whom the government maintains cozy relations. The experts frequently include those who had responsibility for carrying out the government policies that contributed to the occurrence of the crisis in the first place. Thus, no matter how ill fated monetary policy may have been, the government will call on the secretary of the Treasury and the head of the Federal Reserve System to decide, perhaps along with others, what should be done next. In this constricted circle, the range of possible future actions the government might take is almost always no wider than the range of actions taken in the past. Hence, the "experts" are subject to repeating the same errors time and again.

6. **We may trust the government to act responsibly and effectively on the basis of the expertise they command.** The public looks to government officials and their assembled "wise men" to act in the public interest and to organize their actions in an effective manner. If the policymakers lack the requisite knowledge, then such trust is bound to be misplaced because no matter now responsible the policymakers may try to be, they simply don't know what they are doing. If they do have the requisite expertise, however, they may still fail to act on it because of their political, ideological, or material interests and connections. The public tends to think of crises as akin to mechanical problems—the car's engine is not running, and policymakers need to give it a "jump start." Crises, however, are rarely so simple. They more often involve far-reaching relationships among many individuals, groups, and nations, and the lack of productive coordination that the crisis presents can seldom be restored by simple policy actions such as "the government ought to double its spending and rely on borrowed funds to cover

its budget deficit." Complex political, social, and economic breakdowns rarely take a form subject to easy treatment by activist policymakers (though many of them can take care of themselves if only policymakers stand aside from them).

7. The clear benefits of quick government action may be assumed to outweigh its costs and its actual or potential negative consequences. Crisis decision making is not characterized by careful attempts to justify actions on a benefit-cost basis. If the situation is dire, policymakers and many members of the public simply assume that a policy with positive net benefits may be adopted. Little basis exists for this assumption. Even in a crisis, the government may take many actions whose costs and risks greatly outweigh any benefit they may bring. The potential is great for focusing on benefits that are immediate and visible while disregarding costs that are delayed and less easily perceived. Thus, policymakers are likely to plunge almost blindly ahead where more calculating angels fear to tread.

8. Fact finding, deliberation, study, and debate are too time consuming and must be forgone in favor of immediate action. In April 1932, a year before the momentous explosion of New Deal measures after Roosevelt took office, Felix Frankfurter complained in a letter to Walter Lippmann that "one measure after another has been . . . hurriedly concocted. . . . [T]hey have been denominated emergency efforts, and any plea for deliberation, for detailed discussion, for exploration of alternatives has been regarded as obstructive or doctrinaire or both."[7] The events of the spring 1933 congressional session raised all of these attributes by an order of magnitude.

President Obama likewise recently declared that enough debate had occurred on the massive "stimulus" package even though it had been rushed through both houses of Congress, neither of which had paused to hold hearings on it. "We can't posture and bicker. Endless delay and paralysis in Washington in the face of this crisis will only bring deepening disaster."[8]

9. Existing structures and incumbent firms must be preserved; new structures and firms are unthinkable. Existing officeholders, bureaucrats, firm

---

7. Quoted in Larry G. Gerber, *The Limits of Liberalism: Josephus Daniels, Henry Stimson, Bernard Baruch, Donald Richberg, Felix Frankfurter, and the Development of the Modern American Political Economy* (New York: New York University Press, 1983), 267–68.
8. Quoted in Sullum, "Fear Is His Friend."

managers, and owners have a decisive political advantage over possible alternative holders of their positions ("new entrants"). Hence, the overriding theme in any crisis is that current politicians and capitalists must be preserved—propped up, bailed out, subsidized, or whatever it takes to save them and their present organizations. In truth, however, the best way to deal with some crises is by getting rid of the persons and organizations that helped to bring them on. Bankruptcy, for example, is not the end of the world, but simply the end of existing stockholders. If a company still possesses valuable assets, they will be transferred to new and presumably more competent managers.

10. If a policy is not getting the results its proponents expected it to get, more money should be poured into it until it finally "works." This presumption receives application to government policies in general, not simply to crisis policies in particular, but it gains force during a national emergency, when getting results is regarded as especially imperative. By the time Barack Obama became president, the U.S. Treasury and the Fed had made commitments for trillions of dollars in loans, capital infusions, loan guarantees, and other purposes. Yet the economy continued to sink. The president and his senior advisers did not conclude that these measures had failed, but only that they had been too timid. Thus, President Obama told reporters that after Japan's bust in the early 1990s, the Japanese government "did not act boldly or swiftly enough," even though it spent trillions of dollars on construction projects. Likewise, Treasury Secretary Timothy Geithner concluded from his study of the Japanese stagnation that "spending must come in quick, massive doses, and be continued until recovery takes firm root."[9]

11. We must not be deterred by the accumulation of public debt; there is no practical limit to how much the government may safely borrow. Political officeholders prefer to finance their spending by borrowing rather than taxing, if possible. That way, the public does not feel so dispossessed and therefore is less inclined to oppose the spending programs. In a national emergency, the officeholders' preference for deficit finance comes even more boldly to the fore, and throughout history governments have tended to borrow heavily to pay for major wars. With the dawning of the Age of Keynes, deficit financing during a recession acquired an ostensible intellectual rationale, magnifying whatever

---

9. Both Obama and Geithner quoted in Sullum, "Fear Is His Friend."

inclinations the politicians already possessed. At present, the public debt is rising at an unprecedented rate, yet few people raise serious objections to the government's spending programs on this ground. Virtually everyone who matters politically is content to rely on what I call "vulgar Keynesianism"—or at least to pretend to do so.

12. The occasion demands that policymakers put aside partisan or strictly political maneuvering and instead act entirely in the general public interest, and we can expect them to act accordingly. After Woodrow Wilson had sought and gained a congressional declaration of war in 1917, he declared that "politics is adjourned." By this expression, he sought to convey the idea that he would henceforth abstain from the usual partisan maneuvering and devote himself to prosecution of the war in the most effective way and that, he hoped, others would do the same. Whether his announcement of the adjournment was sincere or merely an attempt to paint those who disagreed with his war policies as partisan obstructionists, we do not know. We do know, however, that partisan political actions did not cease on either side.[10]

In a similar way, President Obama recently declared: "We are in one of those periods in American history where we don't have Republican or Democratic problems, we have American problems. My commitment as the incoming president is going to be to reach out across the aisle to both chambers to listen and not just talk, to not just try to dictate but try to create a partnership. . . . [W]e're . . . not going to get bogged down by old-style politics on either side."[11] A month later he reiterated this idea, denouncing "the same old partisan gridlock that stands in the way of action while our economy continues to slide" and promising, "We can place good ideas ahead of old ideological battles, and a sense of purpose above the same narrow partisanship."[12] Even as he made this declaration, however, partisan maneuvering continued as usual on both sides in Congress.

Politics cannot be put aside. Politics is what politicians and political interest groups do. Partisanship is inevitable as political actors who seek conflicting ends struggle for maximum control of the government.

---

10. Seward W. Livermore, *Politics Is Adjourned: Woodrow Wilson and the War Congress, 1916–1918* (Middletown, Conn.: Wesleyan University Press, 1966).
11. Quoted in Baldwin, "Barack Obama Gets to Work."
12. Obama, "The Action Americans Need."

7

The Political Economy
of Crisis Opportunism

IN PERSONAL LIFE, no one relishes a crisis, but in political life many people pray for a crisis as drought-stricken farmers pray for rain. For these people, a societal crisis promises to bring not extraordinary difficulties, dangers, and challenges, but rather, as many now frankly admit, enlarged opportunities. President Barack Obama's chief of staff Rahm Emanuel made no attempt to conceal his appreciation of such latent promise when he averred recently, "You never want a serious crisis to go to waste. . . . [T]his crisis provides the opportunity for us to do things that you could not do before."[1] My first task here is to explain the sense in which a crisis creates new opportunities for political actors and why it does so.

Politicians are not, however, the only ones who perceive opportunity in a crisis. Other types of actors also spring forth to exploit the economic, social, and political changes that crisis brings. These opportunists include ideologues who have previously failed to augment their ranks or to realize their programmatic objectives, seekers of economic privilege who have previously found themselves stymied by public hostility or partisan political opposition, and militarists who see a new opening to promote their favorite foreign adventures and who sometimes tout military spending as a cure for economic malaise and overseas interventions as a tonic for depressed public morale and an avenue to "national greatness." My second task here is both to clarify how these various opportunists

---

1. Quoted in Charles Krauthammer, "Deception at Core of Obama Plans," *Real Clear Politics,* March 6, 2009, at http://www.realclearpolitics.com/articles/2009/03/a_dishonest
_gimmicky_budget.html.

seek to exploit a crisis for the achievement of their particular ends and to identify the conditions that promote or impede their designs.

Anyone who has followed the news in recent years can appreciate the importance of understanding the political economy of crisis opportunism. Since the financial crisis came to a head in the summer of 2008, the nation—and, to a large extent, the whole world—has been buffeted by a tempest of unprecedented government measures ostensibly intended to save large financial firms from bankruptcy; to assist homeowners, businesses, and others affected by the credit stringency, the housing bust, and the recession; and to brake and reverse the overall economic decline with "stimulus" spending. By the end of November 2008, the government (including the Federal Reserve System) had already committed $8.5 trillion to an assortment of financial-assistance measures, "including loans and loan guarantees, asset purchases, equity investments in financial companies, tax breaks for banks, help for struggling homeowners and a currency stabilization fund."[2] The snowball continued to roll, becoming ever larger during the following six months. On June 15, 2009, the *Wall Street Journal* reported:

> Since the onset of the financial crisis nine months ago, the government has become the nation's biggest mortgage lender, guaranteed nearly $3 trillion in money-market mutual-fund assets, commandeered and restructured two car companies, taken equity stakes in nearly 600 banks, lent more than $300 billion to blue-chip companies, supported the life-insurance industry and become a credit source for buyers of cars, tractors and even weapons for hunting.
>
> . . . Government spending as a share of the economy has climbed to levels not seen since World War II. The geyser of money has turned Washington into an essential destination for more and more businesses. Spending on lobbying is up, as are luxury hotel bookings in the capital.[3]

We may debate whether the actual economic conditions warranted such extreme government reactions, but there is little doubt that government officials,

---

2. Kathleen Pender, "Government Bailout Hits $8.5 Trillion," *San Francisco Chronicle*, November 26, 2008.
3. Bob Davis and Jon Hilsenrath, "Federal Intervention Pits 'Gets' vs. 'Get-Nots,'" *Wall Street Journal*, June 15, 2009.

politicians, media commentators, and substantial elements of the public have viewed the economic events of recent years as a national emergency. Thus, in the ominous meaning of the proverbial Chinese curse, we are indeed living in "interesting times." In this crisis, it behooves us more than ever to understand the theory and the historical evidence that bear on the political economy of crisis opportunism. Our subject rises far above the realm of idle intellectual curiosity. Indeed, it has the greatest practical importance for the preservation of our prosperity and our liberties.

Normality Versus Crisis

During normal times in a modern representative democracy, political life involves much pulling and hauling with relatively little to show for all the efforts. Countless individuals and interest groups seek to attain their political ends, but the legislature can attend to relatively few of these matters at the same time, and many proposals must perforce be dismissed or tabled for the time being. Moreover, as a rule (cribbed from Newton's Third Law of Motion), for every political action there is an equal and opposite reaction. Virtually every proposal of substantial consequence has both organized supporters and organized opponents, and in the great majority of cases the opponents are strong enough to block a proposal's adoption or to weaken it substantially.

It's not as though nothing gets done, however. Indeed, even a "do-nothing" Congress may enact hundreds of bills in a session; the regulatory agencies churn out several thousand new or revised regulations each year; and the courts decide a multitude of cases. But nearly all of these actions are fairly inconsequential. The public swallows them without choking, if indeed it has any awareness of them. Lawyers rewrite some contracts; payroll administrators and accountants tweak their software. Life goes on—altered, to be sure, but not altered greatly. As Thomas Jefferson remarked, "The natural progress of things is for liberty to yield and government to gain ground,"[4] but in normal times liberty does not yield greatly, and government does not gain much ground.

---

4. Thomas Jefferson to Edward Carrington, August 4, 1787, in *The Jeffersonian Cyclopedia* (New York: Funk and Wagnells, 1900), entry no. 4683.

We may liken Jefferson's "natural progress of things" to a river's current, which flows invariably toward the sea. Most of the time this current is slow and predictable, and the river does not overflow its banks. The trees that loggers cut, trim, and shove into the river for transportation downstream we may liken to the proposals and cases that interested parties push onto the legislature, the regulatory agencies, and the courts. The floating logs are usually so numerous that when the river's current and water level are normal, logjams form, impeding the passage of nearly all the logs. One may occasionally break away and continue downstream, or the loggers, risking life and limb, may go onto the floating jumble and undertake to loosen the mass of logs and set some of them free to continue downstream.

In politics, the natural flow consists of an ideological current. Especially since the ascendancy of progressivism a century ago, Americans (as well as western Europeans and many others) have viewed the government as the institution of first resort for the solution of perceived social and economic problems. This progressive inclination, however, is not the same as a yearning for totalitarianism. Most people, including progressives, continue to believe that in normal times the government should be limited, though they disagree about where the limits should be placed. People are normally disposed to appreciate that a private sphere ought to be preserved and that, especially in economic life, the invisible hand of market relations can accomplish much good and ought not to be interfered with by the visible hand of the state.

A crisis, however, alters the fundamental conditions of political life. Like a river suddenly swollen by the collapse of an upstream dam, the ideological current becomes bloated by the public's fear of impending dangers and its heightened uncertainty about future developments. Bewildered people turn to the government to resolve the situation, demanding that government officials "do something" to repair the damage already done and to prevent further harm. The public's cry, for the most part, is not for any particular government action; in truth, few have a definite idea of what should be done. Nevertheless, the people demand that the government do something, trusting that government officials will react to the situation intelligently and effectively. In sum, *under modern ideological conditions* the onset of a crisis is marked by heightened deference to government officials, trust in their judgment, and willingness to grant them discretion in selecting and implementing a course of action.[5]

In shaping a response to this public outcry, government officials draw from three major reservoirs. The first holds plans and programs the government was already seeking to implement that had been blocked by public or interest-group opposition (e.g., the USA PATRIOT Act of 2001, for the most part a collection of provisions long sought by the Department of Justice). These policies are already sitting, as it were, on the government's shelf, and government officials need only take them down, whisk off the dust, and put them into operation as soon as they acquire authority to do so. The second reservoir of crisis actions holds proposals put forth by organized interest-group advocates (e.g., the Agricultural Adjustment Act of 1933, for the most part a collection of subsidy schemes long sought by agricultural lobbies and related interest groups). Like the government's own off-the-shelf policies, these plans and programs may have languished for a long time without political success. Finally, the government and the interest groups may bring forward fresh proposals that they have formulated quickly as the crisis has developed—attempts, so to speak, to "strike while the iron is hot" (e.g., proposals to raise the prices of agricultural exports in 1933 by abandonment of the gold standard and devaluation of the dollar in international exchange).

In normal circumstances, all of these proposals would serve only to clog the logjam even tighter, but in a crisis they have a much greater chance of adoption. This enhanced potential arises in part from the public's fear-driven insistence that the government "do something" extraordinary to restore peace, order, or prosperity. Adoption of a slew of new laws and regulations will be widely and favorably perceived as "doing something." In addition, the government and the interest groups may dynamite the logjam by a kind of implicit agreement that every important group may get its most desired policy adopted now if only each group will set aside its normal objection to the other groups' most desired policy. Thus, what political scientists would call a huge "log roll" (i.e., the idea that

---

5. See Robert Higgs, *Neither Liberty nor Safety: Fear, Ideology, and the Growth of Government* (Oakland, Calif.: The Independent Institute, 2007).

an exchange of votes take place) serves to break what I have called the normal logjam. Crisis therefore produces a virtual free-for-all of policies, programs, and plans that expand the government's power in new directions and strengthen it where it previously existed in a weaker form.

Opportunists' Actions Create the Ratchet Effect

In analyzing the crisis-driven growth of government, it is useful to think in terms of a stylized "ratchet phenomenon." Figure 7.1 shows schematically how such episodes pass through five distinct phases, the net effect of which is to lift the trend line of the government's growth to a higher level. We may identify these phases as follows: (1) precrisis normality; (2) expansion; (3) maturity; (4) retrenchment; and (5) postcrisis normality. The most important aspect of this representation is that the retrenchment phase is insufficient to return the true size of government (conceived as a composite index of the government's size,

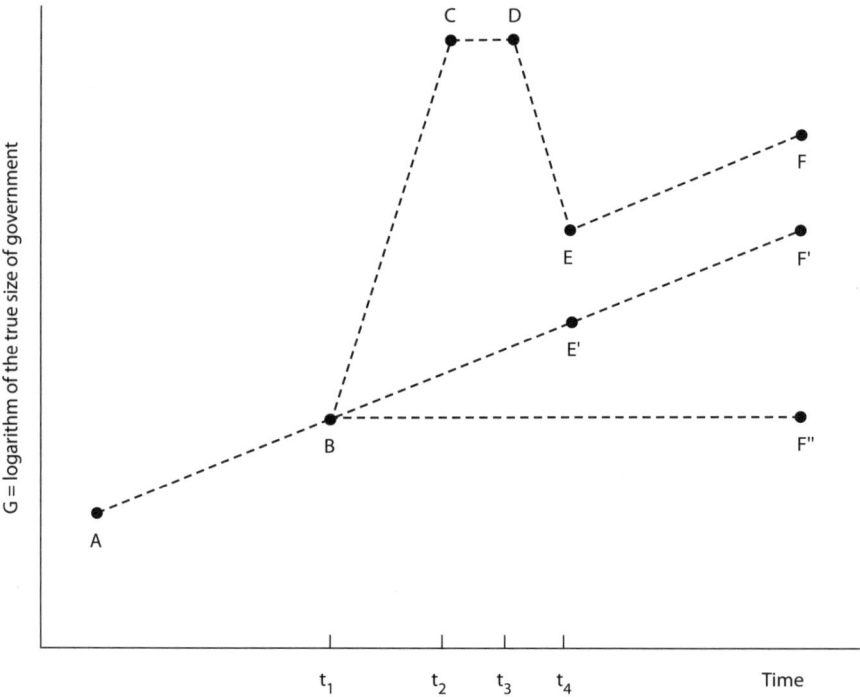

Figure 7.1 Schematic Representation of the Ratchet Phenomenon

scope, and power) to the level that would have been attained if the government had simply continued along the path of its growth during the phase of precrisis normality. Thus, although the government does surrender ground during the retrenchment phase, it does not lose enough to compensate fully for the ground gained during the expansion. It has a net gain, not only as compared with its precrisis size, but also as compared with the position it would have attained if it had continued to grow as it was growing before the onset of the crisis.[6]

Opportunists, both inside and outside the formal state apparatus, play distinctive roles during each of these phases. Indeed, it is fair to say that their actions create the ratchet effect, although, to repeat, this entire phenomenon presupposes an essential condition—a dominant ideology of progressivism or something akin to it—that disposes the public at large to regard the government as the savior of first resort in a national emergency.

During normal periods, interest groups, politically ambitious individuals, and ideological entrepreneurs work assiduously on politics as usual, seeking to gain marginal improvements in their positions, yet understanding that because of the mutually blocking logjam of competing proposals and counterproposals jostling for executive, legislative, and judicial attention and action, they will probably have to be satisfied with half a loaf, if indeed they have any success at all. These supplicants and schemers understand, however, that when a crisis comes along, their prospects will brighten substantially and that success will be more likely to the extent that they have prepared themselves and cultivated the relevant ground well in advance.

Therefore, the various individuals and groups occupy themselves in formulating and refining desired executive, legislative, and judicial actions that are more ambitious than present conditions will accommodate. As they do so, they devote resources to publicizing and promoting their ideas in order to "soften up" opinion leaders and the mass public so that when the propitious day finally comes, people will not react strongly against a scheme that might seem unnecessary or excessive if they had never encountered arguments for it in the past. Thus, for example, if people had never heard proposals for nationalizing health insurance, they might be startled by political attempts to enact such a

---

6. Robert Higgs, *Crisis and Leviathan: Critical Episodes in the Growth of American Government* (New York: Oxford University Press, 1987), 57–74.

plan during an economic emergency, such as the present financial debacle and economic recession.[7] Having softened up the public by promoting this scheme for years, however, the interest groups and ideological entrepreneurs who favor it stand a much better chance of gaining its approval now than they otherwise would have had.

Therefore, even in normal periods when nothing extraordinary seems to be happening in politics, many groups are working hard to lay the groundwork for future gains, appreciating that ultimate success is unlikely except in a crisis, during which a general dissolution of offsetting political blockages will occur as the quickening current of "do something" sentiment alters the calculations of the president, the bureaucrats, the legislators, and even the judges. It was no mere coincidence, for example, that the Supreme Court revolution of 1937 took place in the midst of the nation's greatest peacetime emergency. Judges, too, feel the pressure and are compelled to yield to it. Justice Owen J. Roberts, the "swing man" who more than anyone else bore responsibility for the court's turnaround in 1937, later observed: "Looking back, it is difficult to see how the Court could have resisted the popular urge." He referred obliquely to "the tremendous strain and the threat to the existing Court, of which I was fully conscious."[8] During normal periods, interest groups are looking ahead to the crisis-driven emergence of, among other things, the next swing man on the Supreme Court. Lawyers are honing their arguments for future briefs aimed at him.

Once a crisis breaks out, time becomes all important, and each party who seeks to exploit the occasion rushes to get his nose under the policy tent ahead of the others. Raymond Moley, the most important member of the Brains Trust, recalled that immediately after Franklin D. Roosevelt took office as president in 1933, "Washington became a mecca for the old Socialists, single-taxers, utility reformers, Civil Service reformers, and goo-goos of all types." As Roosevelt's "unofficial sieve on policy," Moley spent hours each afternoon in appointments with "a choice variety of panacea artists." He received, for example, "literally

---

7. "On Healthcare, Obama Pushes for Fast Action," *Boston Globe,* May 29, 2009, at http://www.boston.com/news/nation/articles/2009/05/29/on_healthcare_obama_pushes_for_fast_action/.
8. Quoted in Charles A. Leonard, *A Search for a Judicial Philosophy: Mr. Justice Roberts and the Constitutional Revolution of 1937* (Port Washington, N.Y.: Kennikat Press, 1971), 144, 155.

dozens" of "plans for industrial rehabilitation." "Official Washington," he wrote, "was in the grip of a war psychology as surely as it had been in 1917."[9]

In the mad scramble, it is easy for even powerful interest-group advocates to get lost in the crowd. The decisive advantage rests with the executive branch of government, especially with the president and the small number of persons who have access to or influence over him. At such times, the president's autonomy and discretion reach a maximum, and hence his capacity for shaping events to suit his own desires also peaks. In the spring of 1933, wrote Moley, "Congress was in the mood to give [President Roosevelt] power as great as that of any other President in history."[10] But even the president's extraordinary capacity will not last indefinitely, and if he does not move quickly, opponents of his favored measures may succeed in marshalling enough counterforce to foil him. Hence, all delays, even those required for gathering and assessing the most important facts about the crisis, must be avoided in favor of, as Roosevelt expressed it in his first Inaugural Address in March 1933, "action, and action now." It came as no surprise, then, that President Barack Obama declared on February 5, 2009: "The time for talk is over. The time for action is now, because we know that if we do not act, a bad situation will become dramatically worse. Crisis could turn into catastrophe for families and businesses across the country."[11]

Like President Obama, proponents of particular government actions after the onset of a crisis generally claim that the proposed action is imperative: unless it is adopted, horrible consequences will ensue. Therefore, they insist that delays to weigh their proposal's costs against its benefits or studies to identify adverse longer-term effects or careful considerations of who will gain and who will lose are intolerable. They urge that the government must act immediately. In such a frenzied atmosphere, the usual efforts to deliberate, to hear different sides, to adhere to procedural due process, and to attend to due diligence before making expenditures are likely to be set aside in favor of quick action. In the recent financial debacle, for example, trillions of dollars in loans, guarantees,

---

9. Raymond Moley, *After Seven Years* (New York: Harper and Brothers, 1939), 128, 167, 185, 191.

10. Moley, *After Seven Years,* 221.

11. Quoted in William A. Niskanen, *Slow Down the Political Response to a Perceived Crisis* (Washington, D.C.: Cato Institute, February 9, 2009), at http://www.cato.org/pub_display .php?pub_id=9951.

capital infusions, and other forms of financial aid were committed without the knowledge even of members of Congress. Senator Byron Dorgan complained on the floor of the Senate on February 3, 2009: "We've seen money go out the back door of this government unlike any time in the history of our country. Nobody knows what went out of the Federal Reserve Board, to whom and for what purpose. How much from the FDIC [Federal Deposit Insurance Corporation]? How much from TARP [Troubled Assets Relief Program]? When? Why?"[12]

This situation strongly favors the political insiders, especially the president and those closest to him. It is no accident, therefore, that crisis has been associated not only with the growth of government, but also with the centralization of government power and fiscal resources. A crisis is a president's time in the sun. As Jimmy Carter wrote to an adviser, "When a president has authority to act unilaterally (as in a crisis), his leadership can be exerted. Otherwise, compromise, delay and confusion are more likely."[13] All modern presidents understand this reality, and most of them strive to exploit it to the maximum. The so-called imperial presidency has grown for the most part out of "bold" presidential actions during national emergencies and from the subsequent institutionalization of such crisis-time precedents.

As the president and others closest to the pinnacle of political power act, they undertake to rationalize their actions and to marshal mass support for those actions. Hence, they typically mount unusual efforts to propagandize the public and to intimidate opponents by suggesting that they are "slackers" or otherwise lacking in patriotism and, in extreme cases, by jailing dissidents or expelling them from the country. To ensure that opponents are not undermining the chosen emergency policies, the government usually undertakes to place many more people under surveillance, often justifying this action as an effort to ferret out spies, saboteurs, or terrorists, even though such surveillance invariably extends much more widely than indicated and often targets completely peaceful persons and groups, such as pacifists and people who oppose the government's actions on

---

12. Quoted in Mark Pittman and Bob Ivry, "U.S. Taxpayers Risk $9.7 Trillion on Bailout Programs (Update 1)," *Bloomberg.com,* February 9, 2009, at http://www.bloomberg.com/apps/news?pid=20601087&sid=aGq2B3XeGKok.
13. Quoted in Michael Gerson, "Obama's Crisis: Credibility," *Washington Post,* September 9, 2009.

religious grounds. As more and more people fall under the government's watchful eye, some who might have spoken out or organized others in opposition to the government's emergency measures are silenced, and such muzzling helps the government to create the impression that no real opposition exists except for that of traitors, subversives, and "wreckers."[14] Government may also organize the mass public to turn them into de facto informers, putting even greater pressure on opponents of its program to keep silent lest they expose themselves to malicious reports by unfriendly neighbors or acquaintances.[15]

Meanwhile, the government paints the sacrifices and costs entailed by its chosen emergency policies as patriotic, beneficial, and even heroic. Policies that may bring benefits to only a chosen few are depicted as required by the "public interest" or by pressing economic or social necessity. Proponents invite those who remain hostile to the chosen policies to shut up unless they have "something better" to propose or "something constructive" to say. Such debating tactics help to quiet criticism and, again, to create the impression that the government's crisis policies enjoy near-universal public approbation.

During the third, or maturity, phase of the ratchet phenomenon, the government has implemented an array of emergency plans and programs, and it occupies itself primarily in making them work passably well while the crisis persists. To call this phase the "maturity phase" does not mean that the government's actions have settled into an enduring pattern or system; indeed, constant changes, adjustments, reversals, and accommodations of various sorts always

---

14. The actions described in this paragraph were most notable during the War Between the States and the two world wars, but the government also took similar egregious actions under the COINTELPRO rubric between 1956 and the early 1970s. For a well-documented survey, see Michael Linfield, *Freedom Under Fire: U.S. Civil Liberties in Times of War* (Boston: South End Press, 1990). See also Higgs, *Neither Liberty nor Safety,* 1–22, which gives evidence running up to the present "war on terror." Peacetime emergencies brought forth less of this kind of government action, but by no means a complete absence of it. During the early New Deal, for example, the government strove to whip up mass support for the National Industrial Recovery Act and to stigmatize as "slackers" and "chiselers" those who declined to cooperate with this national cartelization scheme. See Higgs, *Crisis and Leviathan,* 179 and sources cited there.

15. For example, the government's on-again, off-again Operation Terrorism Information and Prevention System (TIPS); for a brief account, see "Operation TIPS," *Wikipedia,* at http://en.wikipedia.org/wiki/Operation_TIPS.

occur. This flux reflects the "disequilibrium" that the government has created by imposing its power on a population disposed to act differently. If, for example, the government imposes price controls, it will have to devise ways to placate persons placed at a disadvantage by such controls, to make exceptions to its rules in cases where the rules are proving especially counterproductive to the government's own purposes, and to refine the program's substantive details and its administrative setup.[16]

In this phase, the opportunists who have succeeded in gaining implementation of their favored plans and programs occupy themselves in defending their schemes against critics (many of them insiders operating elsewhere, perhaps somewhat competitively, within the government), consolidating their newly gained powers, enlarging their budgets, and generally striving to entrench their operations within the government and the overall society. In a sense, these actions take place within a crisis setting that has itself, for the time being, become the "normal" situation for the government's operations. So, to some extent, logjams similar to those that characterize the precrisis normal period may develop, although they will differ in their details, reflecting the way in which the crisis has brought forth an assortment of emergency programs to deal with the prevailing situation. Thus, for example, at the peak of a war, interservice rivalry may characterize the military budgeting process just as it did before the war began, but now its dimensions will be greatly enlarged—the army, navy, and air force may be fighting over the division of 10 or 20 percent of gross domestic product (GDP) rather than the division of only 3 percent.

As the crisis continues, the emergency programs will benefit from the general public's accommodation to the new realities of the government's enlarged role. People not only will learn how to avoid the worst disadvantages of the new arrangements but more generally will to some extent accommodate their thinking to those arrangements as well. To people who had not been subject to military conscription (e.g., Americans between 1919 and 1939), the initiation of a draft may seem to be an outrageous imposition on their liberties. Once this system of involuntary military service has operated for years, however, people

---

16. See, for example, George P. Shultz and Kenneth W. Dam, "The Life Cycle of Wage and Price Controls," in *Economic Policy Beyond the Headlines* (New York: Norton, 1977), 65–85.

may come to regard it much as they regard destructive weather—an act of nature that must be endured in the event that it happens. (When I was growing up in the 1950s, the young men of my acquaintance thought about the draft much as they thought about the possibility that a drunk driver might crash into them and kill them on the highway: bad things happen sometimes. They did not organize protests against the draft, and when selected, virtually everybody went quietly, resigned to having his life derailed for a couple of years. I never knew anyone who tried to evade the draft in those days. Of course, once the Vietnam War began, conditions began to change in this regard.)

When the crisis ends or at least wanes significantly, many people will naturally expect that some, if not all, of the government's extraordinary measures adopted ostensibly in response to the crisis will be terminated or greatly scaled back. After all, one invariant aspect of the government's actions during the expansion phase of the ratchet phenomenon is that significant new burdens are placed on the general public. Even if people have accepted the government's measures as desirable or necessary in combating the crisis, their enthusiasm for them will eventually wear thin, especially when the measures' rationale seems to have evaporated. At this point, the government will feel itself under pressure to "return to normalcy," as Warren G. Harding expressed the idea during his campaign for the presidency in 1920. Now, as we enter the fourth, or retrenchment, phase of the ratchet phenomenon, the opportunists who gained so much ground in the second phase and successfully defended it during the third phase will be placed unavoidably on the defensive.

Although some emergency-program managers may themselves be keen for a return to normal conditions, many others will not be. During the crisis, a variety of new "iron triangles" will have been created, and the old ones strengthened. Each triangle consists of government oversight and appropriations committees in the legislature, a government bureau responsible for making purchases or for administering regulations or controls, and a set of private-sector beneficiaries who have profited somehow from the emergency program's operation during the crisis. The leaders of these three groups and to a lesser extent their rank and file stand to lose positions of substantial value in the event that the program is abolished or greatly diminished. They are therefore likely to search for and to find reasons why such retrenchment should not occur at all or at least should not be carried out on a drastic scale.

One time-honored tactic is to redefine the threat against which their crisis-time operations presumably were directed. So, for example, after the surrender of German and Japanese forces in 1945, the U.S. armed forces, which had grown spectacularly between 1940 and 1944, faced the prospect of returning to a budget of 1 percent of GDP (approximately the amount spent on the military in fiscal year 1940), after having reached a level of more than 40 percent of GDP at the peak of the war effort.[17] Not only would the military's cash flow be squeezed to a relative trickle, but—not to be ignored in this context—the number of required flag officers would be diminished commensurately, which would mean the involuntary retirement of hundreds of generals and admirals who had only recently attained these high commands. Is it any surprise, then, that military leaders immediately perceived that in order to face down the alleged threat posed by the Soviet Union, they needed an armed force much larger than the one the nation had maintained in 1940?[18]

Another tactic is to shift missions while keeping the emergency agency or powers intact. So, for example, after the armistice in 1918 and the peace treaty in 1919, the U.S. War Finance Corporation, which had operated during the war to steer financial capital to enterprises given high priority by the government's economic mobilization plans, was retained when Eugene Meyer, its wartime managing director, and others perceived that it could be used to finance U.S. exports, especially agricultural exports, to Europe at a time when the European purchasers were hard pressed to arrange their own financing.[19] The Emergency Fleet Corporation, created to build merchant ships to carry U.S. supplies to Europe during World War I, similarly continued to build ships after the armistice,

---

17. Robert Higgs, "Introduction: Fifty Years of Arms, Politics, and the Economy," in *Arms, Politics, and the Economy: Historical and Contemporary Perspectives,* edited by Robert Higgs (New York: Holmes and Meier, 1990), xvii.

18. I say "alleged threat" not because I take a benign view of the Soviets or minimize the genuine threat they posed to many Europeans and Asians, but because the threat they posed to *U.S.* national security was a much more problematic matter. The literature on the origins of the Cold War is immense, but with special relevance to the "switching missions" point I am making here, see Arlene Lazarowitz, "Promoting Air Power: The Influence of the U.S. Air Force on the Creation of the National Security State," *The Independent Review* 9, no. 4 (Spring 2005): 477–99.

19. Higgs, *Crisis and Leviathan,* 153–54.

and under the Merchant Marine Act of 1920 this same agency, now called the Merchant Fleet Corporation, put the ships to use by transforming itself into a government-owned shipping line.[20]

Attempts to eliminate or diminish emergency programs run up against a fundamental principle of political action: people will fight harder to keep an established benefit than they will fight to obtain an identical benefit in the first place. This asymmetry assists every effort to hang on to iron triangles created or enlarged during a crisis. Legislators do not enjoy taking benefits away from constituents; doing so may cost them votes down the line. Political actors thrive on the creation of programs with concentrated benefits and dispersed costs. By the same token, they try to avoid actions that entail dispersed benefits and concentrated costs because those on whom the concentrated losses will fall are certain to howl and to scratch and claw with every resource they can command to avoid the loss. After a crisis has clearly ended, it is not possible for beneficiaries of crisis-oriented programs to hang on to everything they have gained during the emergency, but they can in many instances stage an organized retreat that allows them to retain some of the ground they previously occupied.

When the dust of the retrenchment fights has settled, the politicoeconomic system finds itself endowed with an altered dynamic. Some emergency agencies (perhaps renamed or redirected to permanent departments) remain in operation; some emergency laws remain in force; and some court decisions reached during the crisis stand as precedents for future decisions, including decisions made in normal times. Above all, the population goes forward with its political sensibilities altered from their precrisis configuration. If the government's crisis management can be plausibly represented as having been successful, as it often can be, then people may be more likely to trust the government to take on more tasks or to engage old problems more energetically than it did previously. Which is to say, the experience gained by having passed more or less successfully (or so people believe) through a crisis in which the government took a variety of extraordinary actions is likely to move the dominant ideology in a direction more favorably disposed toward new government initiatives in the future. We may think of this kind of change as ideological learning from experience (and propaganda).

---

20. Higgs, *Crisis and Leviathan*, 153.

Of course, such learning will not be left for people to arrive at on their own. The crisis-program managers are virtually certain to write memoirs recounting their heroic emergency performance and proclaiming the virtues of the extraordinary government activities they oversaw during the crisis. Ideologues who prefer bigger, more powerful government in any event will seize on the apparent lessons to be taken from the just-concluded crisis and the surge of government action that came forth in response to it. And many progressives will seek to use wartime experiences as springboards for similar, permanent government activities.

The Crisis Opportunists' Priority List

As we have seen, the opportunists who emerge to exploit a national emergency have a variety of options at their disposal. It is helpful in understanding their actions to recognize that some options serve their purposes better than others, even if they pursue simultaneously all feasible avenues to achieve their ends. The general arrangement of these options, in increasing order of potency, is as follows:

- New government personnel
- New government policies
- New government agencies
- New statutes
- New court decisions, especially Supreme Court decisions

Another option, difficult to rank because it may take a multitude of specific forms, consists of new precedents in government action, response to problems created by crisis policies, and accommodation of opponents and other aggrieved parties; generally speaking, all of these forms amount to new precedents for dealing with the negative feedback that crisis-time government actions may generate. If new government actions are to succeed, the government must somehow sooth the people who are irate about its actions. Simply telling them "we've got the guns and you don't" only stimulates the opposition to work harder.

As a well-known political aphorism informs us, "Personnel is policy." Even if the laws, regulations, and judicial precedents have not changed, new officeholders can move the substance of the government's policy substantially in new directions by choosing to ignore certain issues or to pour more resources into them. Benign neglect of enforcement is a time-honored way for regulators to gut a regulation, even though it remains formally in force. Regulators or judges alternatively may begin to come down hard on violators of rules that no one was bothering to enforce previously.

So the first and usually the easiest thing government officials (backed, as usual, by their supporting coalition of interest groups inside and outside the government) can do in a crisis is to replace existing officeholders with "our people." Within the federal executive branch, this sort of replacement goes back at least to Andrew Jackson's administration, with its forthright embrace of the spoils system. The civil-service system eventually reined in such replacements for the bulk of the executive branch's personnel, but at the upper reaches, where the most important officeholders are, they continue to serve at the president's pleasure, and every president begins his tenure in office with a thorough "housecleaning" and installation of his own appointees. The onset of a national emergency often calls for another housecleaning, sometimes as a gesture of national unity (e.g., Franklin D. Roosevelt's appointment of leading Republicans Henry Stimson and Frank Knox to head the War and Navy Departments in 1940, when the president was striving to win over Republicans in general and Republican industrialists in particular to support his preparation for war).

Even better than replacing personnel at the outset of a crisis is the alteration of policies. To some extent, such changes, even when highly important, require nothing but executive orders as authorization. Many policies can be changed without any formal proceedings at all; department heads simply announce that henceforth certain matters are to be handled differently. Policy changes are likely to be more durable than personnel changes because policies that remain in place for some time create vested interests in their preservation—new sets of beneficiaries who stand to lose power, jobs, contracts, subsidies, or other privileges if the existing policy is abandoned. Such vested interests will work hard to prevent a policy reversal in the future, so they will help to ensure that the emergency policy, perhaps with some reconfiguration of its public rationale, continues after the emergency has passed. On May 21, 2009, the *Wall Street Journal* reported that although some big banks were seeking to repay TARP funds to the government, "many of the other emergency measures created to prop up the financial system are developing an air of permanence."[21]

For a crisis opportunist, even better than a new policy is a new government agency, especially one with a new, designated function that effectively institutionalizes support for an interest-group agenda inside the apparatus of government itself. Such agencies may be created by executive order, as Woodrow Wilson created the War Industries Board during World War I. Agencies first created by the presidential order may then proceed to acquire statutory authority. Thus, the Federal Energy Office, created by President Richard Nixon to deal with the energy crisis in 1973, became the statutorily authorized Federal Energy Administration in 1974 and ultimately the Department of Energy in 1977.

Although such a progression may appear in retrospect to have developed sequentially in response to an ongoing series of events, crisis opportunists sometimes foresee and work to bring about this kind of permanent institutionalization from the very beginning. Thus, as Broadus Mitchell writes, "though the framers of the [Agricultural Adjustment Act of 1933], to overcome congressional objections, presented it as an emergency measure, there is abundant evidence that all along they intended it to be the basis of long-time policy."[22] Although the Agricultural Adjustment Administration, which administered the act's provisions during the 1930s, was later eliminated (and the 1933 act itself was overturned by the Supreme Court in 1936), its functions were folded into the Department of Agriculture, and under authority of statutes enacted in 1936, 1938, and later years the latter has continued to administer a system of agricultural income and price supports since the 1930s.

For a crisis opportunist, even better than a new agency is a new law. Once a policy and its administrative agency have received statutory authority, the burden of discontinuing the policy weighs heavily on the policy's opponents. In Congress, it is much easier to pass a new statute than to repeal an existing one. Legislative procedures give the defenders an advantage (e.g., single senatorial objection to a bill, traditional filibuster, etc.). Vested interests invariably lobby to retain their statutory privileges. Rarely does the general public take much

---

21. "U.S. Rescue Aid Entrenches Itself," *Wall Street Journal,* May 21, 2009.
22. Broadus Mitchell, *Depression Decade: From New Era Through New Deal, 1929–1941* (New York: Harper Torchbooks, 1969), 187.

interest in a law's repeal, and public apathy fosters legislative inertia. Laws often remain on the books long after they have become completely obsolete or even absurd. Ronald Reagan famously quipped that "nothing is as permanent as a temporary government program." He might well have added, "Especially if it rests on statutory authority."

For a crisis opportunist, even better than a new statute is a new court decision, especially one by the Supreme Court. Statutes mean nothing if the courts of appeal declare them unconstitutional. During a crisis, of course, the courts are likely to be especially accommodating to the government's programs: "*inter arma enim silent leges*" (in times of war, the laws fall silent). Although the courts may not become completely mute or totally submissive during a peacetime crisis, as the great court fight of the 1930s illustrates, they are always more likely to concede extraordinary powers to the government during a perceived national emergency than they would be to do so in normal times. Once the court has rendered an obliging decision, however, that decision remains on the record and may serve as a precedent for subsequent cases in which the government's power during normal times is contested. If statutes are difficult to overturn, Supreme Court decisions are even more difficult. Constitutional revolutions occur only at long intervals. For this reason, crisis opportunists especially prize their court victories during episodes of national emergency. To this day, for example, the Supreme Court's favorable decisions on rent controls and military conscription during World War I continue to carry weight in court cases.

Finally, crisis opportunists may value (above everything else they achieve during a national emergency) the lessons they learn about how to manage new powers so that opponents do not obstruct the operation of those powers or somehow nullify them. Crisis managers learn how to deal with dissent: some opponents may be clapped in prison or deported; others may be silenced by vaguely worded warnings against unpatriotic obstructionism. Thus, in December 2001 Attorney General John Ashcroft wasted no words on nuance, declaring: "To those who . . . scare peace-loving people with phantoms of lost liberty, my message is this: Your tactics only aid terrorists for they erode our national unity and diminish our resolve."[23] Each time the crisis managers navigate through a new

---

23. "Ashcroft: Critics of New Terror Measures Undermine Effort," *CNN News,* December 7, 2001, at http://archives.cnn.com/2001/US/12/06/inv.ashcroft.hearing/.

storm, they learn more about where the rocks are and how to avoid them (or to blow them out of the water).

During World War II, for example, the government strictly censored news from the battlefields and for most of the war even forbade publication of photographs of dead American servicemen. In Vietnam, in contrast, the reporters got into the thick of the fighting and sent back gory, unsettling videotape that, being shown regularly on the nightly news programs, helped to undermine the usual lies and distortions being distributed by the military authorities. Taking this lesson to heart, the armed forces in the U.S. attack on Iraq in 2003 put into effect a system of "embedding" reporters in military units, thereby effectively preventing them from going where they might need to go to find out about the most important developments and helping to ensure that they would bond with their de facto protectors and report the news from these soldiers' point of view.[24]

Can Anything Be Done?

Having recognized the dangers that inhere in the government's responses to perceived national emergencies, we might well ponder whether anything can be done to prevent or moderate the harms they cause. Although an ironclad guarantee against such harms is inconceivable, apart from the dissolution of the government that causes them, we can imagine several ways in which the government's worst crisis-time excesses might be checked.

All crisis policymaking springs fundamentally from widespread public fear or even panic, and little can be done to prevent such hysteria except by challenging the government propaganda and the inaccurate news reports that magnify it. Efforts to rein in the government's overreaching must concentrate, first, on affecting the public's thinking about how the government ought to act during an emergency and, second, on changing the machinery of government so that ill-considered or poorly justified measures cannot be adopted so easily. In short, protective efforts may be directed, first, toward policy education and ideological change and, second, toward institutional change.

---

24. See, for example, Center for Media and Democracy, "Embedded," *SourceWatch,* at http://www.sourcewatch.org/index.php?title=Embedded; and "Embedded Journalism," *Wikipedia,* http://en.wikipedia.org/wiki/Embedded_journalism.

Policy education might well seek to reveal the great extent to which past government emergency measures have proved counterproductive at the time of their implementation and, even worse, when they persisted after the emergency had passed. Analysts might well emphasize the extent to which these policies have been driven by special interests posing as friends of the general public interest, often by advancing transparently fallacious arguments. Studies might well focus on the distribution of benefits and costs. A showing that some group, perhaps even a seemingly large one, benefited from a crisis-driven policy should never be accepted as a sufficient justification for the policy's adoption: analysts should reveal the policy's costs, the distribution of these costs across the entire population, and the various pecuniary and nonpecuniary forms the costs took; and they should trace how these aspects of the policy changed over the entire period in which the policy remained in effect or continued to have discernible consequences. To a large extent, these efforts amount to little more than systematically fleshing out Frédéric Bastiat's teachings about taking into account both the seen and the unseen as well as Henry Hazlitt's insistence that economic analysis, properly performed, must relate to how an action affects not simply some, but all groups and not simply the immediate situation, but the long-run future as well.

Above all, the government should never be given a pass merely because in someone's estimation government officials "cared" about the people even as they acted in ways that harmed the very people about whom they allegedly cared. Franklin D. Roosevelt and the New Deal constitute the classic case of this sort of faulty evaluation by historians and other policy analysts. Giving government officials credit for caring rather than for actually promoting the general public interest encourages emotional posturing and the public shedding of crocodile tears instead of the implementation of public policies that actually benefit the people as a whole (e.g., protection of private-property rights, enforcement of voluntary private contracts, noninterference with domestic and international trade, maintenance of sound money or, better, relinquishment of monetary matters to the private sector).

In reforming government institutions to guard against harmful government actions during a crisis, anything done to restore the classic protections of federalism and the separation of powers—fundamental aspects of U.S. governmental design that have eroded dangerously over the ages—will prove helpful. Many of the mistakes the government makes during a national emergency spring from excessively hasty action and from the excessive discretion ceded to the executive branch by the other branches of government. One may grant that emergencies may justify quicker government action yet still insist that even in such circumstances actions may be taken *too* hastily. What is the point of acting very quickly if the government can do so only in a biased, ill-considered, and ultimately (on net) harmful way? Gridlock is not an altogether bad thing, even in a crisis. By allowing time for competing points of view to be heard and for potentially adversely affected interests to mount and voice opposition, gridlock means that more balanced and better justified measures may be designed before bad policy provisions become locked in place, perhaps forever.

All emergency measures should have sunset provisions, lest special interests and other opportunists use the pretext of crisis to get a permanent foot in the door. If the government's crisis measures have explicitly stated dates of expiration in the near future (say, in two years or less), special interests will have less incentive to push for them because their long-term duration will be less certain and because the prospect of having to gain their future reapproval, probably under calmer conditions, will lower their prospective benefits and increase their prospective costs to the special interests.

Conclusion

Crisis brings opportunists running, both from inside and from outside the government, because crisis alters the fundamental forces that impel and constrain political action. It thereby creates unusual opportunities for extraordinary government actions, plans, and programs to be implemented. That crisis has this effect is widely understood by political actors inside and outside the government. Opportunism is therefore to be expected and to be guarded against—especially by the general public, which is likely to be saddled with the crisis programs' burdens and injustices. Throughout U.S. history, national emergencies have served as outstanding occasions for the (ratcheting) loss of liberties. If government is by its very nature an institution that allows some people to benefit from what others have created, then national emergency creates the context in which this nature becomes expressed to the maximum. Of course, the crisis opportunists invariably claim that every move they make actually serves the broad public interest—we would scarcely expect them to say anything else. But these reassurances ring hollow when contrasted with the political logic and the historical facts that pertain to national emergencies. Everyone understands that a crisis, virtually by definition, is a time of great danger, but too few understand that the greatest danger often resides not so much in the perceived threat as in the government's ostensible measures to fend it off. The public needs a greater understanding that in a crisis not all the barbarians are outside the walls.

8

War Is Horrible, but . . .

ANYONE WHO HAS done even a little reading about the theory and practice of war, whether in political theory, international relations, theology, history, or common journalistic commentary, has encountered a sentence of the form "War is horrible, but . . . ." In this construction, the phrase that follows the conjunction explains why a certain war was (or now is or someday will be) an action that ought to have been (or still ought to be) undertaken notwithstanding its admitted horrors. The frequent, virtually formulaic use of this expression attests that nobody cares to argue, say, that war is a beautiful, humane, uplifting, or altogether splendid course of action, and therefore the more often people fight, the better.

Some time ago—in the late nineteenth and early twentieth century, for example—one might encounter a writer, such as Theodore Roosevelt, who forthrightly affirmed that war is manly and invigorating for the nation and the soldiers who engage in it: war keeps a nation from "getting soft." Although this opinion is no longer expressed openly with great frequency, something akin to it may yet survive, as Chris Hedges argues in *War Is a Force That Gives Us Meaning*.[1] Nowadays, however, even those who find meaning for their lives by involvement in war, perhaps only marginal or symbolic involvement, do not often extol war as such.

They are likely instead to justify a nation's engagement in war by calling attention to alternative, even more horrible outcomes that, retrospectively, would have occurred if the nation had not gone to war or, prospectively, will occur if it does not go to war. This seemingly reasonable "balancing" form of argument

---

1. Chris Hedges, *War Is a Force That Gives Us Meaning* (New York: Public Affairs, 2002).

often sounds stronger than it really is, especially when it is made more or less in passing. People may easily be swayed by a weak argument, however, if they fail to appreciate the defects of the typically expressed "horrible, but" apology for war.

Rather than plow through various sources on my bookshelves to compile examples, I have availed myself of modern technology. A Google search for the exact phrase "war is horrible, but" on September 11, 2006, identified 1,450 instances; the same search on January 7, 2011, yielded 30,400 instances. Rest assured that this larger, more recent number is still smaller than the entire universe of such usage—some instances have yet to be captured electronically. Among the examples I drew from the World Wide Web are the following fourteen statements. I identify the person who made the statement only when he is well known.

1. **"War is horrible. But no one wants to see a world in which a regime with no regard whatsoever for international law—for the welfare of its own people—or for the will of the United Nations—has weapons of mass destruction"** (U.S. Deputy Secretary of State Richard Armitage).

This statement was part of a speech Armitage gave on January 21, 2003, shortly before the U.S. government unleashed its armed forces to inflict "shock and awe" on the nearly defenseless people of Iraq. The speech repeated the George W. Bush administration's standard prewar litany of accusations, including several claims later revealed to be false, so it cannot be viewed as anything but bellicose propaganda. Yet it does not differ much from what many others were saying at the time.

On its own terms, the statement scarcely serves to justify a war. A regime's disregard of international law, its own people's well-being, and the will of the United Nations, combined with possession of weapons of mass destruction— these conditions apply to several nations. They no more justified a military attack on Iraq than they justified an attack on Pakistan, France, India, Russia, China, the United Kingdom, Israel, or the United States itself.

2. **"War is terrible, war is horrible, but war is also at times necessary and the only means of stopping evil."**

The *only* means of stopping evil? How can such singularity exist? Has evil conduct never been stopped except by war? For example, has shunning—

exclusion from commerce, financial systems, communications, transportation systems, and other means of international cooperation—never served to discipline an evil nation-state? Might it do so if seriously tried? (If these questions give the impression that I am suggesting the possibility of resort to embargo or blockade, that perception is not exactly correct. Although I support various forms of voluntary, peaceful withdrawal of cooperation with evil-doing states, I do not endorse state-enforced—that is, violent or potentially violent—embargoes and blockades.) Why must we leap to the conclusion that only war will serve, even though other measures have scarcely been considered, much less been seriously attempted? If war is really as horrible as everyone says, then it would seem that we have a moral obligation to try very hard to achieve the desired suppression of evil doing by means other than resort to warfare, which is itself always a manifest evil, even when it is seemingly the lesser one.

3. **"No news shows [during World War II] were showing German civilians getting fried and saying how sad it was. It was war against butchers and war is horrible, but it's war, and to defend human decency, sometimes war is necessary"** (Ben Stein).

Stein is a knowledgeable man. He surely knows that the U.S. government imposed draconian censorship of war news during World War II. Perhaps the censors had their reasons for keeping scenes of incinerated German civilians away from the U.S. public. After all, even if Americans in general had extraordinarily cruel and callous attitudes toward German civilians during the war, many Americans had relatives and friends in Germany.

Stein appears to lump *all* Germans into the class of "butchers" against whom he claims the war was being waged. He certainly must understand, however, that many persons in Germany—children, for example—were not butchers and bore absolutely no responsibility for the actions of government officials who were. Yet these innocents, too, suffered the dire effects of, among other things, the terror bombing that the U.S. and British air forces inflicted on many German cities.

To say, as Stein and many others have said, that "war is war" gets us nowhere; in a moral sense, this tautology warrants nothing. Many people, however, evidently consider all moral questions about the conduct of war to be settled simply by their having labeled or by their having accepted someone else's labeling of certain actions as a "war." Having chanted this exculpatory incantation over the state's organized violence, they believe that all transgressions associated with that violence are automatically absolved—as the saying goes, "All's fair in love and war." It does not help matters that regimes treat some of the most egregious transgressors as heroes.

Finally, Stein's claim that "to defend human decency, sometimes war is necessary" is at best paradoxical because it says in effect that human indecency, which war itself surely exemplifies, is sometimes necessary to defend human decency. Perhaps he had in mind the backfires that firefighters sometimes set to help them extinguish fires. This metaphor, however, seems farfetched in connection with war. It is difficult to think of anything that consists of as many different forms of indecency as war does. Not only is its essence the large-scale wreaking of death and destruction, but its side effects and its consequences in the aftermath run a wide range of evils as well. Whatever else war may be, it surely qualifies as the most indecent type of action people can take: it reduces them to the level of the most ferocious beasts and often accomplishes little more than setting the stage for the next, reactive round of such savagery. In any event, considered strictly as a way of sustaining human decency, it gets a failing grade every time because it invariably magnifies the malignity that it purports to resist.

4. "War is horrible, but slavery is worse" (Winston Churchill).

Maybe slavery is worse, but maybe it's not; it depends on the conditions of the war and the conditions of the slavery. Moreover, if one seeks to justify a war on the strength of this statement, he had best be completely certain that but for war, slavery will be the outcome. In many wars, however, slavery was never a possibility because neither side sought to enslave its enemy. Many wars have been fought for limited objectives, if only because more ambitious objectives appeared unattainable or not worth their cost. No war in U.S. history may be accurately described as having been waged to prevent the enslavement of the American people. Some people talk that way about World War II or the Cold War, if it can be counted as a war, but such talk has no firm foundation in facts.

Some may object that the War Between the States was fought to prevent the ongoing slavery of the blacks then held in thrall. But however deeply this view may be embedded in American mythology, it is contrary to fact. As Abraham Lincoln made crystal clear in his letter of August 22, 1862, to *New York Tribune* editor Horace Greeley, he did not mobilize the armed forces to free the slaves, but only to prevent the seceding states from leaving the Union: "My paramount object in this struggle *is* to save the Union, and is *not* either to save or to destroy slavery. If I could save the Union without freeing *any* slave I would do it, and if I could save it by freeing *all* the slaves I would do it; and if I could save it by freeing some and leaving others alone I would also do that." When Lincoln brought forth the Emancipation Proclamation—a document carefully drawn so that at the time of its promulgation it freed not a single slave—he issued it only because at that time it seemed to be a useful means for the attainment of his "paramount object," preserving the Union. The slaves, including those in states that had not seceded, were ultimately freed for good by ratification (at gunpoint in the former Confederate states) of the Thirteenth Amendment in 1865, which is to say as a ramification of the war, which itself had not been undertaken in 1861 in pursuit of this then-unforeseen outcome.

5. "You may think that the Iraq [W]ar is horrible, but there may be some times when you can justify [going to war]."

Perhaps war *can* be justified at "some times," but this statement itself in no way shows that the Iraq War can be justified, and it seems all too obvious that it cannot be. If it could have been justified, the government that launched it would not have had to resort to a succession of lame excuses for waging it, each such excuse being manifestly inadequate or simply false. The obvious insufficiency of any of the reasons put forward explains why so many of us put so much time and effort into trying to divine exactly what *did* impel the Bush administration's rush to war.

6. "War is horrible, but sometimes we need to fight."

Need to fight for what? The objective dictates whether war is a necessary means for its attainment. If the objective was to preserve Americans' freedoms and "way of life," the U.S. government certainly did not need to fight most of the enemies against whom it waged war during the past two centuries. Oddly enough, the only time the enemy actually posed such a threat, during the Cold

War, the United States did *not* go to war against that enemy directly, although it did fight (unnecessarily) the enemy's less-menacing allies—North Korea, China, and North Vietnam. In the other wars, the United States might well have remained at peace had U.S. leaders been sincerely interested in peace rather than committed to warfare.

7. "Of course war is horrible, but it will always exist, and I'm sick of these pacifist [expletive deleted] ruining any shred of political decency that they can manage."

Many people have observed that wars have recurred for thousands of years and therefore will probably continue to occur from time to time. The unstated insinuation seems to be that in view of war's long-running recurrence, nothing can be done about it, so we should all grow up and admit that war is as natural and hence as unalterable as the sun's rising in the east each morning. Warfare is an inescapable aspect of "how the world works."

This outlook contains at least two difficulties. First, many other conditions also have had long-running histories: for example, reliance on astrologers as experts in foretelling the future; affliction with certain cancers; submission to rulers who claim to dominate their subjects by virtue of divine descent or appointment; and many others. People eventually overcame each of these long-established conditions. Science revealed that astrology is nothing more than an elaborate body of superstition; scientists and doctors discovered how to control or cure certain forms of cancer; and citizens learned to laugh at the pretensions of rulers who claim divine descent or appointment (at least, they *had* learned until George W. Bush successfully revived this doctrine among the benighted rubes who form the Republican base). Because wars spring in large part from people's stupidity, ignorance, and gullibility, it is conceivable that alleviation of these conditions might have the effect of diminishing the frequency of warfare, if not of eliminating it altogether.

Second, even if nothing *can* be done to stop the periodic outbreak of war, it does not follow that we ought to shut up and accept every war without complaint. No serious person expects, say, that evil can be eliminated from the human condition, yet we condemn it and struggle against its realization in human affairs. We strive to divert potential evildoers from their malevolent course of action. Scientists and doctors continue to seek cures for cancers that have afflicted humanity for millennia. Even conditions that cannot be wholly eliminated can sometimes be mitigated, but only if someone tries to mitigate them. War may belong to this class of events.

Finally, whatever else one might say about the pacifists, one may surely say that if everyone were a pacifist, no wars would occur. Pacifism may be criticized on various grounds, as it always has been and still is, but to say that pacifists "lack any shred of political decency" seems itself to be indecent. Remember: war is horrible, as everybody now concedes, but many immediately put out of mind.

8. **"Every war is horrible, but freedom and justice cannot be allowed to be defeated by tyranny and injustice. As hideous as war is, it is not as hideous as the things it can stop and prevent."**

This statement assumes that war amounts to a contest between freedom and justice on one side and tyranny and injustice on the other. One scarcely commits the dreaded sin of moral equivalence, however, by observing that few wars present such a stark contrast, in which only the children of God fight on one side and only the children of Satan fight on the other. One reason why war is so horrible is that it invariably drags into its charnel house many—again, the children are the most undeniable examples—who must be held blameless for any actions or threats that might have incited the war.

Even if we set aside such clear-cut innocents and consider only persons in the upper echelons of the conflicting sides, it is rare to find only angels on one side and only demons on the other. In World War II, for example, the Allied states were led by such angels as Winston Churchill, who relished the horrific terror bombing of German cities; Josef Stalin, one of the greatest mass murderers of all time; Franklin D. Roosevelt, of whose moral uprightness the less said the better; and Harry S Truman, who took pleasure in annihilating hundreds of thousands of defenseless Japanese noncombatants initially with incendiary bombs and ultimately with nuclear weapons. Yes, the other side had Adolf Hitler, whose fiendishness I have no desire to deny or minimize, but the overall character of the leadership on both sides sufficiently attests that there was enough evil to go around. As for the ordinary soldiers, of course everyone who knows anything about actual combat appreciates that the men on both sides quickly become brutalized and routinely commit atrocities of every imaginable size and shape.

So it is far from clear that war is always or even typically "not as hideous as the things it can stop and prevent." On many occasions, refusal to resort to war, even in the face of undeniable evils, may still be the better course. When World War II ended, leaving more than 62 million dead, most of them civilians, and hundreds of millions displaced, homeless, wounded, sick, or impoverished, the survivors might well have doubted whether conditions would have been even more terrible if the war had not taken place. (The dead were unavailable for comment.) To make matters worse, owing to the war the monster Stalin gained control of an enormous area stretching from Czechoslovakia to Korea; and because of the defeat of the Japanese Empire, the monster Mao Zedong would soon take complete control of China and impose a murderous reign of terror on the world's most populous country that cost the lives of perhaps another 60 million persons (possibly as many as 77 million, according to one plausible estimate). It is difficult to believe that the situation in China would have been so awful even if the Japanese had succeeded in incorporating China into the Greater East Asia Co-Prosperity Sphere.

9. **"I grant you the war is horrible, but it is a war, after all. You have to compare apples to apples, and when I do that, I see this war is going well."**

This statement about the U.S. war in Iraq exemplifies what some call the "not as bad as Hamburg-Dresden-Tokyo-Hiroshima-Nagasaki" defense of brutal warfare. If we make such pinnacles of savagery our standard, then, sure enough, everything else pales by comparison. But why should anyone adopt such a grotesque standard? To do so is to concede that anything less horrible than the very worst cases is "not so bad." In truth, warfare's effects are sufficiently hideous at every level. What the Israelis did in Lebanon a few years ago bears no comparison with the February 1945 Allied attack on Dresden, of course, but the sight of even one little Lebanese child dead, her bloody body gruesomely mangled by an explosion, ought to be enough to give pause to any proponent of resort to war. Try putting yourself in the place of that child's mother.

10. "[Certain writers] all agreed that war is horrible but said the Bible gives government the authority to wage war to save innocent lives."

Biblical scholars have been disputing what Christians may and may not do in regard to war for two thousand years. The dispute continues today, so the matter is certainly not resolved among devout Christians. Even if Christians may go to war to save innocent lives, however, a big question remains: Is the government going to war for this purpose or for one of the countless other purposes that lead governments to make war? Saving the innocent makes an appealing excuse, but it is often, if not always, only a pretext. "Just war" writers from Augustine to Thomas Aquinas to Grotius to the latest contributors have agonized over the ready availability of such pretexts and warned against the wickedness of advancing them when the real motives are less justifiable or even plainly immoral.

For centuries, European combatants on all sides invoked God's blessing for their wars against one another. As recently as World War II, the Germans had "Gott mit Uns," a declaration that adorned the belt buckles of Wehrmacht soldiers in *both* world wars. Strange to say, in 1917 and 1918 Christian ministers of the gospel in pulpits across the United States were assuring their congregations that *their* nation-state was engaged in a "war for righteousness" (the title of Richard M. Gamble's splendid book[2] about this repellent episode). So the invocation of biblical authority really doesn't get us very far: the enemy may be invoking the same authority.

Nowadays, of course, one side invokes the Jewish and Christian God, whereas the other calls upon the blessing of Allah. Whether this bifurcated manner of gaining divine sanction for the commission of mass murder and mayhem represents progress or not, I leave to the learned theologians.

11. "War is horrible, but thank God we have men and women who are willing and able to protect our people and our freedom."

These men and women may be willing and able to supply such protection, but do they really end up doing so? Our leaders constantly proclaim that

---

2. Richard M. Gamble, *The War for Righteousness: Progressive Christianity, the Great War, and the Rise of the Messianic Nation* (Wilmington, Del.: Intercollegiate Studies Institute, 2003).

their wars are aimed at protecting us and our freedoms—"We go forward," declared George W. Bush, "to defend freedom and all that is good and just in our world"—but one has to wonder, considering that in the entire history of warfare each major U.S. war (with the possible exception of the War for Independence) left the general run of the American people with fewer freedoms after the war than they had enjoyed before the war.

In my book *Crisis and Leviathan*,[3] I document this ratchet effect in detail for the two world wars. After World War I, the U.S. government not only kept taxes far above their prewar levels but also retained newly court-sanctioned powers to conscript men for foreign wars, to interfere with virtually any private transaction in international trade and finance (Trading with the Enemy Act of 1917), and to suppress free speech in a draconian manner (Sedition Act of 1918). After World War II, the government again kept taxes much higher they had been before the war, retained for the first time a large peacetime military apparatus, created the Central Intelligence Agency as a sort of personal presidential intelligence and quasi-military outfit, continued to draft men for military service even during peacetime, and engaged much more pervasively in central management and manipulation of the private economy. The people for their part gained not freedom, but the privilege of living with the very real threat of nuclear holocaust hovering over them for four decades while the U.S. government kept the Cold War pot boiling.

The so-called war on terror has struck deeply into Americans' right to privacy by vastly enhancing the government's surveillance activities and virtually gutting the Fourth Amendment's protection against warrantless searches and seizures. It has also led the government to create an agency now empowered to commit acts in U.S. airports that if committed by others would be prosecuted as sexual assault and battery and as criminal molestation of children. This "war" has also served to justify one of the greatest military spending run-ups in U.S. history, leaving U.S. military-related spending—if correctly measured—greater than the comparable spending of all other nations combined. Nevertheless, Americans are no safer because of these sweeping infringements of their liberties, many of which have been de facto pork-barrel projects and others of which have been

---

3. Robert Higgs, *Crisis and Leviathan: Critical Episodes in the Growth of American Government* (New York: Oxford University Press, 1987).

nothing more than security theater. War, whether real or make-believe, serves to justify huge increases in government spending, taxing, borrowing, and exertion of power over private affairs, and such government surges attract opportunists galore but do little or nothing to improve people's real security. Indeed, in the war on terror the government has added fuel to the fire of Muslim rage against Americans in the Middle East but has achieved nothing positive to compensate for this heightened threat.

Every time the rulers set out to protect the village, they decide that the best way to do so is to destroy it in the process. Call me a cynic, but I can't help wondering whether protection of the people and their freedoms was really the state's objective in each of these cases, and after fifty years of thinking about the matter, I've come up with some pretty attractive alternative hypotheses. One of them is that, as marine general Smedley Butler famously expressed it, "war is a racket,"[4] but I have other alternative hypotheses, too.

12. "War is horrible, but some economic good came out of World War II. It brought the United States out of one of the greatest slumps in history, the Great Depression."

This venerable broken-window fallacy refuses to die, no matter how many times a stake is driven through its heart. Most Americans believe it. Worse, because less excusable, nearly all historians and even a large majority of economists do so as well. I've been whacking at this nonsense for several decades, but, so far as I can tell, I've scarcely made a dent in it. Should anyone care to see a complete counterargument, I recommend the first five chapters of my book *Depression, War, and Cold War*.[5]

In brief, the government did not—indeed, could not—create wealth simply by spending vast amounts of money (much of it newly created as a result of cooperative Federal Reserve policies) on soldiers and weapons. The government did wipe out unemployment during the war, but only by putting millions of men in the armed forces. During World War II, these forces absorbed, primarily

---

4. Smedley D. Butler, *War Is a Racket* (New York: Round Table Press, 1935), at http://www.lexrex.com/enlightened/articles/warisaracket.htm.
5. Robert Higgs, *Depression, War, and Cold War: Challenging the Myths of Conflict and Prosperity* (Oakland, Calif.: The Independent Institute, 2006).

by conscription, 16 million persons at one time or another (about three times the number of persons officially counted as unemployed in 1941) and caused a similar number of people to be employed in military-supply industries. The economy looked prosperous because everybody was working and (except those in the armed forces) earning seemingly good wages and salaries. Yet the supply of civilian goods and services actually shrank, and many ordinary goods were not available at all (e.g., new cars) or were available only in limited, rationed amounts (e.g., meats, sugar, canned foods, gasoline, and tires). Private investment also dropped sharply as the government took over the allocation of capital, directing it into arms-related projects. So the apparent "wartime prosperity" was spurious. Only when the war ended and the military machine was largely dismantled did genuine prosperity return, for the first time since 1929.

13. "War is horrible, but whining about it is worse. Either put up or shut up."

Some people always reject the denunciation of any familiar social institution or conduct unless the denouncer offers a "constructive criticism"—that is, unless he puts forward a promising plan to eliminate the evil he denounces. I admit at once that I have discovered no cure for the human tendency to resort to war even when much more intelligent and humane alternatives are available. I have been trying to convince people that on nearly all such occasions they are allowing their rulers to bamboozle them and to turn them into cannon fodder for purposes that serve the rulers' interests, not the people's. I'm getting nowhere in this effort, but I'm going to keep trying. I'm also going to continue to denounce stupidity, ignorance, ugliness, bullying, and cruelty, even though I don't expect to succeed on those fronts, either.

14. "Of course, war is horrible, but at present it's still the only guarantee to maintain peace."

The statement as it stands is self-contradictory because it affirms that the only way to make sure that we will have peace is by going to war. Perhaps, if we are feeling generous, we may interpret the statement as the time-honored exhortation that to maintain the peace, we should *prepare* for war, hoping that by dissuading any aggressor from moving against us, our preparation will preserve the peace. Although this policy is not self-contradictory, it is dangerous because the preparation we make for war may itself move us toward actually going to war. For example, preparation for war may entail increasing the number of military officers and allowing the top brass to exert greater influence in making foreign policy. Those officers may believe that without war, their careers will go nowhere, and hence they may tilt their advice to civilian authorities toward risking or actually making war, even when peace might easily be preserved. Military suppliers may likewise use their political influence to foster international suspicions and fears that otherwise might be allayed. Wars are not good for business in general, but they are good for the munitions contractors. Certain legislators may develop an interest in militarism; perhaps it helps them to attract campaign contributions from arms contractors, veterans' groups, and members of the national guard and military reserve organizations. Pretty soon we may find ourselves dealing, as President Dwight D. Eisenhower did, with a military-industrial-congressional complex, and we may find that it packs a great deal of political punch and acts in a way that, all things considered, diminishes the chance of keeping the country at peace.

Conclusion

From the foregoing commentary, a recurrent theme may be extracted: those who argue that "war is horrible, but . . ." nearly always use this rhetorical construction not to frame a genuinely serious and honest balancing of reasons for and against war, but only to acknowledge what cannot be hidden—that war is horrible—and then to pass on immediately to an affirmation that notwithstanding the horrors, whose actual forms and dimensions they neither specify nor examine in detail, a certain war ought to be fought.

The reasons given to justify fighting this particular war, however, generally amount to claims that cannot support a strong case. They are often not even bona fide reasons, but mere propaganda, especially when they emanate from official sources. They sometimes even rest on historical errors, such as the claim that the armed forces in past wars have somehow kept foreigners from depriving us of our liberties. The case for war rests most often on ill-founded speculation about what will happen if we do not go to war.

People need to recognize, however, that government officials and their running dogs in the media, among others, are not soothsayers. None of us knows the future, but these interested parties lack a disinterested motive for making a careful, well-informed forecast. They have, as the saying goes, an agenda of their own. "The best and the brightest" of our leaders and their kept experts generally amount to little more than what C. Wright Mills called "crackpot realists," and on occasion, such as the one since the attacks of September 11, 2001, they don't meet even that standard. Hence, these geniuses, equipped with all of that secret information they constantly emphasize their critics don't possess, have lately put forward forecasts of a "cake walk" through Iraq, a "slam dunk" on finding lots of weapons of mass destruction there, and liberal-democratic dominoes falling across the Middle East—forecasts that fit more comfortably in a lunatic asylum than in a discussion among rational, well-informed people.

In arguing that we should go to war, the government generally relies on marshalling patriotic emotion and reflexive loyalty rather than on making a sensible case. Much of the discussion that does take place is a sham because the government officials who pretend to listen to other opinions, as U.S. leaders did most recently during 2002 and early 2003, have already decided what they are going to do, no matter what other people may say. These rulers know that once the war starts, nearly everybody will fall into line and "support the troops."

If someone demands that the skeptic about war offer constructive criticism, here is my proposal: always insist that the *burden of proof* should rest heavily on the warmonger. This protocol, which is now anything but standard operating procedure, is eminently judicious precisely because, as we all recognize, war is horrible. Given its horrors, which in reality are much greater than most people appreciate, it only makes sense that those who propose to enter into those horrors make a very, very strong case for doing so. If they cannot—and I submit that they almost never can—then people will serve their own interests best by declining an invitation to war. As a rule, the most rational, humane, and auspicious course of action is indeed to give peace a chance.

PART II

Closer Looks at Key Actors and Critical Events

9

Who Was Edward M. House?

EDWARD M. HOUSE, a man now almost completely forgotten, was one of the most important Americans of the twentieth century. Given the sorry state of historical knowledge in the United States—for example, most high school seniors do not know that the War Between the States was fought sometime between 1850 and 1900[1]—we cannot reasonably expect many people today to identify House, much less to know anything about him. I suspect that scarcely anyone except a smattering of history teachers and a few history mavens can accurately state why he was an important figure in U.S. history. Yet he arguably had a greater impact on the past century than all but a handful of other actors.

Political history tends to be written primarily with reference to formal state leaders—pharaohs, Caesars, kings, prime ministers, presidents, and their most notable civilian and military officers. Yet probably at all times and places much less prominent individuals have exerted potent influence out of the limelight or completely behind the scenes. I have long been interested in what we might call the general theory of gray eminence and in leading specimens of the genus. The typical American at present knows little or nothing, for example, about Eliju Root, Bernard M. Baruch, John J. McCloy, Clark Clifford, and David Rockefeller, although each of these men played a powerful role in shaping the world in which we now live. I do not mean to suggest that all such unofficial movers and shakers are rich and use their wealth as the key that admits them to the inner sanctums of official power. Some, such as House, were not outrageously

---

1. Kat Long, "Survey: U.S. Students Fail History: Many High School Seniors Don't Know Basic Historical Dates or Events," February 27, 2008, at http://americanaffairs.suite101 .com/article.cfm/us_students_get_a_d_in_history.

rich, and some who were rich, such as Baruch, had great influence not simply because of their wealth, although having great gobs of money at one's disposal certainly never hurts when one sets out to cultivate so-called statesmen.

Edward Mandell House (1858–1938) grew up in Houston, Texas. His father, Thomas William House, an English immigrant who had made a fortune as a blockade runner during the War Between the States, died the third-richest man in the state in 1880, leaving to his children an estate valued at $500,000. Edward managed his share of the inheritance astutely, even though he spent much of his time engaged in politics—never running for an elective office or seeking an appointive one, but helping other men to gain office and make policy. Though a sickly man and certainly not a flamboyant one, he had a flair for making friends who appreciated his discretion, respected his views, and valued his counsel. This talent for winning friends and influencing people would remain the basis of his remarkable achievements in politics throughout his life. He was, in today's lingo, a very smooth operator, appreciated all the more because he clearly had no desire to displace the king he had just helped to place on the throne. The power he sought was the power behind the throne.[2]

By the first decade of the twentieth century, House was seeking a new, wider stage for his political activities. He had played an important part in getting four governors elected in Texas and in guiding their policies in office—the first of them, Jim Hogg, had given him the entirely honorific title of "colonel," by which he was known thereafter—but he was losing interest in the local scene.

From 1886 on, House maintained a capacious residence in Austin, where he wined and dined local politicos, but in 1902 he added an apartment in New York City, where he had many friends and contacts. He also spent a great deal of time in the summers at a rented house on the shore near Boston and in Europe. Wherever he went, doors were opened to him, and he and his wife, Loulie, entertained actively in return. The range of his friendships, acquaintances, and social connections was extraordinary. His recent biographer, Godfrey Hodgson, reports: "[House's] diary records meals with Henry James, Edith Wharton, and Rudyard

---

2. Murray N. Rothbard refers to the soft-spoken Texan as "the mysterious House" and describes him as President Woodrow Wilson's "foreign policy Svengali." Murray N. Rothbard, *Wall Street, Banks, and American Foreign Policy* (Burlingame, Calif.: Center for Libertarian Studies, 1995), 15, 18.

Kipling, as well as with the virtuoso pianist Ignazy Jan Paderewski, who became president of Poland. He mingled with politicians, generals, bankers, academics, journalists, and society hostesses in New York, Paris, and London. He knew J. P. Morgan Jr. well enough to call him 'Jack,' and he dined with Henry Clay Frick in the house that became his great art museum."[3] Not a bad showing for a man who had left Cornell before graduating and whose annual income ranged only from $20,000 to $25,000 (approximately $450,000 to $560,000 in today's dollars).

In 1911, House spied what he took to be a potentially rising star to which he might hitch his idle political wagon, a man with no prior experience as a politician until his election as governor of New Jersey in November 1910. Woodrow Wilson (1856–1924) had been, except for a brief stint as a fledgling lawyer, a lifelong academic; he spent his life prior to 1910 as a student, professor, and university administrator, serving from 1902 to 1910 as president of Princeton University, an office in which he gained a well-deserved reputation for self-righteous unwillingness to compromise. After his election as governor, a number of Democrats began to tout him as the party's next candidate for the presidency, and in the winter of 1910–11 House decided to join this movement, "to do what I could to further Governor Wilson's fortunes."[4]

House played an important role as campaign strategist and intraparty peace-maker in 1911 and 1912, and he deserves part of the credit for getting Wilson first the nomination and then the presidency. Of course, the principal person responsible for Wilson's election was Theodore Roosevelt, whose insatiable craving for power had led him to bolt the Republican Party and run as a Progressive Party (Bull Moose) candidate, thereby splitting the opposition to Wilson and ensuring a Democratic victory. House played an even more important role after Wilson's election because the president-elect had little interest in the nuts and bolts of party politics, including the distribution of patronage and the selection of men for cabinet and other high-level positions, and he left these decisions largely in House's hands. Wilson offered House himself any cabinet position he wanted, except secretary of state, which had been reserved for William Jennings

---

3. Godfrey Hodgson, *Woodrow Wilson's Right Hand: The Life of Colonel Edward M. House* (New Haven, Conn.: Yale University Press, 2006), 9.
4. Quoted in Hodgson, *Woodrow Wilson's Right Hand,* 56.

Bryan, but House declined, preferring to work in the shadows as the president's most trusted adviser.

In this capacity, House quickly developed an extraordinarily intimate relationship with the president as his political adviser, personal confidant, and frequent social companion. He engaged actively in the extended politicking that ultimately led to passage of the Federal Reserve Act and in the ticklish conduct of U.S. relations with Mexico, then in the throes of violent revolution. As war clouds began to gather over Europe, House, with Wilson's approval, undertook to head off hostilities by bringing about an understanding among the United States, Great Britain, and Germany, making them jointly the guarantors of world peace. He met with Kaiser Wilhelm II and separately with British foreign secretary Sir Edward Grey, among others, to work up interest in the plan, but this attempt at preemptive reconciliation obviously never came to fruition.

During the war, House actively engaged in efforts to bring the fighting to an end. He shared Wilson's view that the most desirable outcome would be one that left the postwar world drastically reshaped in a way that eliminated or greatly diminished militarism, promoted national self-determination, spread democracy, left the United States standing astride the international political system, and brought about the recognition of Wilson as the world's savior. In short, House shared Wilson's peculiar megalomania and undertook to make its main objective a reality. At the same time, House, ever the practical deal maker and compromiser, understood that the United States could not simply impose its will on the world and that the Americans would have to yield to other powerful nations, especially Great Britain and France, some of the prizes they sought to gain from the war. As Hodgson writes, both "Wilson and House were willing to bargain territories and populations for the particular peace they wanted," even if they had to sacrifice "national self-determination" along the way.[5]

After the war began in 1914, Wilson proclaimed that the United States would remain neutral in word and deed, but Wilson and House's natural inclination was to favor the British, and as various provocations by both sides ensued, the president and his right-hand man dealt with them in a fashion that tilted the United States increasingly toward frank support of the Allies and

5. Hodgson, *Woodrow Wilson's Right Hand,* 106.

opposition to the Central Powers. As early as the *Lusitania*'s sinking in May 1915, House advised Wilson that Americans could "no longer remain neutral spectators," but Wilson moved toward war more hesitantly.[6]

When Secretary of State Bryan refused to abandon honest neutrality, sensibly holding the British starvation blockade of Germany to be as reprehensible as the German torpedoing of (arms-carrying) passenger liners, he was pushed out of the government and replaced by Robert Lansing. From the outset, however, Lansing was allowed little real discretion, and House acted as the de facto foreign minister. A joke went around in Washington:

Question: How do you spell "Lansing"?
Answer: H-O-U-S-E.

House began to preach "preparedness," which meant building up a great U.S. army and navy. Hodgson writes: "While the president dreamed of saving the world, House was beginning to contemplate the implications for the American state of being a world power. In this activity between 1915 and 1917 it is not fanciful to see a first, sketchy draft of what would become the national security state." Although House continued his efforts to bring the warring parties to a truce, he admitted early in 1916 that "in spite of all he was doing, a break with Germany could not be averted but only deferred."[7] According to French foreign minister Jules Cambon, House told him in February 1916 that U.S. entry into the war on the Allied side was inevitable and awaited only a serviceable incident that would cause the American people to rally behind the president's call for war.[8] Needless to say, a peacemaker who is already resigned to war is unlikely to bring about peace, and, indeed, House's efforts failed to halt the massive, pointless bloodletting in Europe.

When Wilson ran for reelection in 1916, House played a much greater role than he had played in the campaign in 1912. He had "no official role in the campaign, yet he planned its structure; set its tone; guided its finance; chose speakers, tactics, and strategy; and, not least, handled the campaign's greatest asset and

---

6. Hodgson, *Woodrow Wilson's Right Hand,* 109.
7. Hodgson, *Woodrow Wilson's Right Hand,* 113, 115.
8. Hodgson, *Woodrow Wilson's Right Hand,* 116.

greatest potential liability: its brilliant but temperamental candidate."[9] After campaigning on the slogan "He kept us out of war," Wilson narrowly won the election, garnering 277 electoral votes to Charles Evans Hughes's 254.

Shortly after beginning his second term, however, Wilson asked Congress for a declaration of war.[10] We may properly attribute a substantial share of the credit (or blame) for this action to House's subtle and persistent efforts to move the president toward it during the preceding two years.[11] As House confided to his diary, he had worked from the start of his relationship with Wilson to influence him in a certain direction: "I began with him before he became President and I have never relaxed my efforts. At every turn, I have stirred his ambition to become the great liberal leader of the world."[12] In Wilson, a man whose grotesquely swollen conception of his own importance had few equals, House's guidance had encountered a highly receptive pupil.

Once the United States became a declared belligerent, the prospect of an Allied victory increased greatly, and House occupied himself actively not only in engineering a vehicle to end the fighting, but also in planning the contours of the postwar world. Like Wilson, House "believed that the war had been imposed on the peoples of Europe by the monarchies and their aristocracies," and therefore both men maintained that a postwar settlement should include, among other things, the destruction of the German and Austro-Hungarian empires and the creation of a number of new, democratic states in central Europe.[13] To fill in the details of this vision, Wilson accepted House's proposal to assemble a group of experts.[14] The resulting project was known as "the Inquiry," and the plan it created became the basis for Wilson's Fourteen Points and for his principal proposals at the Versailles conference. The Inquiry ultimately placed

---

9. Hodgson, *Woodrow Wilson's Right Hand,* 126.

10. In Rothbard's estimation, "Woodrow Wilson's decision to enter the war may have been the single most fateful action of the 20th century, causing untold and unending misery and destruction" (*Wall Street, Banks, and American Foreign Policy,* 21).

11. Besides Hodgson, *Woodrow Wilson's Right Hand,* see Rothbard, *Wall Street, Banks, and American Foreign Policy,* 18–19.

12. Quoted in Hodgson, *Woodrow Wilson's Right Hand,* 139.

13. Hodgson, *Woodrow Wilson's Right Hand,* 150.

14. Council on Foreign Relations, "Continuing the Inquiry," n.d., at http://www.cfr.org /about/history/cfr/inquiry.html.

126 scholars on its payroll. Although each of them had substantial credentials, hardly any of them had expertise on European politics—a shortcoming that helped to doom the president's dealings with the likes of David Lloyd George and Georges Clemenceau at Versailles. Indeed, as one ponders this big committee's hubristic attempt to redraw the map of much of Europe and other parts of the world, such as the Middle East, F. A. Hayek's idea of the "pretense of knowledge" springs to mind.[15] According to Hodgson, "Few [members of the Inquiry] had any detailed knowledge of, for example, the disputed frontiers of Romania, Hungary, or Bulgaria, still less of the history and ethnography of Poland or the Ottoman Empire. One who was assigned to work on Italy confessed later that he was 'handicapped by a lack of knowledge of Italian.' . . . [W]hen it came to what we would now call the Middle East, the Inquiry more or less gave up."[16] Is it any wonder, then, that the arrangements made at Versailles for the Middle East proved to be the source of what has aptly been called "a peace to end all peace" and that almost a century later the world continues to pay a horrible price for the statesmen's bungling in 1919?[17]

House contributed probably more than anyone else to the formulation of Wilson's Fourteen Points, which served as the Germans' understanding of how they would be treated when they silenced their guns in November 1918. On the night of January 5, 1918, Wilson and House had sat down together at 10:30 to sketch out a major speech by Wilson on his vision for a postwar settlement. Two hours later they had, as House wrote in his diary, "finished remaking the map of the world."[18] When Wilson delivered his speech, however, he "conspicuously ignored complexities the Inquiry had recognized."[19] (Of course, politicians

---

15. See F. A. Hayek, "The Pretense of Knowledge," in *New Studies in Philosophy, Politics, Economics, and the History of Ideas* (Chicago: University of Chicago Press, 1978), 23–24.
16. Hodgson, *Woodrow Wilson's Right Hand,* 160.
17. David Fromkin, *A Peace to End All Peace: Creating the Modern Middle East, 1914–1922* (New York: Henry Holt, 1989). After the Treaty of Versailles was signed, the Inquiry quickly transformed itself, with funding from leading figures in American business and banking, into the Council on Foreign Relations (CFR), officially established in 1921 (see the source cited in note 15). The CFR has arguably been the most influential private group in the foreign-policy realm since its inception—and thus another of House's significant enduring legacies.
18. Quoted in Hodgson, *Woodrow Wilson's Right Hand,* 165.
19. Hodgson, *Woodrow Wilson's Right Hand,* 167.

always ignore complexities; if they don't, they won't last long as politicians.) Later, after the Treaty of Versailles had been hammered out—and Wilson's amateurish attempt at direct diplomacy was hammered pretty severely in the process—the Germans justly complained that they had been hoodwinked into the armistice by Wilson's promise to make the Fourteen Points the basis of a postwar settlement. As English diplomat and author Harold Nicolson, a member of the British delegation, wrote, "It is difficult to resist the impression that the Enemy Powers accepted the Fourteen Points as they stood; whereas the Allied Powers accepted them only as interpreted by Colonel House. . . . Somewhere, amid the hurried and anxious imprecisions of those October [1918] days, lurks the explanation of the fundamental misunderstanding which has since arisen."[20] And what a momentous misunderstanding it was! Even James Brown Scott, a legal expert in the U.S. delegation, said of the ultimate treaty that "the statesmen have . . . made a peace that renders another war inevitable."[21] In light of this history, we might credit House with having made an important contribution to ending the fighting in 1918 *and* to establishing the preconditions for its resumption in 1939.

House and three others joined Wilson himself to compose the five-man American delegation to the high-level negotiations at Versailles that began in December 1918. House shared Wilson's vision of a League of Nations, and at the conference he did as much as anyone to make this vision a reality, albeit one born with a congenital defect owing to the Senate's ultimate rejection of U.S. membership. Twenty-six years later the creation of the United Nations, a second attempt to establish an effective international peacekeeping league, may therefore be traced back in part to House's efforts.

When Wilson departed France in mid-February 1919, he left House at the conference "to act in his place and with his full confidence."[22] In the president's absence, House proceeded to do what he had been doing successfully for decades: he made deals, compromising where necessary to gain the other parties' agreement and creating the best possible arrangements he could make in an extremely

---

20. Quoted in Hodgson, *Woodrow Wilson's Right Hand,* 190.
21. Quoted in Hodgson, *Woodrow Wilson's Right Hand,* 243.
22. Hodgson, *Woodrow Wilson's Right Hand,* 215.

complex and challenging situation. Although he kept Wilson informed as he went along, the president seems not to have comprehended fully the agreements that House was making in France. When Wilson returned to Versailles in mid-March and absorbed the details, he reacted with dismay, if not with horror, to what he viewed as the betrayal of his high ideals for the settlement.

Although House continued to negotiate specific matters at Versailles, he never again acted as the chief U.S. delegate, and the intimate relationship between House and Wilson quickly dissolved: "[T]heir friendship never recovered from the events of February and March 1919. It ended in bitterness and mutual incomprehension, with grave consequences for both of them and ultimately—it really is no exaggeration to say—for the peace of the world."[23] After the Germans signed the treaty in June, House saw the president off for his return voyage to the United States. Their conversation on that occasion was the last they would ever have.

"Wilson's entourage [consisting of his wife, Edith; his personal physician, Admiral Cary T. Grayson; his press secretary, Ray Stannard Baker; and that grayest of gray eminences, Bernard Baruch], then and for the rest of their lives, interpreted House's entirely intelligible and honorable diplomatic maneuvers as the blackest treason."[24] Edith Wilson, whom the widowed president had married in 1915, had disliked House from the beginning. She evidently resented him because of the intimacy he shared with her new husband. After the president became incapacitated by a major stroke in September 1919, Edith, besides acting as de facto president of the United States for much of the remainder of his term, made sure that no communication from House reached the bedridden Wilson. For years, the two men had been so close that Wilson trusted House to speak for him, confident that his own thoughts would be expressed precisely. "Mr. House," the president had once said, "is my second personality. He is my independent self. His thoughts and mine are one."[25] But now House found himself completely cut off. It is a dangerous thing to disappoint a vainglorious and vindictive man, but no less dangerous to vex his ruthless, scheming wife.

---

23. Hodgson, *Woodrow Wilson's Right Hand*, 217.
24. Hodgson, *Woodrow Wilson's Right Hand*, 225.
25. Quoted in Hodgson, *Woodrow Wilson's Right Hand*, 6.

House lived another twenty years after the war. He continued to circulate in the highest circles in the United States, especially among the ringmasters of the Democratic Party, and in Europe, but he never again exercised the kind of influence he had exercised from 1912 to 1919 by virtue of his close association with Woodrow Wilson. He went to considerable lengths to tell his side of the story and to vindicate his actions, while Edith Wilson and the other members of Wilson's entourage continued to demonize the erstwhile gray eminence and to blame him for the president's postwar failures. House still traveled in style and socialized with European aristocrats and American plutocrats. He was, in Hodgson's expression, "a grandee on a world scale."[26] He never publicly criticized Woodrow Wilson, and even in private, where he did criticize, he always professed loyalty. When Wilson died in 1924, House wished to attend the funeral, but Baruch told him that he would not be admitted. After advising Franklin D. Roosevelt in the 1920s and early 1930s, House became a peripheral figure in the Brains Trust in 1932 and 1933 and contributed to bringing about Roosevelt's election as president. Only in his final few years did he finally withdraw into his private affairs.

He never became bitter. In old age, he developed greater infirmities and grew tired of living, but he was satisfied that he had played a significant role in great events. As he said, "My hand has been on things."[27] Indeed, it had been—to a degree that in our day very few Americans appreciate.

26. Hodgson, *Woodrow Wilson's Right Hand,* 263.
27. Quoted in Hodgson, *Woodrow Wilson's Right Hand,* 272.

10

How U.S. Economic Warfare Provoked Japan's Attack on Pearl Harbor

ASK A TYPICAL AMERICAN how the United States got into World War II, and he will almost certainly tell you that the Japanese attacked Pearl Harbor and the Americans fought back. Ask him why the Japanese attacked Pearl Harbor, and he will probably need some time to gather his thoughts. He might say that the Japanese were aggressive militarists who wanted to take over the world or, at least, the Asia Pacific part of it. Ask him what the United States did to provoke the Japanese, and he will probably say that the Americans did nothing: we were just minding our own business when the crazy Japanese, completely without justification, mounted a sneak attack on us, catching us totally by surprise in Hawaii on December 7, 1941.

You can't blame him much. For more than sixty years, such beliefs have constituted the generally accepted view among Americans, the one taught in schools and depicted in movies—what "every schoolboy knows." This orthodox view is unfortunately a tissue of misconceptions. Don't bother to ask the typical American what U.S. economic warfare had to do with provoking the Japanese to mount their attack because he won't know. Indeed, he will have no idea what you're talking about.

In the late nineteenth century, Japan's economy began to grow and to industrialize rapidly. Because Japan has few natural resources, many of its burgeoning industries had to rely on imported raw materials, such as coal, iron ore or steel scrap, tin, copper, bauxite, rubber, and petroleum. Without access to such imports, many of which came from the United States or from European colonies in Southeast Asia, Japan's industrial economy would have ground to a halt. By engaging in international trade, however, the Japanese had built a moderately advanced industrial economy by 1941.

At the same time, they had also built a military-industrial complex to support an increasingly powerful army and navy. These armed forces allowed Japan to project its power into various places in the Pacific and East Asia, including Korea and northern China, much as the United States used its growing industrial might to equip armed forces that projected U.S. power into the Caribbean, Latin America, and even as far away as the Philippine Islands.

When Franklin D. Roosevelt became president in 1933, the U.S. government fell under the control of a man who disliked the Japanese and harbored a romantic affection for the Chinese because, some writers have speculated, Roosevelt's ancestors had made money in the China trade.[1] Roosevelt also disliked the Germans in general and Adolf Hitler in particular, and he tended to favor the British in his personal relations and in world affairs. He did not pay much attention to foreign policy, however, until his New Deal began to peter out in 1937. He thereafter relied heavily on foreign policy to fulfill his political ambitions, including his desire for reelection to an unprecedented third term.

When Germany began to rearm and to seek *Lebensraum* aggressively in the late 1930s, the Roosevelt administration cooperated closely with the British and the French in measures to oppose German expansion. After World War II commenced in 1939, this U.S. assistance grew ever greater and included such measures as the so-called destroyer deal and the deceptively named Lend-Lease program. In anticipation of U.S. entry into the war, British and U.S. military staffs secretly formulated plans for joint operations. U.S. forces sought to create a war-justifying incident by cooperating with the British navy in attacks on German U-boats in the northern Atlantic, but Hitler refused to take the bait, thus denying Roosevelt the pretext he craved for making the United States a full-fledged, declared belligerent—an end that the great majority of Americans opposed.

In June 1940, Henry L. Stimson, who had been secretary of war under William Howard Taft and secretary of state under Herbert Hoover, became secretary of war again. Stimson was a lion of the Anglophile, northeastern upper crust and no friend of the Japanese. In support of the so-called Open Door Policy

---

1. Harry Elmer Barnes, "Summary and Conclusions," in *Perpetual War for Perpetual Peace: A Critical Examination of the Foreign Policy of Franklin Delano Roosevelt and Its Aftermath*, edited by Harry Elmer Barnes (Caldwell, Idaho: Caxton Printers, 1953), 682–83.

for China, Stimson favored the use of economic sanctions to obstruct Japan's advance in Asia. Treasury Secretary Henry Morgenthau and Interior Secretary Harold Ickes vigorously endorsed this policy. Roosevelt hoped that such sanctions would goad the Japanese into making a rash mistake by launching a war against the United States, which would bring in Germany because Japan and Germany were allied.

The Roosevelt administration, while curtly dismissing Japanese diplomatic overtures to harmonize relations, accordingly imposed a series of increasingly stringent economic sanctions on Japan. In 1939, the United States terminated the 1911 commercial treaty with Japan. "On July 2, 1940, Roosevelt signed the Export Control Act, authorizing the President to license or prohibit the export of essential defense materials." Under this authority, "[o]n July 31, exports of aviation motor fuels and lubricants and No. 1 heavy melting iron and steel scrap were restricted." Next, in a move aimed at Japan, Roosevelt slapped an embargo, effective October 16, "on all exports of scrap iron and steel to destinations other than Britain and the nations of the Western Hemisphere." Finally, on July 26, 1941, Roosevelt "froze Japanese assets in the United States, thus bringing commercial relations between the nations to an effective end. One week later Roosevelt embargoed the export of such grades of oil as still were in commercial flow to Japan."[2] The British and the Dutch followed suit, embargoing exports to Japan from their colonies in Southeast Asia.

Roosevelt and his subordinates knew they were putting Japan in an untenable position and that the Japanese government might well try to escape the stranglehold by going to war. Having broken the Japanese diplomatic code, the Americans knew, among many other things, what Foreign Minister Teijiro Toyoda had communicated to Ambassador Kichisaburo Nomura on July 31: "Commercial and economic relations between Japan and third countries, led by England and the United States, are gradually becoming so horribly strained that we cannot endure it much longer. Consequently, our Empire, to save its very life, must take measures to secure the raw materials of the South Seas."[3]

2. All quotations in this paragraph are from George Morgenstern, "The Actual Road to Pearl Harbor," in Barnes, ed., *Perpetual War for Perpetual Peace*, 322–23, 327–28.
3. Quoted in Morgenstern, "The Actual Road to Pearl Harbor," 329.

Because American cryptographers had also broken the Japanese naval code, the leaders in Washington also knew that Japan's "measures" would include an attack on Pearl Harbor.[4] Yet they withheld this critical information from the commanders in Hawaii, who might have headed off the attack or prepared themselves to defend against it. That Roosevelt and his chieftains did not ring the tocsin makes perfect sense: after all, the impending attack constituted precisely what they had been seeking for a long time. As Stimson confided to his diary after a meeting of the War Cabinet on November 25, "The question was how we should maneuver them [the Japanese] into firing the first shot without allowing too much danger to ourselves." After the attack, Stimson confessed that "my first feeling was of relief . . . that a crisis had come in a way which would unite all our people."[5]

Appendix

After publication of the foregoing article in *The Freeman* (May 2006), Bettina Bien Greaves wrote a letter to *The Freeman* challenging my conclusions.[6] Greaves objects, in particular, that "[w]hen Higgs says Washington *knew* that Japan's efforts to secure raw materials from the South Seas would involve Pearl Harbor specifically, he goes too far." She notes that I relied on Robert Stinnett's *Day of Deceit,* but she does not say why, according to her, such reliance led me astray, except perhaps by saying that Stinnett's book "is based on many documents, obtained under the Freedom of Information Act, that he *claimed* were intercepted pre-attack and that specifically named Hawaii and Pearl Harbor as intended Japanese targets" (my emphasis). Stinnett's book is one of the most deeply researched and carefully documented works of historical research I have seen; anyone who doubts his characterization of the documents he obtained is free to obtain them as he did and to check his reading.

In any event, I replied briefly to Greaves's letter:

---

4. Robert B. Stinnett, *Day of Deceit: The Truth About FDR and Pearl Harbor* (New York: Free Press, 2000).
5. Quoted in Morgenstern, "The Actual Road to Pearl Harbor," 343, 384.
6. Bettina Bien Greaves, "What Did FDR Know?" (letter to the editor), *The Freeman* (July–August 2006): 46.

No short reply can do justice to the comment by my friend Bettina Greaves, but perhaps I can clarify some points.

First, in my article, I aimed to show how the U.S. government took a series of actions to put Japan's economy in a stranglehold, knowing full well that the Japanese might respond to these actions militarily.

Second, I did not seek to resolve the hoary question of exactly what Franklin D. Roosevelt knew and exactly when he knew it. I relied on Robert Stinnett's *Day of Deceit* because it contains a large body of new evidence bearing on this point and related ones. I highly recommend that readers absorb that evidence and reach their own conclusions.

Even if Roosevelt himself did not know for certain on December 6 or earlier that a Japanese attack force was heading for Hawaii, his top military commanders in Washington had solid reasons, based on intercepted Japanese radio messages, to expect an attack there. Perhaps they withheld that information from the president, but I doubt very much that they did so. Still, to my knowledge, no smoking gun directly implicates Roosevelt in certain knowledge that the Japanese would attack Pearl Harbor on December 7.

We should not allow this particular ambiguity in our historical facts to divert us, however, from an appreciation of the bigger picture. The Roosevelt administration took a series of deliberately provocative actions against Japan, knowing that the Japanese might attack in response and knowing the possible targets of such an attack, including Hawaii. That the eventual attack did include Pearl Harbor, along with many other places in the Pacific and southeast Asia, could not have come as a complete surprise to FDR and his top commanders.[7]

---

7. "Robert Higgs Replies" (letter to the editor), *The Freeman* (July–August 2006): 46.

11

Truncating the Antecedents

*How Americans Have Been Misled
About World War II*

WHEREAS HISTORIANS obsessively trace every event's causal lineage further and further into the past, those who are not historians tend toward the opposite extreme: they assume in effect that the world began immediately before the event they have in mind. I call this unfortunate tendency "truncating the antecedents." Among the general public, it has given rise to mistaken interpretations of historical causation in cases too numerous to mention, and mistakes of this sort continue to occur frequently, in part because politicians and other conniving parties have an interest in propagating them.

I was recently struck by this tendency while reading comments at a group blog associated with the History News Network. A commentator there had mentioned that the blame for World War II is not as cut and dried as Americans typically assume it to be, and hence some revisionism is long overdue. In response, another discussant, whose previous contributions to the blog show that he is an intelligent man, expressed bafflement: "Yes, obviously some revisionism regarding the 'great allied leaders' of WWII is called for. But an attempt to be revisionist about the justness of a war where U.S. territory is attacked by one opponent and war is declared on the U.S. by the other opponent is sort of like justifying the War on Iraq on the basis of mythical WMD."

Like Americans in general, this man takes the Japanese attack at Pearl Harbor on December 7, 1941, and the German declaration of war on December 11, 1941, as dispositive evidence that Japan and Germany started the war that ensued between these nations and the United States, and therefore he concludes that they should be held responsible for it. In a later post, he persists in this interpretation by saying: "Nation X attacks Nation Y. One or the other is right. Either

Nation Y is a victim or the attack was a 'justified pre-emptive attack.' Yes, the response may be disproportionate, etc., but those really aren't reasons to declare Nation Y 'wrong.' Or the two 'equally wrong.'" This view represents a classic case of truncating the antecedents.

Many people are misled by formalities. They assume, for example, that the United States went to war against Germany and Japan only after its declarations of war against these nations in December 1941. In truth, the United States had been at war for a long time before making these declarations. Its war making took a variety of forms. For example, the U.S. Navy conducted "shoot [Germans] on sight" convoys, which might include British ships, in the North Atlantic along the greater part of the shipping route from the United States to Great Britain, even though German U-boats had orders to refrain (and did refrain) from initiating attacks on U.S. ships. The United States and Great Britain entered into arrangements to pool intelligence, combine weapons development, test military equipment jointly, and undertake other forms of war-related cooperation. The U.S. military actively cooperated with the British military in combat operations against the Germans, for example, by alerting the British navy of aerial or marine sightings of German submarines, which the British then attacked. The U.S. government undertook in countless ways to provide military and other supplies and assistance to the British, the French, and the Soviets, who were fighting the Germans. The U.S. government provided military and other supplies and assistance, including warplanes and pilots, to the Chinese, who were at war with Japan.[1] The U.S. military actively engaged in planning with the British, the British Commonwealth countries, and the Dutch East Indies for future combined combat operations against Japan. Most important, the U.S. government engaged in a series of increasingly stringent economic warfare measures that pushed the Japanese into a predicament that U.S. authorities well understood would probably provoke them to attack U.S. territories and forces in the Pacific region in a quest to secure essential raw materials that the Americans, British, and Dutch (government in exile) had embargoed.[2]

---

1. See "Flying Tigers," *Wikipedia,* at http://en.wikipedia.org/wiki/Flying_Tigers.
2. Robert Higgs, "How U.S. Economic Warfare Provoked Japan's Attack on Pearl Harbor," *The Freeman* 56 (May 2006): 36–37 (Chapter 10 in this volume).

Consider two summary statements by George Victor, by no means a Roosevelt basher, in his well-documented book *The Pearl Harbor Myth:*

> Roosevelt had already led the United States into war with Germany in the spring of 1941—into a shooting war on a small scale. From then on, he gradually increased U.S. military participation. Japan's attack on December 7 enabled him to increase it further and to obtain a war declaration. *Pearl Harbor is more fully accounted for as the end of a long chain of events,* with the U.S. contribution reflecting a strategy formulated after France fell. . . . In the eyes of Roosevelt and his advisers, the measures taken early in 1941 justified a German declaration of war on the United States—a declaration that did not come, to their disappointment. . . . Roosevelt told his ambassador to France, William Bullitt, that U.S. entry into war against Germany was certain but must wait for an "incident," which he was "confident that the Germans would give us." . . . Establishing a record in which the enemy fired the first shot was a theme that ran through Roosevelt's tactics. . . . He seems [eventually] to have concluded—correctly as it turned out—that Japan would be easier to provoke into a major attack on the Unites States than Germany would be.[3]

> The claim that Japan attacked the United States without provocation was . . . typical rhetoric. It worked because the public did not know that the administration had expected Japan to respond with war to anti-Japanese measures it had taken in July 1941. . . . Expecting to lose a war with the United States—and lose it disastrously—Japan's leaders had tried with growing desperation to negotiate. On this point, most historians have long agreed. Meanwhile, evidence has come out that Roosevelt and [Secretary of State Cordell] Hull persistently refused to negotiate. . . . Japan . . . offered compromises and concessions, which the United States countered with increasing demands. . . . It was after learning of Japan's decision to go to war with the United States if the talks "break down" that Roosevelt decided to break them off. . . . According to Attorney

---

3. George Victor, *The Pearl Harbor Myth: Rethinking the Unthinkable* (Dulles, Va.: Potomac Books, 2007), 179–80, 184, 185, emphasis added.

General Francis Biddle, Roosevelt said he hoped for an "incident" in the Pacific to bring the United States into the European war.[4]

These facts and numerous others that point in the same direction are for the most part anything but new; many of them have been available to the public since the 1940s. As early as 1953, anyone might have read a collection of heavily documented essays on various aspects of U.S. foreign policy in the late 1930s and early 1940s that showed the numerous ways in which the U.S. government bore responsibility for the country's eventual engagement in World War II—that showed, in short, that the Roosevelt administration wanted to get the country into the war and worked craftily along various avenues to ensure that it sooner or later would get in, preferably in a way that would unite public opinion behind the war by making the United States appear to have been the victim of an aggressor's unprovoked attack.[5] As Secretary of War Henry Stimson testified after the war, "[W]e needed the Japanese to commit the first overt act."[6]

At present, however, seventy years after these events, probably not one American in 1,000—nay, not one in 10,000—has an inkling of any of this history. So effective has been the pro-Roosevelt, pro-American, pro–World War II faction that in this country it has utterly dominated teaching and popular writing about U.S. engagement in the "Good War." Only a few years ago, when an essay of mine was included in a collection being considered for publication by the University of Chicago Press, the press's "expert" outside reader expressed shock that I had mentioned in passing Roosevelt's pre–Pearl Harbor maneuvers to bring the country into the war, and he declared that crackpot statements of this sort would discredit the entire volume. (In deference to the editor and to discourage the volume's rejection by the press, I removed the single obnoxious sentence, which was not central to my purposes in the essay in any event, and the book was eventually published, notwithstanding this ignorant "expert's" negative appraisal of my own contribution to it.)

---

4. Victor, *The Pearl Harbor Myth*, 15, 202, 240.
5. See Harry Elmer Barnes, ed., *Perpetual War for Perpetual Peace: A Critical Examination of the Foreign Policy of Franklin Delano Roosevelt and Its Aftermath* (Caldwell, Idaho: Caxton Printers, 1953).
6. Quoted in Victor, *The Pearl Harbor Myth*, 105.

Observations such as the foregoing ones tend to elicit angry accusations of "Holocaust denial" and "moral equivalence," among many others. For the record, then, let me avow that I do not deny the Holocaust, nor do I regard the Roosevelt administration as morally equivalent to Hitler's regime. While I am making my innocence plain, let me also avow that I do not regard the Roosevelt administration as morally equivalent to Stalin's regime. This latter comparison comes up surprisingly seldom, however, given that the two regimes were close allies in the war and, most important, that the major outcome of the war was to leave Stalin and his puppet regimes astride the greater part of the European continent in an area that stretches from the Urals to Bohemia and from Estonia to Azerbaijan. In short, if anyone deserves to be recognized as the war's "winner," that person is Stalin. This fact has somehow never seemed to me to fit comfortably into a characterization of this horrible conflict as the "Good War."

The fate of the European Jews also requires mention, inasmuch as after the war many people professed to believe that saving the Jews was the war's prime justification. Aside from the fact that none of the Allied leaders held that view—Roosevelt himself was a genteel anti-Semite of the sort typical in his time, place, and class—the undeniable truth is that the Jews were not saved: approximately 80 percent of them perished by the end of the war. Little wonder, too, considering that U.S. and British war plans did not give high priority to saving them; as a rule, those plans completely disregarded the urgent need to rescue the surviving Jews.

Few Americans have ever entertained the idea that their country ought not to have entered World War II. They persist in believing that they—the ordinary people of the country, as distinct from its political leaders and their foreign legionnaires—were genuinely threatened by the Japanese and the Germans and therefore that the war "had to be fought." Even George Victor, from whose honest and useful book *The Pearl Harbor Myth* I quoted earlier, has brought himself to believe that Roosevelt had excellent motives for his persistent provocation of Germany and Japan. Thus, he writes: "As Germany began to prepare for conquest, genocide, and destruction of civilization, the leader of only one major nation saw what was coming and made plans to stop it. As a result of Roosevelt's leadership, a planned sequence of events carried out in the Atlantic and more decisively in the Pacific brought the United States into one of the world's greatest cataclysms. The American contribution helped turn the war's tide and saved the world from a destructive tyranny unparalleled in modern history."[7]

Unparalleled? What about Stalin's tyranny or Mao's? Regardless of one's answer to this question, however, another question remains—whether Nazi Germany, as evil as it certainly was, had the ability to defeat the United States, much less to "destroy civilization." Americans love to speculate about German acquisition of atomic weapons, intercontinental ballistic missiles, and other military capabilities that the Nazis in fact never came close to acquiring. As things actually stood, Germany lacked the capability to invade and conquer even Great Britain. Conquering the United States, thousands of miles across the Atlantic, was realistically out of the question. Whatever else one may take U.S. leaders' motives for war to have been in the early 1940s, national self-preservation could not have been among them, unless they were shockingly ill advised as to the economic, logistical, and technological constraints on the German war machine. In reality, that machine had its hands more than full in dealing with the Soviets on the eastern front, not to mention the British and others who were pestering it on other fronts.

Thirty-nine years ago Bruce M. Russett's little book *No Clear and Present Danger* was published. Russett notes at the outset that "[p]articipation in the war against Hitler remains almost wholly sacrosanct, nearly in the realm of theology." In this regard, nothing has changed since 1972. Yet Russett argues forcefully, with logic and evidence, that this orthodoxy rests on shaky grounds. He concludes that World War II "may well have been an unnecessary war that did little for us and that we need not have fought." Nor does he concede that although the war may have been imprudent on instrumental grounds, it was well justified on moral grounds: "it is precisely moral considerations that demand a reexamination of our World War II myths," he insists.[8] Although much has been added to the corpus of World War II scholarship since the publication of Russett's book, this little volume remains unjustly neglected, and its argument deserves serious consideration even now.

---

7. Victor, *The Pearl Harbor Myth*, 16.
8. Bruce M. Russett, *No Clear and Present Danger: A Skeptical View of the U.S. Entry into World War II* (New York: Harper and Row, 1972), 12, 20, 21.

Of course, many other great events in American history might be examined as I have suggested U.S. participation in World War II ought to be examined— by taking the relevant antecedents fully into account. For historians, this advice should be unnecessary: if they know anything, they know that history did not begin yesterday. The American people at large, however, remain extremely vulnerable to misleading descriptions of the government's actions, especially its plunges into foreign wars—accounts of which generally disregard many relevant antecedents, in particular those that cast blame on the United States for stirring up enmities abroad. Yet any honest account of U.S. foreign policy reveals that this country's government has engaged again and again in foreign interventions whose official justifications cannot withstand critical scrutiny.[9] Many of these interventions amounted to little more than armed errand running for privileged American business interests seeking to beat foreigners in line and, not coincidentally, to line their own pockets.[10] This aspect of U.S. foreign policy famously led General Smedley Butler to declare that war is a racket.[11]

Time, some wit has said, is God's way of keeping everything from happening at once. Taking this idea to heart, we may remind ourselves and others that whenever the U.S. government launches a new war abroad, we would be well advised to look into what happened in that part of the world previously, perhaps over the course of several decades. We may well discover that the locals have legitimate grievances against our government or some of its corporate cronies. Or we may simply discover that the situation is more complicated than it has been made out to be. We know one thing for certain at the outset, however: we cannot rely on the government to tell us the truth, the whole truth, and nothing but the truth. Unvarnished truth is to our rulers as holy water is to vampires.

---

9. See John V. Denson, ed., *The Costs of War: America's Pyrrhic Victories*, 2nd exp. ed. (New Brunswick, N.J.: Transaction, 1999).

10. See Stephen Kinzer, *Overthrow: America's Century of Regime Change from Hawaii to Iraq* (New York: Times Books, 2006).

11. Smedley D. Butler, *War Is a Racket* (New York: Round Table Press, 1935), at http://www.lexrex.com/enlightened/articles/warisaracket.htm.

Addendum on 9/11 and the U.S. Wars
in Afghanistan and Iraq

If Franklin D. Roosevelt had been as artless as George W. Bush in his ora-
tory, he might have dispensed with his speech about the "date which will live in
infamy" and so forth and simply told the country on December 8, 1941, that the
Japanese attack on Pearl Harbor had "changed everything." Of course, the Bush
administration's account of the "unprovoked" attacks on September 11, 2001,
allegedly carried out only because some fanatical Muslims "hate our freedoms,"[12]
is another classic case of truncating the antecedents, which in this instance
stretch back through more than sixty years of U.S. interventions in the Middle
East and include a litany of U.S. outrages, from the overthrow of an elected
Iranian government in 1953 to unconditional support for repeated Israeli aggres-
sions and land grabs to the present military occupations of Afghanistan and
Iraq—more than enough to incite some passionate Middle Easterners to seek
violent retribution against Americans in this country as well as in theirs.[13] Yet
the Bush administration encouraged people to believe that we freedom-loving,
peace-loving, ever-generous Americans were simply sitting here minding our
own business when for no comprehensible reason we were attacked by crazed
Arabs intent on martyrdom. Thus, the government again sought to truncate the
antecedents, and if we may judge by the American public's prevailing ignorance
of those antecedents, the attempt has succeeded.

Like the counterfactual claim that U.S. participation in World War II was
justified by its effect in "saving the European Jews" (even though 80 percent perished), none of the Bush administration's humanitarian rationales for the wars
in Afghanistan and Iraq can withstand critical scrutiny. The establishment of
"democracy" has proved to be nothing but a solemn farce, notwithstanding the
bogus, purple-finger-flaunting elections. In Afghanistan, regional warlords and

---

12. From "Transcript of President Bush's Address [to a Joint Session of Congress]," September 20, 2001, at http://articles.cnn.com/2001-09-20/us/gen.bush.transcript_1_joint
-session-national-anthem-citizens?_s=PM:US.

13. Sheldon L. Richman, *"Ancient History": U.S. Conduct in the Middle East Since World
War II and the Folly of Intervention,* Cato Institute Policy Analysis no. 159 (Washington,
D.C.: Cato Institute, August 16, 1991).

powerful narcobarons effectively control the country, except for Kabul, and combat continues to occur episodically with no end in sight. After Barack Obama became president, the U.S. greatly increased its incursions in Pakistan, especially the aerial assassinations carried out by means of missiles launched from Predator drones. In Iraq, efforts to elevate the downtrodden Shiites gave way to an endless sectarian bloodbath, accompanied by binges of ethnic cleansing in Baghdad and other cities, and the U.S. forces eventually shifted to supporting the previously demonized Sunnis and paying them large sums of money to desist from killing U.S. troops (while they continue to kill their Shiite neighbors, who in turn kill one another).[14] In short, the war's rationales and excuses form an incoherent succession of proffered and then abandoned plausibilities, each of which has served only a public-relations purpose for a brief spell, which may have been all that was expected of it. If the U.S. government ever had a genuine reason for going to war in Iraq, it has yet to make that reason public. Every American who has died in this war has truly died in vain. And the many Iraqi dead, of course, have simply been murdered by unjustified foreign invaders or by other Iraqis whose criminality has been fostered by the lawless and chaotic conditions the occupiers have created.

14. Chris Hedges, "The Calm Before the Conflagration," *Truthdig,* February 25, 2008, at http://www.truthdig.com/report/item/20080225_the_calm_before_the_conflagration.

12

Wartime Origins of Modern Income-Tax Withholding

WARS HAVE ALWAYS been the most important occasions for the introduction of new forms of taxation. At the outset of a war, the state suddenly needs greatly increased revenue to pay for personnel and matériel to prosecute the war. Although governments typically increase the rates of existing explicit taxes and raise the rate of the hidden "inflation tax" by abruptly augmenting the money stock, these measures often prove insufficient, and other means must be devised to extract resources quickly from the public. One way to capture more revenue is to reduce tax evasion by seizing the people's earnings before the earners ever lay hands on them. This procedure has come to be known as "tax withholding at the source" or simply "withholding."

Precedents for withholding U.S. taxes go back as far as the War Between the States, when the Treasury withheld taxes owed by federal employees under the income-tax law adopted in 1862 until an 1864 amendment exempted federal salaries from taxation.[1] The war-spawned income-tax law was repealed in 1872, and an income-tax law enacted in 1894 was quickly declared unconstitutional. Immediately after ratification of the Sixteenth Amendment and passage of income-tax legislation in 1913, taxes were withheld at the source. This system provoked so much complaint from employers, however, that even the secretary of the Treasury, William Gibbs McAdoo, recommended its elimination, and

---

1. Cynthia G. Fox, "Income Tax Records of the Civil War Years," *Prologue Magazine* 18 (Winter 1986), at http://www.archives.gov/publications/prologue/1986/winter/civil-war-tax-records.html.

in 1917 Congress withdrew its authorization.[2] After passage of the Social Security Act in 1935, the payroll taxes it authorized were collected at the source, but income taxes still were not.

Before World War II, individuals who owed federal tax on their income earned in a particular year paid the tax during the following year in quarterly installments. In those days, relatively few people paid income taxes. As late as 1939, fewer than 4 million taxable individual returns were filed, and the filers' total tax bill came to less than $1 billion, or less than 4 percent of their net taxable income.[3] When so few people paid income tax and the amounts due in most cases were so small, the system of deferred payment imposed no great burden and gave rise to few taxpayer complaints.

Beginning in 1940, however, the tax burden increased enormously. As the government began to mobilize for participation in a gigantic global war, its revenue demands grew apace. Federal spending burgeoned from less than $10 billion in fiscal year 1940 to almost $93 billion in fiscal year 1945. Although the greater part of this spending upsurge was financed by borrowing, huge increases in tax collections also took place. For 1945, almost 43 million taxable individual income-tax returns were filed, and the filers owed $17 billion, or almost twenty times the amount that Americans had coughed up for this tax for 1939.[4]

Milton Friedman was an economist at the Treasury Department during the early part of the war. In his 1998 memoirs *Two Lucky People*, written with his wife, Rose, he observed: "It was clear to all of us at the Treasury, as we set out to multiply the amount of revenue to be collected from the personal income tax, that it would be impossible to do so unless we could develop a system to collect the taxes as the income was earned, not a year later."[5]

---

2. U.S. Treasury Department, Division of Tax Research, staff memo, January 9, 1941, at http://www.taxanalysts.com/THP/Civilization/Documents/Withholding/hst29048/29048-1.htm; Charlotte A. Twight, *Dependent on D.C.: The Rise of Federal Control over the Lives of Ordinary Americans* (New York: Palgrave, 2002), 102.

3. U.S. Bureau of the Census, *Historical Statistics of the United States, Colonial Times to 1970* (Washington, D.C.: U.S. Government Printing Office, 1975), 1110, series Y402-411.

4. U.S. Bureau of the Census, *Historical Statistics of the United States,* series Y3913-401; Robert Higgs, "The World Wars," in *Government and the American Economy: A New History,* by Price Fishback and others (Chicago: University of Chicago Press, 2007), 444.

5. Milton Friedman and Rose Friedman, *Two Lucky People: Memoirs* (Chicago: University of Chicago Press, 1999), 120.

The main problem connected with switching to a "pay-as-you-go" system was that when the switch was made, the taxpayers would have to pay two years' taxes in a single year—the amount due under the old system on the previous year's earnings and the amount due under the new system on the current year's earnings. Apart from the vociferous complaints such double taxation was sure to elicit, many people would simply be unable to make all of the payments, especially when tax obligations were being increased drastically.

The transition problem sparked a great deal of debate in the government and among the public.[6] Perhaps the leading proposal in 1942 came from Beardsley Ruml, the treasurer of R. H. Macy & Co. who was also the chairman of the Federal Reserve Bank of New York. Ruml proposed to "forgive" the previous year's tax liability completely when the switch to the pay-as-you-go system was made. The Treasury objected to allowing such a great amount of "forgiveness" and proposed an alternative, less-forgiving design.

After more than a year of wrangling in the bureaucracy and in Congress, the Current Tax Payment Act was signed into law on June 9, 1943. This law provided for a complicated partial-forgiveness transition. As Friedman described the law, it basically "canceled . . . one year's tax obligations of $50 or less and 75 percent of the required tax on the lower of 1942 or 1943 income, requiring the remaining 25 percent to be paid in two equal annual installments."[7] After the system became fully operational, employers withheld almost $8 billion for income taxes in 1944 and more than $10 billion in 1945.[8]

Charlotte Twight, in a revealing chapter of her 2002 book *Dependent on D.C.*, shows that during the extended debate that preceded passage of the withholding law in 1943, its proponents used various tactics to misrepresent its workings, its consequences, and the government's reasons for seeking it. In particular, she documents that "the tax 'cancellation' involved was a sham and was understood to be a sham by a significant number of government officials involved in its passage."[9]

---

6. For an excellent brief discussion, see Friedman and Friedman, *Two Lucky People,* 120–23. See also John F. Witte, *The Politics and Development of the Federal Income Tax* (Madison: University of Wisconsin Press, 1985), 119–20. For the most detailed and penetrating account, see Twight, *Dependent on D.C.,* 87–131.

7. Friedman and Friedman, *Two Lucky People,* 121.

8. U.S. Bureau of the Census, *Historical Statistics of the United States,* 1091, table IV.

9. Twight, *Dependent on D.C.,* 109.

The withholding system has remained in effect continuously ever since 1943, even though the war that prompted its creation ended sixty-six years ago, and the system's perpetuation has contributed greatly to nourishing the postwar Leviathan state. As Twight says, "Withholding is the paramount administrative mechanism that since 1943 has enabled the federal government to collect, without significant protest, sufficient private resources to fund a vastly expanded welfare state."[10]

The Treasury itself publicly acknowledges, in a fact sheet on the history of the U.S. tax system posted at its Web site, that wartime withholding not only "greatly eased the collection of the tax" but "also greatly reduced the taxpayer's awareness of the amount of tax being collected, i.e.[,] it reduced the transparency of the tax, which made it easier to raise taxes in the future."[11] Some evidence: in 2005, more than 130 million individual income-tax forms were filed, yielding the federal government $1,108 billion in revenue, and of that amount $787 billion, or 71 percent, came from withholding.[12]

Friedman, who admitted being "one of the architects" of the Treasury's proposal for a withholding system, correctly noted in his memoirs that the system "would have been introduced had I been involved or not." Withholding was an essential element of the government's wartime revenue grab. "At the time," concluded Friedman, "we concentrated single-mindedly on promoting the war effort. We gave next to no consideration to any longer-run consequences. It never occurred to me at the time that I was helping to develop machinery that would make possible a government that I would come to criticize severely as too large, too intrusive, too destructive of freedom. Yet, that was precisely what I was doing."[13]

---

10. Twight, *Dependent on D.C.,* 96.

11. U.S. Treasury Department, *Fact Sheets: Taxes. History of the U.S. Tax System,* at http://www.therochesterdemocrat.com/index.php/test/print/fact_sheets_taxes_history_of_the_us_tax_system/ (accessed April 7, 2011).

12. U.S. Bureau of the Census, *Statistical Abstract of the United States: 2007* (Washington, D.C.: U.S. Government Printing Office, 2007), 315.

13. Friedman and Friedman, *Two Lucky People,* 123.

13

A Revealing Window on the U.S. Economy in Depression and War

Hours Worked, 1929–1950

MANY YEARS AFTER the Great Depression and World War II, controversy continues to swirl as scholars, pundits, and ordinary citizens look back at the watershed events of the 1930s and 1940s. Economists and economic historians have assessed the economy's condition during these momentous years primarily with reference to the usual macroeconomic indicators, especially the real gross domestic product (GDP) and the rate of unemployment. For these analysts, the Great Depression is almost always defined as the long period when real GDP remained well below its trend high-employment capacity and the rate of unemployment stood persistently above its normal range. The war period, in contrast, stands out in the standard statistical series as a time when real GDP appeared to increase phenomenally and the rate of unemployment fell almost to zero.

Interpretation of economic events in the light of such conventional measures has been complicated, however, by institutional peculiarities unique to these extraordinary times. Both real GDP and the rate of unemployment are difficult to interpret in the usual way for those years, the former because of the operation of a wartime command economy, complete with comprehensive price controls and a multitude of other significant departures from market pricing and resource allocation, and the latter because of large-scale, atypical forms of government employment, especially the emergency work-relief programs during the Depression and the military conscription of labor during the war.

I examine here what we can learn by focusing on a different, seldom considered measure—namely, employment of labor as measured by hours worked. This alternative way of looking at the economy's operation helps us to avoid a number of difficulties, such as the exceptional frequency of reduced-hours employment ("work spreading") during the 1930s[1] and the increased prevalence of overtime work during the peak years of the war. By using hours worked as our measure of employment, we avoid the necessity of distinguishing who is employed and who is unemployed[2] and of arbitrarily imposing a cut-off line for determining who has "full-time work." Not all hours worked are equal in economic significance, of course, so we do not avoid all difficulties of analysis by taking this approach, but some of the remaining difficulties can be reduced by disaggregation of the economy's total hours worked into its component sectors.

Table 13.1 shows the basic data to which I make principal reference here. I have drawn these data from John Kendrick's monumental study *Productivity Trends in the United States*.[3] Kendrick carries more significant digits than I show in the table, reporting his figures for hours in millions, but in my judgment such precision is spurious. Indeed, we are taking a substantial chance by relying even on the figures given here, in billions of hours, with one digit after the decimal point. I make this observation not to criticize Kendrick, who describes in great detail the enormous amount of careful effort that he put into making his estimates, but only to recognize that even an analyst as painstaking as Kendrick could not overcome many problems, especially those stemming from the absence of annual source data for many of his component categories. Errors of various sorts no doubt remain embedded in these figures, not all of them offsetting in the aggregates, and readers are advised to bear this unavoidable situation in mind as they consider the present discussion.

---

1. Leverett S. Lyon, Paul T. Homan, Lewis L. Lorwin, George Terborgh, Charles L. Dearing, and Leon C. Marshall, *The National Recovery Administration: An Analysis and Appraisal* (Washington, D.C.: Brookings Institution, 1935), 830–44; Stanley Lebergott, *Manpower in Economic Growth: The American Record Since 1800* (New York: McGraw-Hill, 1964), 185–86.

2. Lebergott, *Manpower in Economic Growth,* 184–85; Michael R. Darby, "Three-and-a-Half Million U.S. Employees Have Been Mislaid: Or, an Explanation of Unemployment, 1934–1941," *Journal of Political Economy* 84 (February 1976): 1–16.

3. John Kendrick, *Productivity Trends in the United States, 1948–1969* (New York: Columbia University Press, 1961).

Table 13.1 Hours Worked (in Billions) in the United States, 1929–1950

Year	Total — Includes Military	Total — Civilian	General Government — Total	General Government — Military	General Government — Civilian	Private — Total	Private — Farm	Private — Non-farm
1929	120.3	119.8	5.4	0.5	4.9	114.9	25.5	89.5
1930	112.6	112.1	5.6	0.5	5.1	107.1	25.2	81.9
1931	103.8	103.3	5.6	0.5	5.1	98.2	25.8	72.4
1932	92.4	91.9	5.4	0.5	5.0	86.9	24.9	62.1
1933	92.6	92.1	6.5	0.5	6.0	86.1	24.8	61.2
1934	92.6	92.2	8.0	0.5	7.5	84.6	22.3	62.4
1935	97.8	97.3	8.6	0.5	8.1	89.2	23.2	66.0
1936	106.8	106.3	10.9	0.5	10.4	95.9	22.5	73.4
1937	111.4	110.9	9.6	0.6	9.0	101.9	24.3	77.6
1938	103.8	103.2	10.7	0.6	10.1	93.1	22.6	70.5
1939	108.5	107.9	10.7	0.6	10.0	97.9	22.7	75.1
1940	113.0	112.0	10.8	1.0	9.8	102.2	22.8	79.7
1941	124.2	121.0	12.9	3.2	9.7	111.3	22.1	89.3
1942	138.3	129.8	18.3	8.6	9.8	120.0	22.9	97.1
1943	156.3	135.3	31.9	21.1	10.9	124.4	22.8	101.6
1944	160.0	133.5	37.4	26.5	10.9	122.7	22.5	100.1
1945	150.0	126.0	34.1	24.0	10.1	115.9	21.0	94.9
1946	131.5	125.4	14.5	6.1	8.4	116.9	20.3	96.7
1947	130.3	127.5	10.9	2.8	8.1	119.4	19.4	100.1
1948	131.0	128.4	10.9	2.6	8.3	120.1	18.8	101.3
1949	126.4	123.6	11.4	2.8	8.6	115.0	18.2	96.8
1950	128.9	125.9	11.8	3.0	8.8	117.1	16.8	100.4

Source: John W. Kendrick, *Productivity Trends in the United States* (Princeton, N.J.:
Princeton University Press, 1961), 312–13.
Note: Detail may not add to totals because of rounding.

The 1930s

In most discussions of the Great Depression, the macroeconomic profile of the subject is portrayed as follows: steep continuous decline from 1929 to 1933, sharp recovery from 1933 to 1937, severe but short "depression within the depression" from 1937 to 1938, and renewed rapid recovery from 1938 onward, with the economy having fully recovered by 1940 or, at the latest, 1941. With regard to hours worked, the profile looks somewhat different, however.

Total hours worked fell substantially from 1929 to 1932. Then, unlike the standard depiction of the economy's course, they hit bottom and stayed put in a virtually flat-bottomed trough for three years, 1932, 1933, and 1934. They then rose substantially until 1937, dropped by 7 percent in 1938, then rose again thereafter. However, even as late as 1940, total hours remained below the 1929 level by 6 percent, and only in 1941, with the population vigorously engaged in mobilization for war, did total hours exceed the 1929 value, by 3 percent. Meanwhile, of course, the population and the potential labor force had grown substantially, the former by 11.6 million persons, so simply getting back to the 1929 level of hours worked represented something less than a complete triumph.

As table 13.1 shows, military employment remained quite low and did not vary substantially from 1929 to 1939. Farm hours worked likewise varied little, although after remaining fairly steady from 1929 to 1933, they dropped in 1934 and never regained their previous level. This abrupt one-shot drop to a lower level probably represents the effects of the New Deal's agricultural-relief programs, some of which created incentives for farmers to reduce the amount of labor, especially sharecroppers' labor, they used in their operations.[4]

Because neither military nor farm hours varied much between 1929 and 1939, the changes in total hours worked in that period are attributable almost entirely to changes in civilian government hours and private nonfarm hours.

Civilian government hours did not change appreciably from 1929 to 1932. In 1933, however, government civilian hours began to rise quickly, and by 1936 they had more than doubled. They remained more or less at the new, higher level thereafter, with only a modest dip in 1937. These increases arose for the most part from employment in the work-relief programs, such as the Civil Works Administration, the Civilian Conservation Corps, the National Youth Administration, the Works Progress Administration, and others,[5] all of which have the distinguishing characteristic of having been created not for the sake of producing

---

4. Warren C. Whatley, "Labor for the Picking: The New Deal in the South," *Journal of Economic History* 43 (December 1983): 905–29.

5. Lester V. Chandler, *America's Greatest Depression, 1929–1941* (New York: Harper and Row, 1970), 194–98.

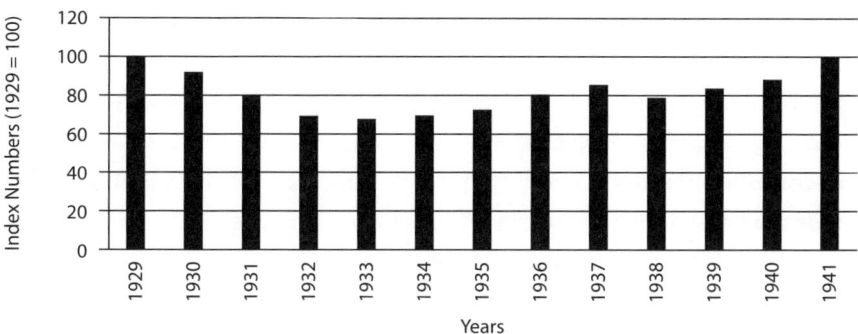

Figure 13.1 Private Nonfarm Hours Worked, 1929–1941

a desired output, but solely for the sake of creating paid employment—they were indeed, as they were widely considered to be at the time, make-work programs. By 1935, even President Franklin D. Roosevelt felt compelled to express publicly his disgust with the "narcotic" of the dole: "I am not willing," he declared, "that the vitality of our people be further sapped by the giving of cash, of market baskets, by a few hours of weekly work cutting grass, raking leaves or picking up papers in the public parks"—although he did approve of public work on the roads and in reforestation projects.[6]

In 1929, private nonfarm hours amounted to three-quarters of all hours worked in the national economy, and their movements thereafter accounted for most of the variation in the economywide total (see figure 13.1). Private nonfarm hours fell by more than 30 percent between 1929 and 1932; they remained almost unchanged at that level in 1933 and 1934 and then increased quickly until 1937, whereupon the economy's reversal brought them back down by 9 percent; and they increased sharply from 1938 to the peak years of the war. Of course, early in the 1930s, hours fell disproportionately in especially hard-hit industries, such as construction and the manufacture of most capital goods and consumer durable goods. The failure of nonfarm hours to revive before 1935 probably owes a great deal to the employment-constricting effects of the National Industrial Recovery Act (NIRA, often simply NRA), which, among other things, raised wage rates

---

6. Quoted in John T. Flynn, *The Roosevelt Myth* (Garden City, N.Y.: Garden City Books, [1948] 1949), 86.

substantially in many industries and set minimum wage rates.[7] Blacks, who in those days worked predominantly in low-wage occupations in the South, took to calling the NRA the "Negro Removal Act" because of its adverse effect on the employment of workers previously employed at wages below the newly prescribed minimums. After the Supreme Court declared the NIRA unconstitutional on May 27, 1935, private nonfarm employment began to grow in earnest.

Private nonfarm hours, however, did not exceed their 1929 level until 1942, when Americans were energetically building up the war-supply industries and a gigantic complex of military facilities to accommodate an armed force that eventually exceeded 12 million men and women in uniform. As late as 1939, Roosevelt's seventh year in the presidency, private nonfarm hours were 16 percent below their total in 1929 and about 21 percent below the trend high-employment level for 1939 (computed on the assumption of a constant rate of growth of such hours between 1929 and 1948). Perhaps no other single comparison expresses so succinctly, so unambiguously, and so irrefutably the New Deal's failure to bring about full economic recovery. Moreover, in 1939 private nonfarm hours no longer represented nearly 75 percent of the total national hours worked, as they had in 1929, but only 69 percent—surely a move in the wrong direction with regard to restoring the pre-Depression level of economic well-being.

The 1940s

Total hours worked increased rapidly from 1940, when in the latter half of the year the United States began to mobilize for war, until the peak in 1944. Hours fell substantially in 1945 and 1946, by 18 percent altogether, before stabilizing on a lower plateau from 1946 to 1950, except for a small dip during the recession year 1949. Government civilian hours and farm hours varied within a relatively narrow range in the 1940s, which means that the large variations in total hours during this decade may be traced for the most part to variations in military hours and private nonfarm hours. (We might note, however, that

---

7. Lyon et al., *The National Recovery Administration*, 317–64, 834; Chandler, *America's Greatest Depression*, 230–32; Harold L. Cole and Lee E. Ohanian, "New Deal Policies and the Persistence of the Great Depression: A General Equilibrium Analysis," *Journal of Political Economy* 112 (August 2004): 779–816.

within the fairly constant number of total civilian government hours, work hours of people in emergency make-work programs were progressively diminished in the first half of the 1940s, and this decline was offset by increases in the hours worked by regular government employees, most notably by the 2.3 million civilians that the armed forces added to their payrolls.[8] Note, too, that farm hours declined slightly each year from 1942 on.)

The rise and fall of military employment during this decade was nothing short of astonishing. By 1945, military hours equaled more than twenty-six times their amount in 1940. At the annual peak, in 1944, they accounted for almost 17 percent of the economy's total hours worked. Then, after slipping somewhat in 1945, when military personnel began to be mustered out of service in the latter part of the year, military hours fell by 75 percent in 1946 as millions of servicemen left the armed forces. Military hours fell still further in 1947, leveling off for four years at somewhat less than three times their amount in 1940—a ratchet effect that reflected the military establishment's (and its private contractors') newly acquired political clout and the incipient Cold War.[9]

The gigantic military buildup was remarkable for many reasons. For present purposes, it is germane to note that the rise in military hours accounted for 54 percent of the rise in the economy's total hours worked between 1940 and 1944. Did you want to get rid of high unemployment? Here was one sure-fire way to do so—not simply because every man enrolled in the military was ipso facto no longer a candidate to be counted as an unemployed civilian, but also because the people in the uniformed military services required an even greater number of people to support them by working in the war-supply industries and as civilian employees of the military services. No wonder the economy's total hours worked in 1944 exceeded the number worked in 1929 by one-third. In this regard, one might declare with confidence that the economy had finally

---

8. Robert Higgs, "The World Wars," in *Government and the American Economy: A New History,* by Price Fishback and others (Chicago: University of Chicago Press, 2007), 443; Alexander J. Field, "The Impact of the Second World War on US Productivity Growth," *Economic History Review* 61 (August 2008), 682, 684.

9. Arlene Lazarowitz, "Promoting Air Power: The Influence of the U.S. Air Force on the Creation of the National Security State," *The Independent Review* 9, no. 4 (Spring 2005): 477–99; Robert Higgs, *Depression, War, and Cold War: Studies in Political Economy* (New York: Oxford University Press, 2006), 126–27.

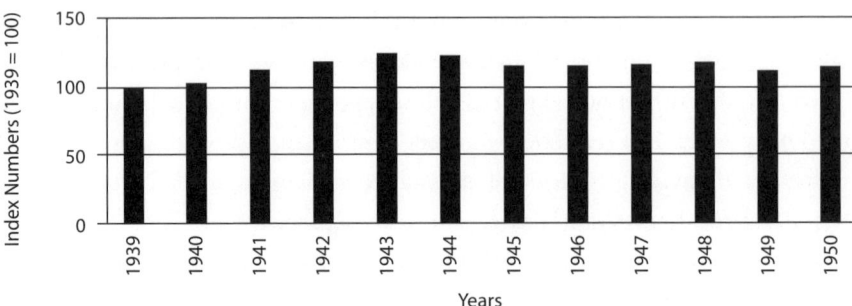

Figure 13.2 Total Civilian Hours Worked, 1939–1950

escaped from the Great Depression—unless, that is, one pauses to consider that many of these "full-employment" hours were being supplied by the 10 million draftees and therefore were not so much being supplied as being extracted.

Certainly, however, private nonfarm hours also shot up during the war, rising by 27 percent between 1940 and their annual peak in 1943. After almost remaining at this elevated level in 1944, private nonfarm hours dropped by 5 percent in 1945, then bounced back slightly after a couple of years to verge on their wartime high. At the wartime peak, however, private nonfarm hours constituted only 65 percent of the national total, in contrast to the nearly 75 percent they had accounted for in 1929—testimony especially to the greatly augmented importance of military employment during the war as well as to the government's bulked-up civilian employment still enduring from its creation during Roosevelt's first term as president.

It is worthwhile to ponder the relation between the increase in total civilian hours during the war (21 percent between 1940 and the peak in 1943; see figure 13.2) and the increase in real GDP (57 percent between 1940 and the peak in 1944, according to Kendrick,[10] but 79 percent according to the Commerce Department's estimate released in 1990,[11] and 74 percent according to the Commerce Department's currently posted estimates[12]). Is it plausible that such

10. Kendrick, *Productivity Trends in the United States,* 291–92.

11. Higgs, *Depression, War, and Cold War,* 65.

12. U.S. Department of Commerce, Bureau of Economic Analysis, National Income and Product Accounts, Table 1.1.3, Real Gross Domestic Product, Quantity Indexes, http://www.bea.gov/National/nipaweb/TableView.asp?SelectedTable=3&Freq=Qtr&First Year=2009&LastYear=2011, accessed June 1, 2011.

a disproportionate increase in output could be brought about by the relatively paltry (19 percent) contemporaneous increase in civilian hours worked?

Consider as well that the civilian hours being added between 1940 and the wartime peak in output were being supplied in large part by teenagers, elderly people, and women with little or no previous experience in the paid labor force, whereas the simultaneous buildup of the armed forces involved almost entirely prime-age male workers. It is true that the private capital stock was used much more intensively (and correspondingly run down) during the war and that the government directly invested $17 billion in war-related manufacturing plants and equipment,[13] which helped to augment measured output in the short run, and civilian workers may have applied themselves with greater diligence than usual as their contribution to victory. Nevertheless, it is extremely difficult for me to find plausible the relation between the measured increase in civilian (or even total) hours worked and the measured increase in real GDP. This apparent mismatch in the input-output data helps to persuade me that the wartime increase in real output has been greatly exaggerated—a conclusion I have reached on other grounds elsewhere as well.[14]

The economic buildup during the war was heavily concentrated in manufacturing, especially the manufacturing of durable goods.[15] Using data on the number of employees and the average hours worked per production worker,[16] I estimate that the number of hours worked in manufacturing increased from 21.0 billion in 1940 to 39.1 billion in 1944, or by 86 percent. This increase accounts for 84 percent of the increase in total civilian hours worked during this period. At this point, we have come face to face with Rosie the Riveter and a legion of her sisters (as well as with a substantial number of teenage boys and elderly men).

Credit where credit is due: these women who took up positions in manufacturing plants could be trained to weld, solder, and tighten bolts as well as anyone,

13. Higgs, *Depression, War, and Cold War*, 44, 93.

14. Higgs, *Depression, War, and Cold War*, 64–68, 102–6.

15. U.S. Bureau of the Budget, *The United States at War: Development and Administration of the War Program by the Federal Government* (Washington, D.C.: U.S. Government Printing Office, 1946), 104; Field, "The Impact of the Second World War on US Productivity Growth," 680–82.

16. U.S. Bureau of the Census, *Historical Statistics of the United States, Colonial Times to 1970* (Washington, D.C.: U.S. Government Printing Office, 1975), 137, 169.

but because most of them lacked work experience, they needed time to acquire and hone their skills. Meanwhile, they remained a drag on productivity, and they were more likely to blunder into an accident. The rate of disabling injuries per hour worked in manufacturing rose by more than 30 percent between 1940 and a wartime peak in 1943.[17] The increase in double-shift and even treble-shift work[18] also diminished the productivity of the additional hours worked in manufacturing. Both of these factors call further into question the "miracle" of the officially estimated increase in output during the war by showing us exactly how the additional hours worked might have been poor substitutes for the hours that would have been worked had the young men not been drafted and removed from the production lines.

Solomon Fabricant, a leading analyst of productivity trends for the National Bureau of Economic Research, wrote at the time: "The new workers are inexperienced; and some are handicapped. . . . Long hours cut the strength of labor and management. As a result [of these factors and others], national output per man hour fails to rise at the peacetime rate. . . . [I]n most peacetime and manufacturing industries . . . actual and palpable declines [in labor productivity] occur. For skilled labor is pulled away, transport is choked, and materials come hesitatingly and in meager quantity."[19]

Similar sorts of questions are raised by the *postwar* mismatch between changes in private hours worked and changes in the private part of real GDP. Whereas the former barely changed between 1945 and 1946, the latter leaped upward by approximately 30 percent. This genuine economic miracle reflects above all the transfer of private workers from war-supply work to the production of civilian goods and services—a shift that the data in table 13.1 do not allow us to track—but it also testifies to the overestimation of the value of war-related goods produced between 1940 and 1945, an overestimation that contributes

---

17. U.S. Bureau of the Census, *Historical Statistics of the United States,* 182.

18. U.S. War Production Board, *American Industry in War and Transition, 1940–1950, Part II: The Effect of the War on the Industrial Economy* (Washington, D.C.: U.S. Government Printing Office, 1945), 7, 32.

19. Quoted in Field, "The Impact of the Second World War on US Productivity Growth," 675.

mightily to the apparent surge in national output during the war that carried output implausibly far above its trend high-employment levels for those years.[20]

In all these areas of doubtful estimation that stems from displacement of private-market pricing, examination of the hours-worked data helps us to keep our focus on a critical variable that is measured relatively unambiguously. Hence, when the hours movement and the movement in a technologically or economically related variable x seem inconsistent, and the government is drastically interfering with the operation of the market system of pricing and resource allocation, chances are good that the change in x is the variable subject to the greater mismeasurement.

Conclusion

A close examination of the data on hours worked helps us to understand better the macroeconomic changes that occurred during the 1930s and 1940s. Perhaps the most arresting conclusions we may reach from this examination are: (1) The profile of the economy's performance between 1929 and 1937 is not clearly V shaped, with a distinct low point in 1933, as it appears in the usual depiction, but more U shaped, with a flat, three-year trough during 1932, 1933, and 1934. (2) Despite (or perhaps because of) the doubling of civilian government hours between 1932 and 1936, which added 5.4 billion annual hours to the total, private nonfarm hours per year increased by only 11.3 billion during that period, leaving them still 18 percent less than their 1929 amount. (3) As late as 1939, private nonfarm hours worked were 16 percent below their 1929 level and about 21 percent below the trend high-employment level for 1939. (4) The tremendous mismatch between the increase in private hours worked and the estimated increase in real GDP from 1940 to 1944 calls into serious question the accuracy of the estimated increase in real output. (5) This question becomes only more thought provoking when we recognize that the growth of private nonfarm hours during the war entailed a substitution of lower-productivity workers for the higher-productivity workers being drained into the armed forces.

---

20. Higgs, *Depression, War, and Cold War,* 105–6.

14

The Economics of the Great Society

Theory, Policies, and Consequences

THE RAPID GROWTH of government and the surge of federal economic interventions that occurred during Lyndon B. Johnson's presidency—the much-ballyhooed Great Society, whose centerpiece was the War on Poverty—differed from the four preceding surges in twentieth-century U.S. history, each of which had been sparked by war or economic depression. No national emergency prevailed when Johnson took office following John F. Kennedy's assassination on November 22, 1963. The nation was not engaged in a major shooting war, and the economy was on the mend after the mild recession of 1960–61. According to historian Paul K. Conkin, the Johnson administration "moved beyond a response to pressing constituency pressures, beyond crisis-induced legislative action, to a studied, carefully calculated effort to identify problems and to create the needed constituencies to help solve them."[1] For the most part, the Great Society represented simply the culmination of economic, political, and intellectual developments, revulsions against the free market, and reformist aspirations stretching back as far as the nineteenth century.

After the Korean War armistice of July 27, 1953, the United States had enjoyed a decade of respite from the rapid growth of government power over economic affairs. The wartime wage, price, and production controls lapsed, although authority to reinstitute the production controls remained. No major extensions of the government's economic controls were enacted. Big government did not disappear, of course; many of the controls and other interventions put in place in the 1930s and 1940s remained in force. But businessmen, according

---

1. Paul K. Conkin, *Big Daddy from the Pedernales: Lyndon Baines Johnson* (Boston: Twayne, 1986), 209.

to economist Herbert Stein, "had learned to live with and accept most of the regulations."[2] Government spending, especially for Social Security benefits, crept upward. All in all, though, the Eisenhower and Kennedy administrations were placid in comparison with their immediate predecessors and successors.

Under Johnson, however, the federal government's intrusion into economic life swelled enormously. In little more than two years after LBJ took office, according to Conkin, "Congress enacted over two hundred major bills and at least a dozen landmark measures. . . . The ferment, the chaos, rivaled that of 1933, and all at a scope at least four times greater than the early New Deal."[3] Major events included enactment of the Civil Rights Act of 1964, the Economic Opportunity Act of 1964, the Food Stamp Act of 1964, the Elementary and Secondary Education Act of 1965, and the Social Security Amendments of 1965 (creating Medicare and Medicaid), as well as establishment of the Office of Economic Opportunity (to oversee programs such as VISTA, Job Corps, Community Action Program, and Head Start), hundreds of community-action agencies, and many other bureaus ostensibly promoting poor people's health, education, job training, and welfare. In addition, during Johnson's presidency broad-gauge economic regulatory measures were adopted in connection with traffic safety, coal-mine safety, consumer-products safety, age discrimination in employment, truth in lending, and other areas. Conkin concludes: "In five years the American government approximately doubled its regulatory role and at least doubled the scope of transfer payments."[4]

Ideological and Political Context of the Great Society

What accounts for this multifaceted outburst? Do its various elements have a common denominator? Some scholars point to an intellectual development that Stein dubs "Galbraithianism," after its leading propagator John Kenneth Galbraith—a loose collection of socioeconomic analysis and evaluation hostile to the free market and favorably inclined toward more sweeping government

---

2. Herbert Stein, *Presidential Economics: The Making of Economic Policy from Roosevelt to Reagan and Beyond* (New York: Simon and Schuster, 1984), 84.
3. Conkin, *Big Daddy from the Pedernales*, 190.
4. Conkin, *Big Daddy from the Pedernales*, 238.

controls. "There was," says Stein, "no demand for a new and different economic system" in the Galbraithian view. Rather, "[t]he ideological case for the old system, the free market, capitalist system, was punctured by the demonstration of exceptions to its general rules and claims, and this opened the way for specific policy interventions and measures of income redistribution without any visible limits."[5]

Galbraithianism's arguments and attitudes gained strength from a spreading conviction that the U.S. economy would continue to grow forever at a fairly high rate, thereby ensuring that new and costly government programs could easily be financed by drawing on the so-called growth dividend.

Economist Henry Aaron's description of the climate of opinion in the 1960s essentially agrees with Stein's. Aaron also traces the widely held Galbraithianism back to previous crises: "The faith in government action, long embraced by reformers and spread to the mass of the population by depression and war, achieved political expression in the 1960s. This faith was applied to social and economic problems, the perceptions of which were determined by simplistic and naïve popular attitudes and by crude analyses of social scientists."[6]

As these observations by the conservative Stein and the left-liberal Aaron illustrate, scholars of diverse ideological persuasions agree that prevailing attitudes among both elites and masses in the mid-1960s favored increased government intervention in the market economy. Thus, ideological postures engendered or fostered by past crises had come once again into political prominence. Such public attitudes reached their high tide during 1964 and 1965, the first two full years of Johnson's presidency. Historian John A. Andrew III describes the mid-1960s as "a liberal interlude unmatched in the twentieth century, except perhaps for the mid-1930s."[7]

Although the 1960s are now often recalled as a sort of radical outburst against established American orthodoxies in economic, social, and political affairs, it would be a mistake to suppose that the business class opposed the dominant strains of political thought and action at that time. Businessmen, observed *Time*

---

5. Stein, *Presidential Economics,* 98.
6. Henry J. Aaron, *Politics and the Professors: The Great Society in Perspective* (Washington, D.C.: Brookings Institution, 1978), 151.
7. John A. Andrew III, *Lyndon Johnson and the Great Society* (Chicago: Ivan R. Dee, 1998), 183–84.

magazine in December 1965, had "come to accept that the Government should actively use its Keynesian tools to promote growth and stability."[8] Thus, as historian Allen J. Matusow has written, when LBJ stood for election in 1964, "the sweetest returns of all came from Wall Street":

> The nation's corporate elite, abandoning its traditional preference for the GOP, voted for the party that had stimulated sales, fueled profits, and lowered corporate taxes. An estimated 60 percent or more of the Business Council—the semi-official link between the corporations and the government—favored LBJ. The lion's share of the big contributions flowed into his campaign coffers. And on September 3 [1964] a group of corporate leaders met in the White House to organize a business committee for Johnson's re-election. Its forty-five founding members included Henry Ford II, Edgar Kaiser of Kaiser Aluminum, Joseph Block of Inland Steel, two members of Eisenhower's Cabinet, and several New York bankers. Corporate liberalism paid big dividends for the Democrats at last.[9]

As usual, when given a choice between free-market ideology and crony-capitalist proceeds, the leaders of big business tended to follow the money.

Moreover, in those days a so-called New Class—composed of scientists, lawyers and judges, city planners, social workers, professors, criminologists, public-health doctors, reporters, editors, and commentators in the news media, among others—viewed new government programs as outlets for their "idealism" and as opportunities to do well while doing good. Thus, a multitude of left-leaning intellectuals and pseudo-intellectuals gave significant leadership, support, and voice to the government's surge during the Johnson years.

More prosaic political developments also played an important role. Lyndon Johnson, who had begun his political career as a New Dealer and political horse trader in Texas, possessed not only boundless energy and ambition, but also keen political instincts and skills; he knew how to move Congress in the direction he wanted it to go. Moreover, the elections of 1964 gave the Democrats huge majorities in both houses of Congress and brought into office an extraordinarily

---

8. "The Economy: We Are All Keynesians Now," *Time,* December 31, 1965, at http://www .time.com/time/magazine/article/0,9171,842353,00.html.

9. Allen J. Matusow, *The Unraveling of America: A History of Liberalism in the 1960s* (New York: Harper and Row, 1984), 151.

leftish group of freshman legislators. According to Aaron, "No administration since Franklin Roosevelt's first had operated subject to fewer political constraints than President Johnson's."[10]

The specific forms the Great Society took reflected the increasing diversity of animals in the political jungle. While longstanding lobbies for business, labor unions, farmers, and middle-class professional groups continued to operate, many new interest groups organized and gained political clout on behalf of so-called oppressed minorities: women, American Indians, Chicanos, students, homosexuals, the handicapped, the elderly, and many others, none of whom had been directly represented as such to an important extent in U.S. politics. These groups demanded that the federal government solve a variety of racial, urban, employment, and consumer problems, real and imagined. As Conkin notes, "Each of [the] Great Society commitments promised benefits to a targeted and often an increasingly self-conscious interest group (blacks, the aged, the educationally deprived, the poor, the unemployed, urban ghetto dwellers, consumers, nature enthusiasts). In no case did the targeted recipients of new favors have either the political clout or the leadership to gain the legislation. But in each case their visibility or their protest helped create broader attention and concern. Passage of each major Great Society bill thus depended upon a broad coalition."[11]

Galbraithianism, Marxism, New Leftism, and other varieties of critical socioeconomic analysis also helped to justify the displacement of antiwar and pro–civil rights enthusiasms onto a diverse set of antimarket causes, giving rise to heightened support for environmental, consumer, and zero-risk regulations. No perceived social or economic problem seemed out of bounds in this cacophonous new political environment. Faith in the government's ability to solve social and economic problems reached a new high. Regardless of the nature of the problem—racial antipathy, unemployment, illiteracy, poor nutrition, inadequate housing, workplace accidents, insufficient cultivation of the arts, unsightly roadsides, environmental pollution, and a thousand other real and perceived problems spanning the full range of social and economic life—both

---

10. Aaron, *Politics and the Professors,* 3; Matusow, *The Unraveling of America,* 151.
11. Conkin, *Big Daddy from the Pedernales,* 213.

intellectual elites and the mass public agreed in large part that the solution took the same general form: the federal government should "do something," or if the government were already engaged in dealing with a problem, it should act more vigorously or on a larger scale. In particular, in one way or another it should spend more money.

Nevertheless, although the Great Society established critically important new federal powers and agencies, it did not cause total federal domestic spending to increase tremendously at first. A portentous sign might have been seen, however, in the quick acceleration of federal transfer payments, which increased from $34.2 billion in 1963 to $65.5 billion in 1969.[12] Over time, this fiscal locomotive gained more and more momentum. Thus, according to Michael D. Tanner, between 1963 and 2010 "the federal government spent more than $13 trillion fighting poverty."[13]

Almost everyone now acknowledges that federal entitlement programs, crowned by the enormously costly healthcare systems the Great Society spawned, have promised much greater benefits than the government can fund indefinitely; hence, many of these benefits will have to be cut, notwithstanding the political fury such cuts surely will elicit. This impending sociopolitical tumult represents one of the Great Society's bitterest fruits.

Economic Analysis and Great Society Programs

Although the Great Society should be understood as primarily a political phenomenon—a vast conglomeration of government policies and actions based on political stances and objectives—economists and economic analysis played important supporting roles in the overall drama. Even when political actors could not have cared less about economic analysis, they were usually at pains

---

12. U.S. Department of Commerce, Bureau of Economic Analysis, "National Income and Product Accounts," table 3.2, at http://www.bea.gov/National/nipaweb/TableView .asp?SelectedTable=87&Freq=Qtr&FirstYear=2008&LastYear=2010, accessed June 1, 2011.

13. Michael D. Tanner, "More Proof We Can't Stop Poverty by Making It More Comfortable," *Investor's Business Daily,* September 17, 2010, at http://www.investors.com/News AndAnalysis/Article/547746/201009171932/More-Proof-We-Canand8217t-Stop-Poverty -By-Making-It-More-Comfortable-.aspx.

to cloak their proposals in some sort of economic rationale. If much of this rhetoric now seems to be little more than shabby window dressing, we might well remind ourselves that the situation in this regard is no better now than it was then—witness, for example, the stampede of mainstream economists back to what I call "vulgar Keynesian" remedies in wake of the economic crisis that assumed panic proportions in the second half of 2008.[14]

Regardless of how political actors in the 1960s might have sought to exploit economic analysis to gain a plausible public-interest rationale for their proposed programs, the most prominent body of economic analysis in those days—the sort taught by the leading lights at Harvard, Yale, Berkeley, and most of the other great universities—virtually cried out to be exploited in this way. During the mid-1960s—as luck would have it, the very years during which I was learning economics in four different colleges and universities—the so-called Neoclassical Synthesis (a name coined by Paul Samuelson) achieved its greatest hold on the economics profession. With "synthesis," the name refers to the combination of a microeconomic part, which contains the theory of individual markets that had been developed during the preceding two centuries, and a macroeconomic part, which contains the ideas about national economic aggregates advanced in John Maynard Keynes's landmark 1936 book *The General Theory of Employment, Interest, and Money* as further developed, systematized, and extended by (some of) Keynes's followers during the three decades after the book's publication. (Note that not all leading economists accepted the Neoclassical Synthesis as an accurate representation of Keynes's own views. Joan Robinson, for example, called it "bastard Keynesianism.")[15]

---

14. See, for instance, Justin Fox, "The Comeback Keynes," *Time,* October 23, 2008, at http://www.time.com/time/magazine/article/0,9171,1853302,00.html; "The Keynes Comeback," *The Economist* (October 1, 2009), at http://www.economist.com/node/14539560; Ben Quinn, "Raising Keynes: An Old Economist Finds New Rock-Star Status," *Christian Science Monitor,* January 13, 2009, at http://www.csmonitor.com/Business/2009/0113/raising-keynes-an-old-economist-finds-new-rock-star-status; Louis Uchitelle, "Economists Warm to Government Spending but Debate Its Form," *New York Times,* January 6, 2009, at http://www.nytimes.com/2009/01/07/business/economy/07spend.html.

15. "Bastard Keynesianism," in *An Encyclopedia of Macroeconomics,* edited by Brian Snowden and Howard R. Vane (Northampton, Mass.: Edward Elgar, 2002), 51.

On the microeconomic side, the Neoclassical Synthesis incorporated the so-called New Welfare Economics that had been developed during the 1930s, 1940s, and 1950s. In this form, microeconomic theory advanced a general equilibrium theory of the economy's various markets, identified the conditions for the attainment of equilibrium in this idealized system, and demonstrated that various "problems"—springing from external effects, collective goods, less-than-perfect information, and less-than-perfect competition, among other conditions—would cause the system to settle in a state of overall inefficiency: the value of total output would fall short of the maximum that would have resulted from systemic efficiency, given the economy's available resources of labor and capital and its existing technology. Attainment of such an inefficient state was characterized as a "market failure," and economists expended enormous efforts in alleging the existence of such market failures in real-world markets and in proposing means (for example, taxes, subsidies, and regulations) by which the government might remedy—in theory, at least—these failures and thus maximize "social welfare."

Had economic theorists rested content with using the microeconomics of the Neoclassical Synthesis strictly as a conceptual device employed in abstract reasoning, it might have done little damage. However, as I have already suggested, this type of theory cried out for application, which in practice was nearly always *mis*application. The idealized conditions required for theoretical general-equilibrium efficiency could not possibly obtain in the real world, yet the economists readily endorsed government measures aimed at coercively pounding the real world into conformity with these impossible theoretical conditions. Closely examined, such efforts represented a form of madness. Moreover, as the great economist James Buchanan observes, the economists' obsession with general equilibrium gives rise to "the most sophisticated fallacy in [neoclassical] economic theory, the notion that because certain relationships hold in equilibrium[,] the forced interferences designed to implement these relationships will, in fact, be desirable."[16] Great Society measures such as the Elementary and Secondary Education Act (1965), the Higher Education Act (1965), the Motor

---

16. James M. Buchanan, "General Implications of Subjectivism in Economics," in *What Should Economists Do?* (Indianapolis, Ind.: Liberty Fund, 1979), 83.

Vehicle Safety Act (1966), and the Truth in Lending Act (1968), as well as many of the consumer-protection and environmental-protection laws and regulations found ready endorsement among contemporary neoclassical economists, who viewed them as proper means for the correction of imagined market failures.

The assumptions that underlay these economic interpretations and applications, however, could be sustained only by wishful thinking. Economists presumed to know where general equilibrium lay or at least to know the direction in which various inputs and outputs should be changed in order to approach general-equilibrium efficiency more closely. But neoclassical economists cannot move the earth with a mathematical lever because they have no place to stand—no "given" information about (presumably fixed) property rights, consumer preferences, resource availabilities, and technical possibilities. What neoclassical economics takes as given is in reality revealed only by competitive processes. "Most modern economists," Buchanan aptly concludes, "are simply doing what other economists are doing while living off a form of dole that will simply not stand critical scrutiny."[17] Yet critics such as Buchanan were hardly numerous during the 1960s. In my own training in economics between 1962 and 1968, I encountered only one of them—Buchanan himself, when he made a seminar presentation at Johns Hopkins while I was a graduate student there. In this regard, my education was typical of what other students were being taught during those years.

If the microeconomic side of the Neoclassical Synthesis fostered government measures to remedy a variety of putative market failures, its macroeconomic side endorsed government measures to remedy the greatest alleged market failure of all—the economy's overall instability and its frequent failure to bring about a condition known as "full employment." The supposition that mass unemployment constituted or reflected a market failure had come easily to young economists who came of age during the Great Depression. In those years of seemingly endless subpar economic performance, all sorts of ideas had been advanced to explain what was wrong and what should be done to repair the economy. Keynes's ideas had many competitors, most of them utterly crackpot. Anglo-American economists' longstanding commitment to classical and neoclassical economics did not collapse completely during the 1930s, but it came

---

17. Buchanan, "General Implications of Subjectivism," 90–91.

under increasing strain, and many good economists who should have known better capitulated to unsound but increasingly influential ideas. In the 1940s, the dam burst completely, at least for the elite members of the economics profession, and by the early 1950s Keynesian ideas had entrenched themselves solidly. Since then, some species of Keynesianism has been either in a dominant position in the profession or clamoring to gain such dominance. *Time* magazine observed in December 1965, "Now Keynes and his ideas, though they still make some people nervous, have been so widely accepted that they constitute both the new orthodoxy in the universities and the touchstone of economic management in Washington."[18] Although the stagflation of the 1970s and the rise of the New Classical school seemed for a while to have banished Keynesianism from the leading circles of the economics profession—at least in its form circa the 1960s— vulgar Keynesianism came back with astonishing vigor in the wake of the panic of 2008 and the subsequent recession.[19]

In the mid-1960s, however, these events lay far in the future, and the Neoclassical Synthesis reigned supreme among American economists in the profession's upper reaches. Thus, John F. Kennedy obtained advice about economic policy from Paul Samuelson in 1960 and 1961, and President Johnson maintained a Council of Economic Advisers headed in succession by three prominent Keynesian macroeconomists—Walter Heller, Gardner Ackley, and Arthur M. Okun— and including others, such as Otto Eckstein and James Duesenberry. Thus, whatever advice Johnson received from his council accorded with the tenets of the Neoclassical Synthesis. Among economists outside the Johnson administration, the Neoclassical Synthesis received its most influential exposition from such lions of the economics profession as Samuelson, John R. Hicks, Robert Solow, James Tobin, Lawrence Klein, and Franco Modigliani—all future winners of the Nobel Prize in economics. In December 1965, *Time* magazine quoted Milton Friedman, whom it described as "the nation's leading conservative economist," as saying: "We are all Keynesians now."[20]

---

18. "The Economy."
19. See sources cited in note 14. See also Robert Higgs, "Recession and Recovery: Six Fundamental Errors of the Current Orthodoxy," *The Independent Review* 14, no. 3 (Winter 2010): 265–72.
20. "The Economy."

The classical economists had regarded long periods of mass unemployment as impossible because such a condition represented a gross, sustained disequilibrium in the labor market, and normal economic changes, especially reductions in the real wage rate, would tend to restore an equilibrium in which the amount of labor services that workers wished to supply equaled the amount that employers wished to demand, so no involuntary unemployment of labor would exist. Keynes and his followers insisted, however, that wages and prices were not as flexible in modern economies as they were assumed to be in classical economics. Real wage rates might not fall (or might not fall enough), notwithstanding extraordinarily great unemployment of labor. In this view, the only way to reduce such sustained mass unemployment was by increasing the demand for products, thereby increasing the quantity of labor services that employers demanded even at the given, rigid level of real wages.

Moreover, to bring about such an increase in "aggregate demand"—the overall amount spent for new final goods and services per period of time—reliance on private consumers and investors might prove unavailing. Consumers, whose incomes would be diminished by the lost earnings occasioned by mass unemployment, would be able to play only a passive role. Investors might fail to save the day because of what Keynes called a lapse of their "animal spirits," which, to be frank, was no explanation at all, but merely a name given to a mysteriously shrunken amount of private demand for new capital goods. In this situation, aggregate demand could be raised sufficiently only from a third source—namely, increased government spending for newly produced goods and services financed by government borrowing. Moreover, such increased government spending would not only raise aggregate demand directly but would also have a so-called multiplier effect, whereby private incomes would be increased, and expenditure of these increased money receipts would set in motion a continuing series of greater demand, increased employment, higher income, and so on, by which the economy might ultimately be pushed to a state of full employment.

In the 1960s, few economists disputed this general framework of analysis. Even critics such as Milton Friedman accepted it, arguing only that certain second-order aspects of the model—for example, aggregate demand's quantitative response to an increase in the quantity of money—differed from what the Keynesians assumed. In the 1960s, few macroeconomists regarded monetary policy changes as important means of pushing an economy out of what they viewed as a mass-unemployment equilibrium. For the typical macroeconomist of those days, fiscal policy—changes in government spending, taxing, and borrowing—held the key to keeping the economy on a stable growth path. As if to certify the completeness of Keynesianism's conquest, the December 1965 issue of *Time* had an image of Keynes on its cover and featured a long, laudatory article titled "We Are All Keynesians Now."

Keynesians recognized that using fiscal policy to alleviate mass unemployment might be overdone, however, raising aggregate demand so high that the main effect of increasing it further would be not so much a further increase in employment as an increase in the rate of (overall consumer price) inflation. To analyze this problem, they developed what became known as the Phillips Curve, an empirically derived, inverse relationship between the rate of unemployment and the rate of inflation. They also made numerous attempts to estimate statistically the precise parameters of this curve. Above all, they assumed its stability over time. If indeed it was stable, it offered policymakers a menu of choices from which to select: combinations of the rate of unemployment and the corresponding rate of inflation. If they were willing to tolerate a higher rate of inflation, for example, they could use increases in deficit-financed government spending to push the rate of unemployment down further. Using fiscal policy in this fashion came to be known as "fine tuning" the macroeconomy. Fine tuning was an economic technocrat's dream come true, assuming that it really worked. However, as economist Edmund S. Phelps noted in 1974, "[T]here was absolutely nothing in economic theory that would have lent significant support to such a belief."[21]

President Johnson was fortunate in regard to economic stabilization and growth during his term in office, although he does deserve credit for pushing Kennedy's stalled tax-cut proposal to quick enactment in February 1964. Nevertheless, the economy was already growing and the rate of unemployment declining when LBJ took office in November 1963, and macroeconomic conditions continued to improve throughout his presidency, although the rate of inflation

---

21. Edmund S. Phelps, "Economic Policy and Unemployment in the 1960s," in *The Great Society: Lessons for the Future,* edited by Eli Ginsberg and Robert M. Solow (New York: Basic Books, 1974), 38–39.

began to edge up after 1965, reaching almost 5 percent during his final year.[22] Between 1963 and 1968, real gross domestic product increased by 29 percent, or by 5.2 percent per year on average.[23] The rate of unemployment declined from 5.7 percent in November 1963, when LBJ became president, to 3.4 percent in January 1969, when he left office.[24] This macroeconomic success owed nothing to policymakers' fine tuning, however, because neither the administration nor the Congress succeeded in making such delicate adjustments of fiscal policy as economic conditions changed. In truth, fine-tuned fiscal policy was impossible in the context of the U.S. government's institutional realities. Even more than Calvin Coolidge, Johnson was simply lucky in the coincidence of his economic policies and the economy's robust performance.

In any event, this remarkable macroeconomic performance probably deserves the lion's share of the credit for the reduction in measured poverty that occurred during the Great Society years. Of course, the administration proposed, enacted, and implemented a plethora of bills aimed in one way or another at reducing poverty. Indeed, for many observers, the Great Society is virtually synonymous with the War on Poverty. In general, however, nearly all of the antipoverty measures, to the extent that they met with any success at all, had only a small effect on the national poverty rate, which fell from 19.5 percent in 1963 to 12.8 percent in 1968.[25] Many of the antipoverty programs had scant funding, and the news coverage they received was out of proportion to the amount of money they received. Some of them, such as the urban-renewal programs, were probably counterproductive; most of them were probably neither fish nor fowl, but

---

22. U.S. Department of Commerce, Bureau of Economic Analysis, "National Income and Product Accounts," table 1.1.9, at http://www.bea.gov/National/nipaweb/TableView.asp?SelectedTable=13&Freq=Qtr&FirstYear=2008&LastYear=2010, accessed June 1, 2011.
23. U.S. Department of Commerce, Bureau of Economic Analysis, "National Income and Product Accounts," table 1.1.6, at http://www.bea.gov/National/nipaweb/TableView.asp?SelectedTable=6&Freq=Qtr&FirstYear=2008&LastYear=2010, accessed June 1, 2011.
24. U.S. Department of Labor, Bureau of Labor Statistics, "Labor Force Statistics from the Current Population Survey," at http://data.bls.gov/pdq/SurveyOutputServlet, accessed April 9, 2011.
25. Carmen DeNavas-Walt, Bernadette D. Proctor, and Jessica C. Smith, "Income, Poverty, and Health Insurance Coverage in the United States: 2008," in U.S. Census Bureau, *Current Population Reports: Consumer Income* (Washington, D.C.: U.S. Census Bureau, September 2009), 44, table B-1, at http://www.census.gov/prod/2009pubs/p60-236.pdf.

only more taxpayer money spent with nothing much to show for their display of good intentions. "[T]hose who most directly benefited," says Matusow, "were the middle-class doctors, teachers, social workers, builders, and bankers who provided federally subsidized goods and services of sometimes suspect value."[26]

As Tanner has recently remarked, apropos of the War on Poverty and its programmatic legacies,

> Throwing money at the problem has neither reduced poverty nor made the poor self-sufficient. Instead, government programs have torn at the social fabric of the country and been a significant factor in increasing out-of-wedlock births with all of their attendant problems. They have weakened the work ethic and contributed to rising crime rates. Most tragically of all, the pathologies they engender have been passed on from parent to child, from generation to generation. In fact, the whole theory underlying our welfare programs is wrong-headed. We focus far too much on making poverty more comfortable, and not enough on creating the prosperity that will get people out of poverty.[27]

The Great Society at least did not bring economic growth to a halt, and therefore it did not preclude a continuation of the long-term reduction in the proportion of Americans living in poverty. As for the Johnson administration's War on Poverty in particular, however, no such benign evaluation is justified. Matusow, who can scarcely be described as a spear carrier for conservative dogma, concludes that "the War on Poverty was destined to be one of the great failures of twentieth-century liberalism."[28]

The Great Society programs—whether for macroeconomic fine tuning, microeconomic remedy of alleged market failures, or redistributions of income and wealth to reduce the incidence of poverty—had an important element in common: the presumption that technocrats possessed the knowledge and capacity to identify what needed to be done, to design appropriate remedial measures, and to implement those measures successfully. In short, the Great Society amounted to social engineering—or, worse, to sheer, groping social

---

26. Matusow, *The Unraveling of America*, 240.
27. Tanner, "More Proof."
28. Matusow, *The Unraveling of America*, 220.

experimentation—on a grand scale. The planners more or less presumed the existence of private-sector problems and took for granted that they could successfully solve those problems through the use of government's coercive power and the taxpayers' money. They did not give much weight—indeed, they often gave no weight whatsoever—to the possibility of what later came to be known in public-choice theory as "government failure." Thus, seeing apparent market failures that left the economy in an inefficient configuration, they supposed that they could identify exactly what to tax, subsidize, or regulate and exactly how much to do so in order to move the economy into an efficient configuration. According to LBJ's biographer Paul Conkin, Johnson "never easily conceded that any except purely private problems did not lend themselves to a political answer. That is, government could directly or indirectly alleviate any distress."[29] As White House aide Joseph Califano later confessed, "We did not recognize that government could not do it all."[30] Yet to describe the Great Society's multifaceted undertakings as merely hubristic would be too kind to their promoters.

All too many of the programs fell short of even this species of defectiveness, amounting to little more than garden-variety efforts to divert taxpayer money in the service of purely personal and political gain for the insiders who designed, operated, and received benefits from the programs. For example, the Community Action Program, unforgettably lampooned by Tom Wolfe in his 1970 story "Mau-Mauing the Flak Catchers,"[31] combined ample components of white middle-class guilt, minority shakedowns, and money thrown around basically to appease the menacing claimants who, having been invited to snatch the money, resorted to whatever form of intimidation would get it for them quickest. "The money" for the program, Conkin concludes, "often seemed to dwindle away, funding little more than the wages of [community-action agency] employees."[32] More generally, as Andrew notes, "Through 'iron triangles' and the use of clientele capture, the very objects of Great Society

29. Conkin, *Big Daddy from the Pedernales,* 193.
30. Quoted in Andrew, *Lyndon Johnson,* 196.
31. See Tom Wolfe, *Radical Chic and Mau-Mauing the Flak Catchers* (New York: Bantam, [1970] 1999).
32. Conkin, *Big Daddy from the Pedernales,* 223.

reforms all too often seized control of the process to block significant change and enhance their own interests."[33]

Level-headed analysts could scarcely have been shocked by this outcome. As Adam Smith long ago remarked, although the "man of system"—preeminent examples of which played leading roles in initiating the Great Society—treats the members of society as if they were but pieces on a chessboard, the people actually have a motive power of their own. In the mid-1960s, the people whom the social and economic planners undertook to "reform" in various ways refused to sit still while the technocrats treated them as lab rats. Instead, they often reacted by resisting, diverting, or seizing control of the "top-down" plans the government sought to impose on them, causing what, from the planners' perspective, seemed to be program failures. One man's failed experiment, however, was often another man's fulfilled political ambition or bulked-up bank account. Across the country, for example, local politicians diverted federal money intended to fund Great Society "reform" measures into support for prosaic, local political priorities.

Conclusion

The economics of the Great Society—whether we consider it from the perspective of economic theory, economic policies, or the consequences of those policies—offers much to criticize and little to praise. The theory it embraced—the Neoclassical Synthesis—combined a microeconomic theory focused on the identification and rectification of market failures and a macroeconomic theory based on primitive, deeply flawed Keynesianism. Although this body of analysis might sometimes arrive at constructive proposals by accident, as it did when it helped to push through the 1964 tax cut, in general it fostered unconstructive or even counterproductive policies whose common element was increased government intervention in the market system. The best thing we can say for the Great Society economic programs as a whole is that they amounted to a gigantic waste of the taxpayers' money. Many programs, however, were worse than wastes; they actually caused harm.

---

33. Andrew, *Lyndon Johnson*, 194.

Viewed from today's perspective, the Great Society seems to have been above all an almost preposterously bloated collection of social-engineering projects. The mentality that underlay this panoply of policies and actions was one of arrogance and presumption: the presupposition that the leadings intellectuals, "the best and the brightest," knew how to rearrange the pieces on the human chess board to construct a better society from the top down and ought to do so. Of course, the politicians who joined in this carnival of folly did not for the most part care one way or another about intellectual presumptions or positions; they simply saw an inviting opportunity to feather the nests of their supporters while accruing wealth, public acclaim, and power for themselves. Opportunists of all sorts, from welfare hustlers to subsidy-seeking real estate developers, naturally came running to the fountain from which such copious quantities of the taxpayers' money were flowing.

After 1965, as the civil rights revolution dissolved into urban riots and violent splinter groups, and as the growing U.S. engagement in Vietnam lengthened American casualty lists and increased Pentagon outlays, the public first soured and then turned increasingly against both LBJ's domestic program and his distant war. By the beginning of 1968, if not earlier, the president had conceded the impossibility of his reelection, and his leading advisers had lost much of their previous enthusiasm for the administration's crusades at home and abroad. Although Richard M. Nixon was elected in 1968, many elements of the Great Society lived on, and some were extended and made ever more expensive, especially the food stamp program, Medicaid, and Medicare. Indeed, the currently looming fiscal train wreck associated primarily with the federal medical-care programs attests that in fundamental ways the U.S. economy continues to suffer grave damage as a consequence of programs initiated as part of the Great Society.

15

Nixon's New Economic Plan

RICHARD NIXON HAD a crisis mentality. In 1962, unhappily out of public office, he wrote an autobiographical account entitled *Six Crises*. Whereas some presidents have faced real crises, however, Nixon's were more the product of his personal sense of siege. As president, he twice declared a state of national emergency, first on March 23, 1970, in response to a strike by postal workers and then on August 15, 1971, when balance-of-payments problems, among other things, led him to adopt an important set of policies called the New Economic Plan. (I do not know whether any of the president's advisers knew that the same name had been given to the policies that Soviet dictator Vladimir Lenin implemented in 1921, but someone among them should have known.)

Like most incumbent politicians, Nixon gladly took advantage of crises to augment his power, but he did not simply sit waiting for an emergency to come along. For him, the risk that he might not be reelected was crisis enough. According to his economic adviser Herbert Stein, he "tended to worry exceedingly about his reelection prospects and so to feel impelled to extreme measures to assure his reelection."[1] Years before the election of 1972, Nixon and his aides began to scheme how they could manipulate the economy to maximize the likelihood of his reelection by creating as much apparent prosperity as possible on the eve of the election.

The New Economic Plan included several important elements, as described in the January 1972 *Annual Report of the Council of Economic Advisers:* "The

---

1. Herbert Stein, *Presidential Economics: The Making of Economic Policy from Roosevelt to Reagan and Beyond* (New York: Simon and Schuster, 1984), 168.

United States suspended the convertibility of the dollar into gold or other reserve assets, for the first time since 1934. It imposed a temporary surcharge, generally at the rate of 10 percent, on dutiable imports. Prices, wages, and rents were frozen for 90 days, to be followed by a more flexible and durable—but still temporary—system of mandatory controls."[2] In no way did this set of policies reflect sound economic principles. Political expediency was its sole driving force.

Nothing illustrates Nixon's political opportunism better than his imposition of mandatory controls over wages, prices, and rents. The president, who had served as a low-level functionary in the Office of Price Administration during World War II, had often expressed an aversion to price controls, which, he declared during the campaign of 1968, "can never be administered equitably and are not compatible with a free economy."[3] Yet, as James Reichley has observed, he was "not prepared to take extreme political risks for the sake of economic dogmas."[4] Having convinced himself that his defeat in the presidential election of 1960 had resulted from the Eisenhower administration's failure to generate favorable macroeconomic conditions on the eve of the election, Nixon was determined not to suffer again from the same kind of mistake. His latent fears were sharply aroused in 1970 and 1971, when the new administration's restrictive fiscal and monetary policies had a more immediate effect in raising the rate of unemployment than in reducing the rate of inflation.

Impatient that the government's macroeconomic policies seemed to be working so slowly, many politically important people began to call for direct price controls: labor union leaders, big businessmen, members of Congress, potential presidential candidates in the next election, high-ranking economists in the Treasury Department, even Federal Reserve Board chairman Arthur Burns—all prodded the president to impose an "incomes policy" because, as Burns put it, "the rules of economics are not working in quite the way they used to."[5] Congress, as if daring Nixon to do what he insisted he would never do, passed the Economic Stabilization Act, authorizing the president to control

2. U.S. Council of Economic Advisers, *Annual Report of the Council of Economic Advisers* (Washington, D.C.: U.S. Government Printing Office, 1972), 22.
3. Quoted in A. James Reichley, *Conservatives in an Age of Change: The Nixon and Ford Administrations* (Washington, D.C.: Brookings Institution, 1981), 205.
4. Reichley, *Conservatives in an Age of Change,* 206.
5. Quoted in Reichley, *Conservatives in an Age of Change,* 220.

all prices, wages, and rents. Nixon signed the bill with apparent reluctance on August 17, 1970.

Late in 1970, the appointment of the flamboyant John Connally as secretary of the Treasury and his subsequent designation as the administration's chief economic spokesman tipped the balance toward more controls. Connally had few economic scruples; he specialized in dramatic political gestures, favoring, in Nixon's football metaphor, the "big play." He supported the imposition of controls because he thought it would appeal to the public as a sweeping, take-charge action by the president.[6]

Nixon liked that aspect of the controls. As he later wrote in his memoirs, imposition of the controls "was politically necessary and immediately popular in the short run."[7] Indeed it was. The stock markets soared. Stein notes that "[t]he Dow-Jones Average rose 32.9 points on Monday after the President's announcement—the biggest one-day increase up to that point."[8] Opinion polls indicated a huge preponderance of approval of the president's action, a response that showed in Stein's view "how shallow was the general support in principle for the basic characteristics of a free market economy."[9] A year later, with rigorous controls still in force, Nixon gained reelection by a huge margin.

Economists, with notable exceptions, can be relied on to testify that price controls "don't work," and in the sense that they have in mind—actually reducing inflation and not simply suppressing its manifestations—their conclusion is correct. From a political perspective, however, this claim misses the point. Price controls do work in another sense—to gain short-run political support for the politicians who impose them. The public seems never to learn that it is being sold a faulty political product. As Stein remarks, even after all of the economic disruptions, artificial scarcities, and inequities of Nixon's price-control program, which finally ended on April 30, 1974, "the experience did not leave the country with a strong commitment to the free market, monetarist way of restraining inflation. The attraction of the direct approach remained."[10] Only

---

6. Richard M. Nixon, *RN: The Memoirs of Richard Nixon* (New York: Grosset and Dunlap, 1978), 518–22, quotation from 518.
7. Nixon, *RN,* 521.
8. Stein, *Presidential Economics,* 180.
9. Stein, *Presidential Economics,* 180.
10. Stein, *Presidential Economics,* 187.

four years later the Carter administration yielded to political temptation and imposed another incomes policy, albeit a half-hearted one entirely reliant on indirect sanctions rather than legal penalties.[11]

The most important legacy of Nixon's wage-price-rent controls was the government's energy-price controls and allocations that persisted long after the comprehensive price controls had expired. When the first "energy crisis" struck, the administration was looking forward to disengagement from its no longer useful incomes policy. But given the lingering presence of the price controls, the Arab oil embargo and the Organization of Petroleum Exporting Countries price hikes of late 1973 and early 1974 quickly led in many areas to shortages that were rationed mainly by the customers' waiting in the infamous gas lines. The inconvenience and uncertainty were more than the American public could bear. There immediately arose, in William Simon's words, "collective hysteria. . . . The political heat was on both Congress and the executive to solve the problem overnight."[12]

Congress "solved" the problem, all right, as anyone who endured the manifold foul-ups of the two "energy crises" (in 1973–74 and 1979–80) will recall. Only with Ronald Reagan's election and the scrapping of all oil-price controls was the mess permitted to clean itself up through market processes. Even then, however, a complex system of price controls lingered for natural gas, a political dragon too fearful for even Sir Ronald to slay. Not until 1993 were the well-head price controls for natural gas terminated fully.[13]

11. Robert Higgs, "Carter's Wage-Price Guidelines: A Review of the First Year," *Policy Review* 11 (Winter 1980): 97–113.

12. William E. Simon, *A Time for Truth* (New York: Berkley Books, 1979), 54.

13. G. Bruce Doern and Monica Gattinger, *Power Switch: Energy Regulatory Governance* (Toronto: University of Toronto Press, 2003), 80.

PART III

Economic Analysis, War, and Politicoeconomic Interactions

16

Recession and Recovery

Six Fundamental Errors of the Current Orthodoxy

AS THE RECESSION that began in early 2008 deepened and the autumn financial debacle passed from one episode to another during the following years, commentary on the economy's troubles swelled tremendously. Pundits pontificated; journalists and editors reported and opined; talk-radio jocks huffed and puffed; public officials spewed out even more double-talk than usual; awkward academic experts, caught in the camera's glare like deer in the headlights, blinked and stumbled through their brief stints as talking heads on TV. We were deluged by an enormous outpouring of diagnosis, prognosis, and prescription, at least 95 percent of which was appallingly bad.

The bulk of it was bad for the same reasons. Most of the people who purport to possess expertise about the economy rely on a common set of presuppositions and modes of thinking. I call this pseudo-intellectual mishmash "vulgar Keynesianism." It's the same claptrap that has passed for economic wisdom in this country for more than fifty years and seems to have originated in Paul Samuelson's *Economics,* first published in the late 1940s, the best-selling economics textbook of all time and the one from which a plurality of several generations of college students acquired whatever they would ever know about economic analysis. This view seeped into educated discourse and writing in the news media and in politics long ago and established itself as an orthodoxy.

Unfortunately, this way of thinking about the economy's operation, in particular its overall fluctuations, is a tissue of errors of both commission and omission. Most unfortunate have been the policy implications derived from this mode of thinking, above all the notion that the government can and should use fiscal and monetary policies to control the macroeconomy and stabilize its fluctuations. Despite having originated more than half a century ago, this view seems to be as vital today as it was in 1949.

Let us consider briefly the six most egregious aspects of this unfortunate approach to understanding and dealing with economic booms and busts.

Aggregation

John Maynard Keynes persuaded his fellow economists and then they persuaded the public that it makes sense to think of the economy in terms of a handful of economywide aggregates: total income or output, total consumption spending, total investment spending, and total net exports. If people remember anything from their introductory economics course, they are most likely to remember the equation

$$Y = C + I + G + (X - M).$$

Sometimes $Q \cdot P$ is equated to the variables on the right-hand side of the equation. So the idea is that aggregate supply (physical output Q times the price level P) equals aggregate demand equals the sum of four types of money expenditure for newly produced final goods and services—private consumption, private investment, government purchases, and net exports.

This way of compressing diverse, economywide transactions into single variables has the effect of suppressing recognition of the complex relationships and differences *within* each of the aggregates. Thus, in this framework the effect of adding a million dollars of investment spending for teddy bear inventories is the same as the effect of adding a million dollars of investment spending for digging a new copper mine. The effect of adding a million dollars of consumption spending for movie tickets is likewise the same as the effect of adding a million dollars of consumption spending for gasoline. And the effect of adding a million dollars of government spending for children's inoculations against polio is the same as the effect of adding a million dollars of government spending for 7.62 mm ammunition. It does not take much thought to conceive of ways in which suppression of the differences within each of the aggregates might cause our thinking about the economy to go seriously awry.

In fact, "the economy" does not produce an undifferentiated mass we call "output." Instead, the millions of producers who bring forth "aggregate supply" provide an almost infinite variety of specific goods and services that differ in countless ways. Moreover, an immense amount of what goes on in a modern market-oriented economy consists of dealings among producers who supply no "final" goods and services at all but instead supply raw materials, components, intermediate products, and services to one another. Because these producers are connected in an intricate pattern of relations, which must assume certain proportions if the entire arrangement is to work effectively, critical consequences turn on what *in particular* gets produced, when, where, and how.

These extraordinarily complex microrelationships are what we are really referring to when we speak of "the economy." It is definitely not a single, simple process for producing a uniform, aggregate glop. Moreover, when we speak of "economic action," we are referring to the *choices* that millions of diverse participants make in selecting one course of action and setting aside a possible alternative. Without choice, constrained by scarcity, no true economic action takes place. Thus, vulgar Keynesianism, which purports to be an economic model or at least a coherent framework of economic analysis, actually excludes the very possibility of genuine economic action, substituting for it a simple, mechanical conception—the intellectual equivalent of a baby toy.

Relative Prices

Vulgar Keynesianism takes no account of relative prices or changes in such prices. After all, in this framework there is only one price, which is called "the price level" and represents a weighted average of all the money prices at which the economy's countless actual goods and services are sold. (There is also the rate of interest, which is treated as a price in a limited and misleading way, about which I say more later.) If relative prices change—which of course they always do to some extent, even in the most stable periods—these changes are "averaged out" and affect the calculated change, if any, in the aggregate price level only in a shrouded and analytically irrelevant manner.

So if the economy expands along certain lines but not along others, while the configuration of relative prices has changed, the vulgar Keynesians know that "aggregate demand" and "aggregate supply" have risen, but they have no idea why or in what manner aggregate demand and supply have risen. Nor do they care. In their view, the economy's aggregate output, the only output they treat as worthy of notice, is driven by aggregate demand, to which aggregate supply responds more or less automatically, and it matters not whether only the demand for cucumbers has risen or, to cite an example Keynes himself used, only the demand for pyramids has risen. Aggregate demand is aggregate demand is aggregate demand.[1]

Because the vulgar Keynesian has no conception of the economy's *structure of output,* he cannot conceive of how an expansion of demand along certain lines but not along others might be problematic. In his view, one cannot have, say, too many houses and apartments. Increasing the spending for houses and apartments is, he thinks, always good whenever the economy has unemployed resources, regardless of how many houses and apartments now stand vacant and regardless of what specific kinds of resources are unemployed and where they are located in this vast land. Although the unemployed laborers may be skilled silver miners in Idaho, it is supposedly still a good thing if somehow the demand for condos is increased in Palm Beach because, for the vulgar Keynesian, there are no individual classes of laborers or separate labor markets: labor is labor is labor. If someone, whatever his skills, preferences, or location, is unemployed, then in this framework of thought we may expect to put him back to work by increasing aggregate demand sufficiently, regardless of what we happen to spend the money for, whether it be cosmetics or computers.

This stark simplicity exists, you see, because aggregate output is a simple increasing function of aggregate labor L employed:

$$Q = f(L), \text{ where } dQ/dL > 0.$$

Note that this "aggregate production function" has only one input, aggregate labor. The workers seemingly produce without the aid of capital! If pressed, the vulgar Keynesian admits that the workers use capital, but he insists that the capital stock may be taken as "given" and fixed in the short run. And—which is

---

1. In *The General Theory of Employment, Interest and Money* (New York: Harcourt, Brace and World, 1936), Keynes wrote: "Pyramid-building, earthquakes, even wars may serve to increase wealth" (129). Provoked by the Keynesian affinity for pyramid building, Paul Cantor quips: "If Keynes liked the pyramids, there had to be something wrong with them, and indeed there seems to be a connection between liking the pyramids and liking Big Government" ("Keynes and the Pyramids," Ludwig von Mises Institute Daily Article, October 14, 2002, at http://mises.org/story/1069).

highly important—his whole apparatus of thought is intended exclusively to help him understand this short run. In the long run, he may insist, we are, as Keynes put it, "all dead,"[2] or he may simply deny that the long run is what we get when we place a series of short runs back to back. The vulgar Keynesian in effect treats living for the moment and only for it as a major virtue. At any given time, the future may safely be left to take care of itself.

The Rate of Interest

The vulgar Keynesian may care about the rate of interest, but only in a restricted sense. For him, the rate of interest is the "price of money"—that is, the rental rate paid on borrowed funds. Such borrowing is always good, and more of it is always better because individuals use borrowed money to purchase consumer goods, thereby "creating jobs," and a job is the finest thing in the known universe. Hence, the lower the rate of interest, the more people will borrow and spend, and the better the economy will function, again so long as any unemployment exists anywhere in the country. Because some unemployment always exists, the vulgar Keynesian always wants the rate of interest to be lower than it is. If it can be lowered artificially by central-bank action, he strongly favors such action. The Federal Reserve System (the Fed) has recently pushed its target for the interest rate on "federal funds"—overnight balances the banks borrow from one another—to a range that begins at zero, and esteemed economists have toyed with the crackpot notion of aiming for a negative rate of interest.[3] (Where do I sign up for a loan?)

The vulgar Keynesian does not understand what the rate of interest really is. He fails to comprehend that it is a crucial *relative price*—namely, the price of goods available now relative to goods available in the future. Remember: he does

---

2. Keynes's oft-quoted statement is actually not quite as ridiculous as it is usually made to seem. His statement in context, in the 1923 *Tract on Monetary Reform,* is: "The long run is a misleading guide to current affairs. In the long run we are all dead. Economists set themselves too easy, too useless a task if in tempestuous seasons they can only tell us that when the storm is past the ocean is flat again." The quotation is available at http://en.wikiquote.org/wiki/John_Maynard_Keynes.
3. N. Gregory Mankiw, "It May Be Time for the Fed to Go Negative," *New York Times,* April 18, 2009, at http://www.nytimes.com/2009/04/19/business/economy/19view.html.

not think in terms of relative prices at all, so it is entirely natural that he fail to recognize how the rate of interest affects the choice between current consumption and saving—that is, acting so as to make possible more future consumption by not consuming current income. In a free market, a reduction in the rate of interest reflects a desire to shift more consumption from the present to the future.

A free market would comprise private suppliers and demanders of loanable funds, and the prevailing market rate of interest would be that at which the amount demanders want to borrow equals the amount suppliers want to lend. Both borrowers and lenders, however, are making their choices in the light of their "time preference," which is to say the rate at which they are willing to trade present goods for future goods. People with a "high rate of time preference" are keen to consume now rather than later, and to induce them to give up present consumption borrowers must compensate them by paying a high rate of interest for the use of their funds.

Although vulgar Keynesians recognize that a lower rate of interest will spur business firms to borrow more money and invest it, they imagine that business investment plans are naturally volatile and essentially irrational—driven, as Keynes said, by the entrepreneurs' "animal spirits."[4] Hence, the degree to which investment responds to a change in the rate of interest is small and may be more or less disregarded. For the vulgar Keynesians, the importance of the rate of interest is that it regulates the amount that individuals will borrow to finance their purchases of consumer goods. Those purchases, in their view, are the essential element in the determination of how much firms want to produce and how much they want to invest in expanding their capacity to produce. Again, however, in this framework it matters not what kind of investment takes place: investment is investment is investment.

Capital and Its Structure

As noted already, the vulgar Keynesian views the capital stock as "given." If he thinks about it at all, he considers it a sort of massive inheritance from the past and assumes that nothing that might be added to or subtracted from it in the short run will change it enough to warrant concern. But if he gives little

---

4. Keynes, *General Theory of Employment*, 161–62.

thought to capital, he gives none at all to its *structure:* the fine-grained patterns of specialization and interrelation among the countless specific forms of capital in which past saving and investment have become embodied. In his framework of analysis, it matters not whether firms invest in new telephones or new hydro-electric dams: capital is capital is capital.

Because the structure of the capital stock is disregarded—even sophisticated economists, such as Frank Knight, have insisted that the capital stock is essentially an undifferentiated glob of monetary value, any part of which may be substituted perfectly for any other part of equal monetary value[5]—no attention is given to how changes in the rate of interest bring about changes in the structure of the capital stock. After all, what possible difference can such a change make? This willful blindness has caused many economists, including the recent Nobel laureate Paul Krugman,[6] to misinterpret the Austrian theory of the business cycle as a theory of "overinvestment," which it definitely is not.

Instead, the theory pioneered by Ludwig von Mises and F. A. Hayek in the first half of the twentieth century—a theory that fell into near oblivion after the Keynesian revolution in macroeconomics—is a theory of *malinvestment,* which is to say a theory of how an artificially reduced rate of interest leads business firms to invest in the *wrong kinds* of capital, in particular the longest-lived capital goods, such as residential and industrial buildings, as opposed to inventories, equipment, and software with a relatively short life. Thus, in the Austrian view, Fed-induced low rates of interest, such as those between 2002 and 2005, lead firms to overvalue longer-term capital projects and to shift their investment spending in that direction, thus producing, for example, booms in building construction. This shift would make economic sense if the interest rate had fallen in a free market, thereby signaling that people wish to defer more consumption by saving more of their current income. But if people have not changed their preferences in this way and continue to prefer present consumption relatively as much as they did previously, then businesses will make mistakes by choosing these kinds of investment projects, which are in effect attempts to anticipate

---

5. K. H. Hennings, "Capital as a Factor of Production," in *The New Palgrave: A Dictionary of Economics,* edited by John Eatwell, Murray Milgate, and Peter Newman (New York: Stockton Press, 1987), 330.
6. Paul Krugman, "The Hangover Theory: Are Recessions the Inevitable Payback for Good Times?" *Slate,* December 4, 1998, at http://www.slate.com/id/9593.

future demands that will never eventuate. When the projects ultimately begin to fail, the boom that the artificially lowered interest rates set in motion will collapse into a bust, with attendant bankruptcies and unemployed labor, as unsustainable projects are liquidated and resources shifted, painfully in many cases, to more viable uses.

Because the vulgar Keynesian is blind to these microdistortions and to the need for their correction in the wake of an artificially induced boom, he fails to see any need for the bankruptcies and unemployment that necessarily attend a substantial economic restructuring. He supposes: if only the government would step in and use its own deficit spending to make up for the reduced private investment and consumption spending, then business would be restored to profitability and workers reemployed *without any economic restructuring.*

It comes as no surprise, then, that people who think along such lines are currently working to continue a policy that contributed greatly to producing the unsustainable boom of 2002–2006: namely, subsidized lending to would-be homeowners who cannot meet normal commercial qualifications for receiving such loans. It does not occur to the vulgar Keynesians that too many resources have been directed into house and condo construction and that lending to homeowners who cannot afford to purchase homes unless they are subsidized to do so signals an uneconomic use of resources at the expense of the taxpayers who directly or indirectly finance these subsidies.

Malinvestments and Money Pumping

With their great, simple faith in the efficacy of government spending as a macroeconomic balance wheel, vulgar Keynesians disregard malinvestment, past and future, and support government spending in excess of the government's revenue, with the difference being covered by borrowing. Of course, they favor central-bank actions to make such borrowing cheaper for the government. In fact, they chronically prefer "easy money" to more restrictive central-bank policies. As noted previously, they prefer easy money not only because it lowers the cost of financing the government's deficit spending, but also because it induces individuals to borrow more money and spend it for consumption goods—such increased consumption spending being viewed as always a good thing, notwithstanding the near-zero rate of saving by individuals in the United

States in the decade or so that preceded the current recession. Reflecting on the vulgar Keynesian attitude toward Fed policy, I keep recalling an old country song whose refrain was "faster horses, younger women, older whiskey, more money."

Vulgar Keynesians do not spend much time worrying about potential inflation; on the contrary, they are obsessed with an irrational fear of even the slightest hint of *de*flation. If inflation should become an undeniable problem, we may count on them to support price controls, which, they are convinced on the basis of sketchy knowledge of such controls during World War II, can be made to work well.

Regime Uncertainty

Vulgar Keynesians are nothing if not policy activists. Like Franklin D. Roosevelt, they believe that the government should "try something," and if that something doesn't work, try something else.[7] Better still would be for the government to try a bunch of things at once, and if they don't turn the trick, then pour more money into them and try something else to boot. The eras the vulgar Keynesians esteem as the most glorious in U.S. politicoeconomic history are Franklin Roosevelt's first term as president and Lyndon B. Johnson's first few years in the presidency. In these periods, we witnessed an outpouring of new government measures to spend, tax, regulate, subsidize, and generally create mischief on an extraordinary scale. The Barack Obama administration's ambitious plans for government action on many fronts filled vulgar Keynesians with hope that a third such Great Leap Forward was in the making.

The vulgar Keynesians do not understand that extreme policy activism may work *against* economic prosperity by creating what I call "regime uncertainty," a pervasive uncertainty about the very nature of the impending economic order, especially about how the government will treat private-property rights in the future.[8] This kind of uncertainty especially discourages investors from putting

---

7. Franklin D. Roosevelt, *Looking Forward* (New York: John Day, 1933), 51.
8. Robert Higgs, "Regime Uncertainty: Why the Great Depression Lasted So Long and Why Prosperity Resumed After the War," *The Independent Review* 1, no. 4 (Spring 1997): 561–90.

money into long-term projects. Such investment, which almost disappeared after 1929, did not recover until after World War II. More than one observer has commented in recent years that regime uncertainty arose from the government's frenetic series of bailouts, capital infusions, emergency loans, takeovers, stimulus packages, and other extraordinary measures crammed into a period of less than a year.[9] With the Obama administration in the saddle, prospects appeared favorable for a continuation of this kind of frantic policy activism. The massive health-care-reform bill and the equally massive financial-reform bill enacted into law recently—each empowering the government to create a multitude of new regulatory bodies and regulations whose yet-undetermined details hang over the economy like a menacing dark cloud—have contributed to the continuation of the regime uncertainty engendered by the government's initial emergency responses to the financial and economic crises in 2008 and 2009. Such unsettling government intervention, which discourages commitments to employ more workers or to invest in new long-term projects, cannot help in restoring prosperity, and it may hurt a great deal.

---

9. See, for example, Peter Boettke, "Regime Uncertainty," *The Austrian Economists,* October 6, 2008, at http://austrianeconomists.typepad.com/weblog/2008/10/regime-uncertai .html; Dave Gonigam, "Regime Uncertainty," *The Daily Reckoning,* March 4, 2009, at http://dailyreckoning.com/regime-uncertainty/; and Carlos Lam, "'Regime Uncertainty' Further Delays Economic Growth," *Seeking Alpha,* April 3, 2009, at http://seekingalpha .com/article/129264-regime-uncertainty-further-delays-economic-growth.

17

Benefits and Costs of the
U.S. Government's War Making

IN 1795, JAMES MADISON observed that "of all the enemies to public liberty, war is, perhaps, the most to be dreaded, because it comprises and develops the germ of every other. . . . No nation could preserve its freedom in the midst of continual warfare."[1] All experience during the past two centuries has confirmed the continuing validity of Madison's observation. Apart from all the sacrifices of life, liberty, and treasure that wars have entailed directly, they have also served as the prime occasions for the growth of the central state, and hence in the United States they have fostered the long-term diminution of civil and economic liberties and the ongoing subversion of civil society.

Every government recognizes that force alone is an inefficient means of propping up its position. At the margin, bamboozlement can be effectively substituted for the use of force, especially in so-called democratic systems, where many ordinary people have embraced the fable that they themselves "are" the government because they cast a ballot every few years. Hence, every government seeks to ease its retention of power by persuading people that it acts only in their interest. A government that goes to war promises its subjects that it is doing so only in defense of those persons' security and freedom. "Yet," as Bruce D. Porter has noted, "having borne the burden of the state for five hundred years, we find that it has rarely fulfilled its twin promises of security and freedom."[2]

Indeed, governments' alluring claim is almost always false. In matters of war making, as elsewhere in their wielding of power, governments act in the

---

1. Quoted in Bruce D. Porter, *War and the Rise of the State: The Military Foundations of Modern Politics* (New York: Free Press, 1994), 10.
2. Porter, *War and the Rise of the State*, 21.

interest of their own leaders, with as many concessions as necessary to retain the support of the coalition of special-interest groups that keeps them in power. In Randolph Bourne's now-hackneyed phrase, "War is the health of the state." This claim is not simply a wild-eyed ideological pronouncement, however; it is as well established as any historical regularity can be. Entire books, such as Porter's *War and the Rise of the State* and my own *Crisis and Leviathan* and *Against Leviathan*,[3] have documented it in excruciating detail.

Aware of this reality, some of us steadfastly resist any claim that war will promote either liberty or security; we do not expect that, notwithstanding what has almost always happened before, nature will change its course on this particular occasion. Although many people can be persuaded that the risks war poses to their own life, liberty, and property rights are justified—necessary and only temporary sacrifices in the service of their own long-term security and liberty—the realistic and well informed among us understand that those who embrace this faith are taking a gamble against very long odds.

In the United States, the government has been at war more or less since 1940, which is to say, in Madison's phrase, engaged in "continual warfare" or in massive preparation for warfare. Can anyone seriously maintain that we Americans are now freer or more secure than we were *before* the sainted Franklin D. Roosevelt and his spiritual descendants took command of the ship of state and steered it into the storm of perpetual war? The U.S. government, which once confined its foreign adventures to ad hoc interventions, most of them in small Caribbean and Central American countries, has acted ever since World War II as a globe-girdling empire, projecting U.S. military and political power here, there, and everywhere with reckless unconcern for a reasonable connection between overall cost and benefit.[4] But why *should* the rulers act prudently, you

---

3. Robert Higgs, *Crisis and Leviathan: Critical Episodes in the Growth of American Government* (New York: Oxford University Press, 1987); and Robert Higgs, *Against Leviathan: Government Power and a Free Society* (Oakland, Calif.: The Independent Institute, 2004).

4. See Ivan Eland, *The Empire Has No Clothes: U.S. Foreign Policy Exposed* (Oakland, Calif.: The Independent Institute, 2004); Chalmers Johnson, *The Sorrows of Empire: Militarism, Secrecy, and the End of the Republic* (New York: Metropolitan, 2004); and Derek Leebaert, *Magic and Mayhem: The Delusions of American Foreign Policy from Korea to Afghanistan* (New York: Simon and Schuster, 2010).

may ask, when they themselves—and, as usual, their supporting cronies—reap whatever benefit is produced, whereas the costs of the interventions take the form of other people's sacrifices of life, liberty, and property rights?

Not least among these sacrifices has been that of the old constitutional structure—the government of checks and balances that once helped to restrain the rulers from launching foreign engagements and suppressing domestic liberties willy-nilly.[5] Owing to the series of hot and cold military emergencies since 1940, the president has become, for all practical purposes, a Caesar. He now goes to war entirely at his own discretion. After all, as his spokespersons tirelessly reiterate, he is the commander in chief of the armed forces (as if this fact simply wiped out the rest of the Constitution).

Congress has become so pusillanimous that it provides no check whatsoever on the president's war making. In "authorizing" the president to attack Iraq or not, entirely as he pleased, Congress recently not only abrogated its clear constitutional duty but did so with grotesquely cavalier disregard for the gravity of the matter at stake. It did not even bother to debate the issue; it simply handed over its power to the executive and returned to the workaday plundering that is its only remaining raison d'être. The president and his subordinate chieftains keep telling us that "we are at war," but that statement is just a turn of phrase for public-relations purposes inasmuch as the clear constitutional requirement of a congressional declaration of war has gone unfulfilled. This form of executive usurpation provokes no great public outcry, however, so conditioned to it have the people become.

To the injury of all past attenuations of our rights under the Constitution, the government has now added the insult of shredding the Fourth, Fifth, and Sixth Amendments.[6] Our rulers declare that by nothing more substantial than

---

5. Higgs, *Against Leviathan,* 201–17.
6. We would scarcely need any special sources to understand these matters, but the government and its handmaidens in the news media have worked hard to obscure them and to persuade us that black is white. The Bill of Rights Defense Committee has prepared an annotated list of "recommended resources," which is available at http://www.bordc .org/recom-resources.htm. In particular, see James Bovard, *Terrorism and Tyranny: Trampling Freedom, Justice, and Peace to Rid the World of Evil* (New York: Palgrave Macmillan, 2003); and Nat Hentoff, *The War on the Bill of Rights and the Gathering Resistance* (New York: Seven Stories Press, 2003).

the emperor's say-so, any person may be arrested and held incommunicado, without trial, and then punished, even put to death. Say good-bye to the writ of habeas corpus, the very bedrock of limited government. Speedy trial? Forget about it. The government has to but whisper those two magic words, *unlawful combatant,* and you may be rendered as much a *desaparecido* as any unfortunate victim of Argentine tyranny. Surely this sort of "defense of our freedom" falls, at best, under the rubric of destroying the village in order to save it. As for due process of law, it's obsolete. Your right to be secure "against unreasonable searches and seizures"? That's ancient history, too, outmoded since September 11, 2001, when, the government insists, "everything changed," including your right to be free of warrantless searches of your premises, Carnivore sweeps of your e-mail, taps of your telephone calls, and airport "security" procedures that, if carried out by anyone but the Transportation Security Agency's personnel, would justify charges of sexual assault and battery and child molestation.

A few things definitely did not change after 9/11, however, and chief among them is the government's lust for greater power and control over every single person in the country—nay, over everyone on the entire earth. Do I fear that the USA PATRIOT Act will be abused? No. I *know* that it has been already and will continue to be because its elastic language allows unscrupulous prosecutors to scratch a variety of itches completely unrelated to terrorism.[7] Apart from these egregious and wholly predictable prosecutorial shenanigans, freedom-loving people ought to recognize that—to borrow a phrase from Edmund Burke—the thing itself is an abuse because it sweeps away fundamental due-process protections of our rights that required centuries to put in place.

In the face of all of this stupendous abuse and too much else even to mention, some people, even some self-described libertarians, persist in arguing that the price we are paying is worthwhile and that we can trust the government to act responsibly and effectively in wielding its new powers. Neither element of that argument can withstand scrutiny.

---

7. Dan Eggen, "Patriot Act Used for More Than Anti-Terror; Justice Report Also Reveals 50 Secretly Detained After 9/11," *San Francisco Chronicle,* May 21, 2003 (reprinted from the *Washington Post*); Eric Lichtblau, "Patriot Act's Reach Has Gone Beyond Terrorism," *Seattle Times,* September 28, 2003 (reprinted from the *New York Times*).

As for trusting the government, the fact—well established in history and in contemporary reality—is that, contrary to what all conservatives seem to believe, the government can be trusted to do the right thing and to do it well even *less* in foreign and defense policy than in matters of domestic policy.[8] Because national-security matters lie outside the immediate experience of the great bulk of the citizens, the government can get away with waste, fraud, brutality, and idiocy far more easily in foreign affairs than it can when prescribing student exams, building houses for poor people, or relieving Grandma's aches and pains. The history of U.S. foreign and defense policy in the past sixty-five years is an unrelieved tale of mendacity, corruption, and criminal blundering.[9] If the government can't fix the potholes in Washington, D.C., it certainly can't build a viable liberal democratic state in Iraq or Afghanistan. No one of sound mind should have supposed that it should even try, much less that it would succeed. These adventures, like so much else that the government undertakes, are a gigantic hoax, and all too many of these efforts verge on racketeering of the sort described by the legendary U.S. Marine general Smedley Butler.[10]

But if the government *were* able and willing to carry out an effective global "war on terrorism" by means of its present policy of empire and naked aggression (politely called "preventive war"), would the benefits of that policy justify the costs being borne? Not for a moment. The costs are real and huge—hundreds of billions of dollars and scores of thousands of dead and wounded so far just for the invasion and occupation of Afghanistan and Iraq, not to mention again the grave injuries to civil and economic liberties here at home. The benefits, to the extent that any exist at all, accrue entirely to a small coterie

---

8. Robert Higgs, "The Cold War Economy: Opportunity Costs, Ideology, and the Politics of Crisis," *Explorations in Economic History* 31 (July 1994), 298–307.

9. See Robert Higgs, ed., *Arms, Politics, and the Economy: Historical and Contemporary Perspectives* (New York: Holmes and Meier for The Independent Institute, 1990); Higgs, *Against Leviathan;* Jonathan Kwitney, *Endless Enemies: The Making of an Unfriendly World* (New York: Penguin, 1984); Derek Leebaert, *The Fifty-Year Wound: The True Price of America's Cold War Victory* (Boston: Little, Brown, 2002); and Leebaert, *Magic and Mayhem.*

10. For Butler's testimony, see Smedley D. Butler, *War Is a Racket* (New York: Round Table Press, 1935), at http://lexrex.com/enlightened/articles/warisaracket.htm.

of political leaders and their supporters among the power elite, for the most part their cronies in the military-industrial, "homeland security," financial, and petroleum sectors. Ideological zealots dedicated to serving the interests of Israel's Likud Party and the members of certain Christian sects thrilled by the prospect of apocalyptic mayhem in the Holy Land go along for the sheer intoxication of the spree, the former serving as high-level conspirators and dis-information specialists and the latter forming a legion of useful idiots, a sort of ten-million-strong Karl Rove Brigade on election day.[11] Can anyone who values the preservation of a free society react except with disgust to any aspect of this criminally lethal and massively destructive government fiasco?

---

11. The most authoritative source on the neocon zealots who operated at the highest levels of the Pentagon hierarchy in the period leading up to the Iraq War is Lieutenant Colonel Karen Kwiatkowski, who "from May 2002 until February 2003 . . . observed firsthand the formation of the Pentagon's Office of Special Plans and watched the latter stages of the neoconservative capture of the policy-intelligence nexus in the run-up to the invasion of Iraq" (Karen Kwiatkowski, "The New Pentagon Papers: A High-Ranking Military Officer Reveals How Defense Department Extremists Suppressed Information and Twisted the Truth to Drive the Country to War," *Salon*, March 10, 2004, at http://www.salon.com/opinion/feature/2004/03/10/osp_moveon). Kwiatkowski, now retired, has written many articles that are accessible on the World Wide Web. Among many other informative sources on the neocon schemers, see especially Jim Lobe, "How Neo-Cons Influence the Pentagon," *Asia Times*, August 8, 2003, at http://www.atimes.com/atimes/Middle_East/EH08Ak01.html; Jim Lobe, "The Neocon Web," December 23, 2003, at http://www.lewrockwell.com/ips/lobe40.html; and Jim Lobe, "CIA Chief Clueless on Neocon Intelligence Channel," March 12, 2004, at http://www.lewrockwell.com/ips/lobe65.html.

18

To Fight or Not to Fight?

*War's Payoffs to U.S. Leaders
and to the American People*

IN A BRIEF COMMENTARY written in 1997,[1] I called attention
to the close association between war and the U.S. presidents ranked as "great" or
"near great" in polls of historians. My essay has gained a fair amount of attention over the years. Even the quintessential establishment historian Arthur M.
Schlesinger Jr. saw fit to cite it with apparent agreement in a 1997 article in the
Political Science Quarterly.[2] After the Ludwig von Mises Institute distributed
my essay again on Presidents' Day in 2007, it was linked and reposted widely
and provoked a considerable amount of comment on the Web.

Although one can hardly quarrel with the close association between the
presidents' intimate involvement in war and their presidential-greatness rank-
ing, one can take issue—and over the years many writers have taken issue—
with my conclusion that "[t]he lesson seems obvious. Any president who craves a
high place in the annals of history should hasten to thrust the American people
into an orgy of death and destruction. It does not matter how ill-conceived the
war may be."[3] For the most part, the disagreement pertains, first, to my general
argument that many, if not all, of the wars from which the most highly ranked
presidents gained their reputed greatness were clearly unnecessary and, second,
to my specific indictment of Abraham Lincoln, Woodrow Wilson, Franklin
D. Roosevelt, Harry Truman, and Lyndon B. Johnson for "their supremely
catastrophic war policies."[4]

---

1. Robert Higgs, "No More 'Great Presidents,'" *The Free Market* 15 (March 1997): 1–3.
2. Arthur M. Schlesinger Jr., "Rating the Presidents: Washington to Clinton," *Political
Science Quarterly* 112 (1997): 179–90.
3. Higgs, "No More 'Great Presidents,'" 1–2.
4. Higgs, "No More 'Great Presidents,'" 2.

Table 18.1 War's Payoffs to the People and the Leaders

U.S. Leaders Choose	Threat to the American People	
	Existential	Lesser or Spurious
Initiate War	American people lose. U.S. leaders lose.	American people lose. U.S. leaders win.
Avoid War	American people win. U.S. leaders ???.	American people win. U.S. leaders ???.

Although we cannot expect to resolve a Great Historical Debate by means of a simple, cut-and-dried approach, we can perhaps clarify our thinking about this matter with the aid of a more systematic representation of the relevant issues. I propose that we organize our thoughts along the lines laid out in the accompanying analytical array, table 18.1, whose content I will explain. The array displays a slightly complicated, two-by-two cross-classification.

At the top, the array shows whether the threat to the American people at large (as distinct from, say, the threat to the government itself or the threat to certain domestic or foreign special-interest groups) is "existential" or "lesser or spurious." Of course, dividing all perceived threats into only these two discrete classes is a crude way to differentiate them, and dividing them into more than two classes or ordering them along a continuum is conceivable, but for my present purposes such additional complications are unnecessary.

By an "existential threat," I mean one that poses a danger to national survival. During World War II, Americans often described the conflict as a "life and death struggle" or a "war for national survival," but I do not believe that it actually was such. None of the enemies of the United States in that war, whether acting alone or in concert with all of the others, had the economic and technological capacity to destroy the American nation, "take over the country," "destroy our way of life," or inflict a comparable amount of harm. Those who dispute my belief should bear the burden of showing, with cogent evidence and argument, that the Axis powers had the capacity to carry out such a takeover or utter destruction. Simply repeating the mantra that Hitler "wanted to take over the world" is not an argument, but an excuse for not making one. An existential threat can arise, however, and, indeed, one prevailed for decades during the Cold War. An all-out nuclear exchange between the United States and the USSR, an apocalypse into which each side was all too prepared to enter at a moment's notice, would have wreaked such horrifying devastation that the survivors probably would have envied the dead, and economic life would have become at best extremely primitive and incapable of sustaining a large population.

In contrast, a threat to the American people may be "lesser or spurious"—in other words, it may not be a risk to national survival or even to national flourishing and perhaps not be a real threat at all. Most wars in U.S. history clearly belong in this category, which undoubtedly comprises the War of 1812, the Mexican-American War, the Spanish-American War, the Philippine-American War, World War I, the Korean War, the Vietnam War, both wars against Iraq, and the U.S. war in Afghanistan that has been under way for the past decade, not to mention the many minor U.S. military actions throughout the world, from the attacks on the Barbary Coast more than two centuries ago to the attacks on Serbia twelve years ago.

Although the secession of the Southern states in 1861 threatened the continuation of the existing political union, it need not have caused anyone's death, and the War Between the States became the terribly devastating affair that it was only because Lincoln and those who rallied to his leadership refused to accept the secession peacefully.

Like Bruce Russett,[5] I believe that the Germans and their allies did not constitute a "clear and present danger" to the American people at large prior to U.S. entry into World War II and, hence, that the Roosevelt administration had no compelling public-interest reason to provoke the Japanese Empire with a protracted series of economic sanctions, threats, and demands in order to open a "back door" for entry into the war in Europe.[6] As Garet Garrett wrote in

5. Bruce M. Russett, *No Clear and Present Danger: A Skeptical View of the United States Entry into World War II* (New York: Harper Torchbooks, 1972).
6. All comprehensive accounts of the lead-up to the attack on Pearl Harbor discuss the U.S. sanctions and diplomatic maneuvers. For brief accounts, see William L. Neumann, "How American Policy Toward Japan Contributed to War in the Pacific," in *Perpetual War for Perpetual Peace: A Critical Examination of the Foreign Policy of Franklin Delano Roosevelt and Its Aftermath,* edited by Harry Elmer Barnes (Caldwell, Idaho: Caxton

May 1941, when Roosevelt had already made the country a de facto belligerent in countless ways, "The alternative had been to create here on this hemisphere the impregnable asylum of freedom and let tyranny in Europe destroy itself, as tyranny always has done and is bound to do again."[7] I need hardly add that very few Americans, either scholars or laypersons, now agree with me in regard to the imprudence of U.S. entry into World War II, but this question ought properly to be decided by historical evidence and theoretically informed judgment, not by majority vote. We might well recall that before the attack on Pearl Harbor, an overwhelming majority of the Americans surveyed by public-opinion pollsters said that they did not want the United States to enter the war.[8]

Along the left side of the array in table 18.1, the distinction is between whether U.S. leaders choose to initiate a war or to avoid war. This variable reminds us that "the people" do not make such decisions; only the president and his coterie do so. In earlier times, Congress was deeply involved as well, but even then issues of war and peace usually could be effectively decided prior to any formal congressional involvement by means of presidential allegations and by the creation of certain faits accomplis or incidents—alleged Mexican incursions into U.S.-

---

Printers, 1953), 260–64, and Robert Higgs, "How U.S. Economic Warfare Provoked Japan's Attack on Pearl Harbor," *The Freeman* 56 (May 2006): 36–37 (Chapter 10 in this volume). For more detailed accounts, see George Morgenstern, "The Actual Road to Pearl Harbor," in Barnes, ed., *Perpetual War for Perpetual Peace*, 317–48, and George Victor, *The Pearl Harbor Myth: Rethinking the Unthinkable* (Washington, D.C.: Potomac Books, 2007), 187–261. For a highly detailed and deeply researched recent account of the U.S. economic warfare in particular, see Edward S. Miller, *Bankrupting the Enemy: The U.S. Financial Siege of Japan Before Pearl Harbor* (Annapolis, Md.: Naval Institute Press, 2007). On the critical matter of U.S. code breaking and interception of encrypted Japanese radio transmissions, see the path-breaking research reported in Robert B. Stinnett, *Day of Deceit: The Truth About FDR and Pearl Harbor* (New York: Free Press, 2000). For unusually clear-eyed accounts by a commentator who wrote about these events as they occurred and displayed remarkable prescience about where they ultimately would lead the country, see Garet Garrett, *Defend America First: The Antiwar Nationalist Editorials of the "Saturday Evening Post," 1939–1942,* with an introduction by Bruce Ramsey (Caldwell, Idaho: Caxton Press, [1939–42] 2002).

7. Garrett, *Defend America First*, 165.

8. Robert Higgs, *Crisis and Leviathan: Critical Episodes in the Growth of American Government* (New York: Oxford University Press, 1987), 199.

claimed territory (1846), alleged Spanish sinking of the battleship USS *Maine* (1898), alleged German plots to help the Mexicans recover territory lost in the Mexican-American War (1917), alleged unprovoked German attacks on U.S. warships in the North Atlantic (1941), alleged unprovoked North Vietnamese attacks on U.S. warships in the Gulf of Tonkin (1964), alleged Iranian provision of munitions used to kill U.S. soldiers in Iraq (2007), and so forth. Only an extraordinarily dull presidential clique lacks the imagination to concoct an appealing casus belli.

In the analytical array, the focus on the leaders' decision may also suggest (correctly) that they make their decision in the service of their own interests—and, of course, in the interests of their crucial supporting coalition of power brokers and special-interest groups—not in pursuit of the people's general interest. Of course, they invariably declare that all of their actions reflect nothing but their unsullied attempt to serve the public. Anyone who believes this sort of nursery tale is sorely in need of deeper immersion in the facts of history, not to mention in the discipline of public choice.

Among the many history books one might recommend to those suffering from naïveté about how our glorious leaders make foreign-policy decisions, some of my favorites are John V. Denson's outstanding collection *The Costs of War,* Walter Karp's *The Politics of War,* Harry Elmer Barnes's classic edited volume *Perpetual War for Perpetual Peace,* Thomas Fleming's *The Illusion of Victory* and *The New Dealers' War,* James Bamford's *A Pretext for War,* and Nicholson Baker's priceless work *Human Smoke.*[9] I also heartily recommend that transcripts of the Nixon Whitehouse tapes be read early and often.

---

9. Barnes, ed., *Perpetual War for Perpetual Peace*; John V. Denson, ed., *The Costs of War: America's Pyrrhic Victories* (New Brunswick, N.J.: Transaction, 1997); Thomas Fleming, *The New Dealers' War: F.D.R. and the War Within World War II* (New York: Basic Books, 2002); Thomas Fleming, *The Illusion of Victory: America in World War I* (New York: Basic Books, 2003); James Bamford, *A Pretext for War: 9/11, Iraq, and the Abuse of America's Intelligence Agencies* (New York: Doubleday, 2004); and Nicholson Baker, *Human Smoke: The Beginnings of World War II, the End of Civilization* (New York: Simon and Schuster, 2008); and Walter Karp, *The Politics of War: The Story of Two Wars Which Altered Forever the Political Life of the American Republic (1890–1920)* (New York: Franklin Square Press, 2010).

It is unsettling to find oneself in complete agreement with Hermann Göring, but the Nazi bigwig was certainly correct when, during an evening conversation in his cell at Nuremberg, he told Gustave Gilbert, a German-speaking U.S. intelligence officer and psychologist:

> [O]f course, the *people* don't want war. Why would some poor slob on a farm want to risk his life in a war when the best that he can get out of it is to come back to his farm in one piece. Naturally, the common people don't want war; neither in Russia nor in England nor in America, nor for that matter in Germany. That is understood. But, after all, it is the *leaders* of the country who determine the policy and it is always a simple matter to drag the people along, whether it is a democracy or a fascist dictatorship or a Parliament or a Communist dictatorship. . . . [V]oice or no voice, the people can always be brought to the bidding of the leaders. That is easy. All you have to do is tell them they are being attacked and denounce the pacifists for lack of patriotism and exposing the country to danger. It works the same way in any country.[10]

Given that the people at large and their interests are essentially irrelevant to the decisions the national leaders make, we are well advised to focus on how those leaders believe war or avoidance of war will serve their own interests.

Therefore, in the interior of my analytical array I indicate roughly the expected outcome of each choice in response to the two types of threat. Each cell indicates both the outcome for the American people in general and the outcome for U.S. government leaders.

Consider the outcome of the situation when an existential threat has arisen and the leaders choose to initiate war (northwest cell). I conjecture that the expected outcome is uninviting for both affected parties because in a war against such a truly grave threat, the likely outcome will be horrible for everybody, notwithstanding that the danger the government is attempting to preempt is a great and genuine one. The only existential threat the American people have ever faced was from Soviet nuclear weapons, and fortunately for everyone those weapons were never used against us, as they would have been in retaliation if

---

10. Quoted in G. M. Gilbert, *Nuremberg Diary* (New York: Da Capo Press, [1947] 1995), 278–79.

U.S. leaders had initiated war against the USSR, as General Curtis LeMay and General Thomas Power, among others in the power elite, wished to do.[11]

The beauty of the Cold War, if one may speak of such a thing, is that the threat of Soviet retaliation served to discipline U.S. leaders, who understood that they might be killed in a nuclear war and that even if they survived, they would no longer preside over a pleasant, prosperous country, but over a radiation-poisoned wasteland populated by desperate, sick, and starving survivors—a situation apt to take all the fun out of preeminence in the ruling class. Thus, the northwest cell in the array testifies to the incentives that made the strategic doctrine of mutually assured destruction (MAD) work. Because of the substantial potential for accidental missile launches, warning-signal malfunctions, and command-and-control failures, MAD itself was fraught with terrifying risks, as any system based on launch-ready, nuclear-armed missiles must be.

Dropping down to the southwest cell of the array, we see the likely outcome if an existential threat exists and the leaders avoid war. The people at large clearly benefit greatly; they are able to continue their normal lives and do not have to endure the mass deaths and other grave harms that war against an existential threat would probably bring them. The leaders' outcome, however, is somewhat less obvious. Although they benefit from continued normal life, as the general public does, they gain none of the special acclaim and greatly enhanced power that might attend their "winning" a war against an existential threat, assuming that winning in such a situation is conceivable.

It is conceivable to General "Buck" Turgidson in the classic Cold War film *Dr. Strangelove* (1964), as it was to several generations of the U.S. government's actual nuclear strategists after whom Turgidson and *Strangelove*'s General Jack D. Ripper and Dr. Strangelove himself were modeled. As John Newhouse writes in *War and Peace in the Nuclear Age*, "Over the years, the brotherhood of specialists, mostly civilians, who have made a calling of nuclear strategy has grown. They review all of the unknowns—unknowables really—that underlie the deployment of nuclear weapons and any conceivable use of them. They devise

---

11. See Robert Higgs, "On 'Winning the War,'" *The Independent Review* 11, no. 1 (Summer 2006), 155–56; Fred Kaplan, *The Wizards of Armageddon* (New York: Simon and Schuster, 1983); and Jeffrey Record, *Nuclear Deterrence, Preventive War, and Counterproliferation*, Cato Institute Policy Analysis no. 519 (Washington, D.C.: Cato Institute, July 8, 2004), 14–15.

scenarios for protracted nuclear war and for limited nuclear war." Newhouse refers to "the glib manner in which the civilian priesthood discussed plans for using nuclear weapons in combat situations."[12] According to Daniel McCarthy, Ronald Reagan, as president, "came to have little patience for Strangelovian defense intellectuals who argued that a nuclear war could be won and that disarmament was a mirage. As he later wrote in his memoirs, Reagan was appalled by those advisers who 'claimed nuclear war was "inevitable" and we had to prepare for this reality. They tossed around macabre jargon about "throw weights" and "kill ratios" as if they were talking about baseball scores.'"[13] Much of this more or less insane strategizing originated at the RAND Corporation, a think tank the U.S. Air Force created in 1946 to serve the needs of its mad bombers. Besides playing a reference role in *Strangelove* as "the Bland Corporation," RAND inspired Malvina Reynolds's blackly humorous lyrics for "The Rand Hymn," which begins:

> Oh, the Rand Corporation's the boon of the world,
> They think all day long for a fee.
> They sit and play games about going up in flames;
> For counters they use you and me, honey bee,
> For counters they use you and me.[14]

I suppose that relatively few top U.S. leaders have thought they would personally come out ahead by initiating a nuclear war, but some leaders undoubtedly have enjoyed initiating wars against threats they falsely claimed might be existential ones, as George W. Bush administration officials insinuated by their "mushroom cloud" allusions to Saddam Hussein's alleged "weapons of mass destruction." This fraudulent pretext for unprovoked aggression fooled the bulk of the electorate, made Bush and company heroes for a season (till the chickens undeniably came home to roost during the protracted U.S. occupation of Iraq), and pushed Bush and Vice President Dick Cheney to reelection

---

12. John Newhouse, *War and Peace in the Nuclear Age* (New York: Knopf, 1989), 298–99.

13. Daniel McCarthy, "Revising Ronald Reagan: Was the 40th President a Peace-Loving Moderate?" *Reason* (June 2007), at http://reason.com/archives/2007/05/09/revising-ronald -reagan.

14. Malvina Reynolds, "The Rand Hymn," 1961, at http://letras.terra.com/malvina-reynolds /755363/.

in 2004. Note in contrast, however, the Bush administration's patient resort to diplomacy in dealing with North Korea, a country whose regime it feared might *actually* possess or soon acquire a few nuclear weapons and some crude delivery vehicles. In recent years, U.S. leaders, knowing that the Iranian regime cannot effectively retaliate directly against them, have been seriously contemplating the use of nuclear weapons against targets in Iran—a scheme that appears to reflect complete detachment from geopolitical and economic reality and human decency, not to mention the possibility that the tail in Jerusalem is wagging the dog in Washington, D.C.

Moving to the southeast cell of the array, we see again that the people win if their leaders refrain from launching a war even against a lesser or spurious threat. Such wars may still cost a great deal of money, devour many thousands of lives, and entail repression of civil and economic liberties. Moreover, because they allay little or no actual threat to the people, they have no genuine value except to the extent that the leadership's propaganda can bamboozle the people into imagining a benefit—for example, that the war in Vietnam would keep the Communist dominoes from falling across all of Southeast Asia; that the war in Iraq would keep Saddam Hussein from "destabilizing" the entire Middle East; blah, blah, blah.

Again, however, the outcome for the leaders is not clear. If they avoid wars against less-than-existential threats, they get little or no credit for doing so, and they sacrifice the enhanced powers, public acclaim, and historians' credit for greatness that victory in such a war may bring. Worse, their political opponents may *blame* them for not going to war. Lyndon Johnson, for example, worried that the conservatives would accuse him of being "soft on communism" unless he escalated the U.S. military engagement in Vietnam in a visible attempt to "win the war" there.[15]

Presidents may profit greatly by initiating war against less-than-existential or completely spurious threats. Knocking down a third-rate power and stealing a big chunk of its land in the Mexican-American War left James K. Polk ensconced among the historians' "near greats." Having helped to instigate the war

---

15. Paul K. Conkin, *Big Daddy from the Pedernales: Lyndon Baines Johnson* (Boston: Twayne, 1986), 257; Allen J. Matusow, *The Unraveling of America: A History of Liberalism in the 1960s* (New York: Harper and Row, 1984), 149–50.

with Spain, Theodore Roosevelt rode to the vice presidency and thence, after William McKinley's assassination, to the presidency itself on the strength of his harebrained romp among the corpses strewn across the Cuban hills.[16] Many Americans love him to this day, undisturbed that he was an ambition-addled protofascist whose insatiable craving for power over his fellow men expired only when he took his last breath. Thus, any threat less than a manifestly existential and personally dangerous one may present an irresistible temptation to U.S. leaders itching for "greatness."

Surrender to this temptation finds its place in the northeast cell of my array, which indicates that the leaders win by initiating war, although, again, the people at large lose. In all actual U.S. wars, the people have been net losers; in each instance, they would have been better off if the war had not been fought. Most Americans will vigorously dispute this claim, of course, proclaiming above all that World War II was not only just, but necessary—nay, unavoidable. As I have already observed, I think they are wrong, but I cannot make a compelling case for my conclusion here, and in any event, others, including Russett and several of the contributors to Barnes's collection *Perpetual War for Perpetual Peace,* have already done so better than I can.[17] Even if I were to concede the orthodox opinion of World War II, however, the rest of the U.S. wars would nevertheless remain strong evidence in support of my claim.

In no event will I concede the necessity or desirability of the U.S. government's going to war against the Confederate States of America in 1861. The usual argument that it did so to destroy slavery does not hold water. As Abraham Lincoln himself made crystal clear in his famous August 22, 1862, letter to Horace Greeley, his only reason for fighting was to preserve the union, with or without slavery.[18] Although the war did result in slavery's destruction as a by-product—the only good to come out of the war—it was not initiated or continued for that purpose. Moreover, even that splendid result might not have been worth the war's cost because, as some serious scholars have argued (most notably Jeffrey Rogers

---

16. Edmund Morris, *The Rise of Theodore Roosevelt* (New York: Random House, 1979), 654–61.

17. But see Chapters 10 and 11 in this volume.

18. Abraham Lincoln, letter to Horace Greeley, August 22, 1862, at http://showcase.netins .net/web/creative/lincoln/speeches/greeley.htm .

Hummel[19]), slavery in North America would probably have ended soon anyhow, without violence, as it did in all of the other countries of the New World (except Haiti), despite its having been institutionalized there for centuries.

Except during the Cold War, when, although top U.S. leaders exposed the country to grave risks, they strove to avoid direct, open warfare with the Soviet Union, the American people have lived for more than two hundred years in the southeast and all too often the northeast cells of my analytical array. Because of the country's fortunate geographical location, protected on the east and the west by broad oceans and bordered on the north and the south by militarily weak states, the American people did not have to face existential threats prior to the nuclear age. Nonetheless, their leaders have again and again given in to their personal ambitions for fame and power and have initiated wars in which the people at large have suffered great losses of economic resources, lives, and liberties—all for benefits that for the masses have fallen grossly short of the sacrifices borne.

Perhaps we ought to admit that many Americans have gained and continue to gain great psychic benefit from the U.S. government's dishing out death and destruction to the foreign devils du jour. Adding that benefit to the calculus, we might have to alter our analysis accordingly in recognition of this red-white-and-blue savagery. Or we might alternatively insist that despite certain vicious strains in the national character and despite the undeniable presence of a perennially bloodthirsty element in the population, most Americans have simply been misled by their leaders,[20] who sought not the people's benefit, but gains for themselves and for their supporting coalition of special-interest groups. Although the national character may be a topic for endless debate, relatively little doubt attaches to the claim that the leaders time and again have sought to attain their own goals by taking the nation to war, however much their doing so might require great sacrifices of the people's lives, liberties, and property.

---

19. Jeffrey Rogers Hummel, *Emancipating Slaves, Enslaving Free Men: A History of the American Civil War* (Chicago: Open Court, 1996).

20. David Gordon, "The Ruses for War: American Interventionism Since World War II," *Mises Review* 13 (Summer 2007), at http://mises.org/misesreview_detail.aspx?control=313; Robert Higgs, "To Make War, Presidents Lie," in *Resurgence of the Warfare State: The Crisis Since 9/11,* 133–36 (Oakland, Calif.: The Independent Institute, [2002] 2005).

19

Military-Economic Fascism

How Business Corrupts Government and Vice Versa

> The business of buying weapons that takes place in the Pentagon is a corrupt business—ethically and morally corrupt from top to bottom. The process is dominated by advocacy, with few, if any, checks and balances. Most people in power like this system of doing business and do not want it changed.
> —Colonel James G. Burton, *The Pentagon Wars*[1]

IN COUNTRIES SUCH as the United States, whose economies are commonly though inaccurately described as "capitalist" or "free market," war and preparation for war systematically corrupt both parties to the state–private transactions by which the government obtains the bulk of its military goods and services. On one side, business interests seek to bend the state's decisions in their favor by corrupting official decision makers with outright and de facto bribes. The outright bribes include cash, gifts in kind, loans, entertainment, transportation, lodging, prostitutes' services, inside information about personal investment opportunities, overly generous speaking fees, and promises of future employment or consulting patronage for officials or their family members. The de facto bribes include campaign contributions (sometimes legal, sometimes illegal), sponsorship of political fund-raising events, and donations to charities or other causes favored by the relevant government officials. Reports of this sort of corruption appear from time to time in the press under the rubric

---

1. James G. Burton, *The Pentagon Wars: Reformers Challenge the Old Guard* (Annapolis, Md.: Naval Institute Press, 1993), 232.

"military scandal."[2] On the other and much more important side, the state corrupts businesspeople by effectively turning them into co-conspirators in and beneficiaries of its most fundamental activity—plundering the general public.

Participants in the military-industrial-congressional complex (MICC) are routinely blamed for mismanagement; they are frequently accused of waste, fraud, and abuse; and from time to time a few of them are indicted for criminal offenses.[3] All of these unsavory actions, however, are typically viewed as

---

2. See, for example, Wayne Biddle, "Audit Cites Pentagon Contractors," *New York Times,* April 29, 1985; Michael Wines, "Ex-Unisys Official Admits Paying Bribes to Get Pentagon Contracts," *New York Times,* March 10, 1989; Michael D. Hinds, "Top Republican on House Panel Is Charged with Accepting Bribes," *New York Times,* May 6, 1992; "National Briefing: Washington: Ex–Pentagon Officials Sentenced," *New York Times,* December 13, 2003; Andy Paztor and Jonathan Karp, "Northrop Papers Indicate Coverup: Documents from '80s Show Accounting Irregularities Were Hidden from Pentagon," *Wall Street Journal,* April 19, 2004; Laura M. Colarusso, "Revolving Door Leads to Jail: Former Acquisition Official Convicted of Steering Business to Boeing for Personal Gain," *Federal Times,* October 11, 2004; Dean Calbreath and Jerry Kammer, "Contractor 'Knew How to Grease the Wheels': ADCS Founder Spent Years Cultivating Political Contacts," *San Diego Union-Tribune,* December 4, 2005; David Wood, "Graft Lurks Within Pentagon's 'Black Budget': Top-Secret Items Escape Oversight," *New Orleans Times-Picayune,* November 30, 2005; Charles R. Babcock, "Contractor Pleads Guilty to Corruption: Probe Extends Beyond Bribes to Congressman," *Washington Post,* February 25, 2006; Brian Ross, "From Cash to Yachts: Congressman's Bribe Menu; Court Documents Show Randall 'Duke' Cunningham Set Bribery Rates," *ABC News,* February 27, 2006, at http://abcnews.go.com/Politics/story?id=1667009&page=1; "Defense Contractor Guilty in Bribe Case," *New Orleans Times-Picayune,* February 25, 2006; William R. Levesque, "There's No Watchdog for Secret Budgets: A Deal Between SOCom and eTreppid Raises Questions, but Is Hard to Track," *St. Petersburg Times,* March 9, 2007; "5 Americans Indicted in Iraq Bid Probe; 3 Officers Among Those Accused of Taking Cash, Gifts Tied to Projects," *MSNBC.com,* February 7, 2007, at http://www.msnbc.msn.com/id/17025277; and "Feinstein Quits Committee Under War-Profiteer Cloud; Report Documents Military Contracts for Firms Owned by Senator's Husband," *World Net Daily,* March 28, 2007, at http://www.worldnetdaily.com/news/article.asp?ARTICLE_ID=549322007.

3. See Robert Higgs, "Military Scandal, Again," *Wall Street Journal,* June 27, 1988; Robert Higgs, "Introduction: Fifty Years of Arms, Politics, and the Economy," in *Arms, Politics, and the Economy: Historical and Contemporary Perspectives,* edited by Robert Higgs (New York: Holmes and Meier, 1990), xx–xxiii. See also Robert Higgs "The Cold War Is Over but U.S. Preparation for It Continues," in *Against Leviathan: Government Power and a*

aberrations—misfeasances to be rectified or malfeasances to be punished while retaining the basic system of state–private cooperation in the production of military goods and services.[4] I maintain, in contrast, that these offenses and even more serious ones are not simply unfortunate blemishes on a basically sound arrangement, but superficial expressions of a thoroughgoing, intrinsic rottenness in the entire setup.

It is regrettable in any event for people to suffer under the weight of a state and its military apparatus, but the present arrangement—a system of military-economic fascism as instantiated in the United States by the MICC—is worse than full-fledged military-economic socialism. In the latter, people are oppressed because they are taxed, conscripted, and regimented, but they are not co-opted and corrupted by joining forces with their rapacious rulers; a clear line separates them from the predators on the "dark side." With military-economic fascism, however, the line becomes blurred, and many people actively hop back and forth across it: members of advisory committees, such as the Defense Science Board and the Defense Policy Board,[5] and university administrators meet regularly with Pentagon officials,[6] and the revolving door spins furiously. According to a September 2002 report, "[t]hirty-two major Bush appointees are former executives, consultants, or major shareholders of top weapons contractors," and a much greater number crosses the line at lower levels.[7]

Free Society (Oakland, Calif.: The Independent Institute, 2004), 247–68; Ernest Fitzgerald, *The Pentagonists: An Insider's View of Waste, Mismanagement, and Fraud in Defense Spending* (New York: Harper and Row, 1989); William E. Kovacic, "Blue Ribbon Defense Commissions: The Acquisition of Major Weapon Systems," in Higgs, ed., *Arms, Politics, and the Economy,* 61–103; and William E. Kovacic, "The Sorcerer's Apprentice: Public Regulation of the Weapons Acquisition Process," in Higgs, ed., *Arms, Politics, and the Economy,* 104–31.

4. For an explicit example of the "aberration" claim, see Fitzgerald, *The Pentagonists,* 197–98.

5. For Defense Science Board and Defense Policy board information, see, respectively, http://www.acq.osd.mil/dsb/charter.htm and http://fl1.findlaw.com/news.findlaw.com/hdocs/docs/dod/dpbac80201chrtr.pdf.

6. For a report of an especially remarkable meeting, see Julian Borger, "'Dr. Stangeloves' Meet to Plan a New Nuclear Era," *The Guardian,* August 7, 2006.

7. Michelle Ciarrocca, "Post-9/11 Economic Windfalls for Arms Manufacturers," *Foreign Policy in Focus* 7, no. 10 (September 2002), 2. See also Richard Stubbing, *The Defense*

Moreover, military-economic fascism, by empowering and enriching wealthy, intelligent, and influential members of the public, removes them from the ranks of potential opponents and resisters of the state and thereby helps to perpetuate the state's existence and its intrinsic class exploitation of people outside the precinct of the state and its major supporters. Thus, military-economic fascism simultaneously strengthens the state and weakens civil society, even as it creates the illusion of a vibrant private sector patriotically engaged in supplying goods and services to the heroic military establishment (the Boeing Company's slickly produced television ads, among others, splendidly illustrate this propagandistically encouraged illusion).

Garden-Variety Military-Economic Corruption of Government Officials

We need not dwell long on the logic of garden-variety military-economic corruption. As pots of honey attract flies, so pots of money attract thieves and con men. No organization has more money at its disposal than the U.S. government, which attracts thieves and con men at least in full proportion to its control of wealth. Unscrupulous private parties who desire to gain a slice of the government's booty converge on the morally dismal swamp known as Washington, D.C., and take whatever actions they expect will divert a portion of the loot into their own hands. Anyone who expects honor among thieves will be sorely disappointed by the details of these sordid activities.

Although headlines alone cannot convey the resplendently lurid details, they can suggest the sorts of putrid sloughs that drain into the swamp:[8]

Game: An Insider Explores the Astonishing Realities of America's Defense Establishment (New York: Harper and Row, 1986), 90, 96; Nick Kotz, *Wild Blue Yonder: Money, Politics, and the B-1 Bomber* (New York: Pantheon Books, 1988), 230; Tom Hamburger, "Perle's Conflict Issue Is Shared by Other Defense Panel Members," *Wall Street Journal,* March 27, 2003; Jamie Doward, "'Ex-Presidents Club' Gets Fat on Conflict; High-Flying Venture Capital Firm Carlyle Group Cashes in When the Tanks Roll," *The Observer,* March 23, 2003, at http://observer.guardian.co.uk/iraq/story/0,12239,919897,00.html; and Donald L. Barlett and James B. Steele, "Washington's $8 Billion Shadow," *Vanity Fair* (March 2007), at http://www.vanityfair.com/politics/features/2007/03/spyagency200703.
8. For these headlines, see note 2.

- "Audit Cites Pentagon Contractors [for Widespread Abuse of Overhead Charges]"
- "Ex-Unisys Official Admits Paying Bribes to Get Pentagon Contracts"
- "Top Republican on a House Panel Is Charged with Accepting Bribes"
- "Ex–Pentagon Officials Sentenced [for Taking Monetary Bribes and Accepting Prostitutes' Services from Contractors]"
- "Northrop Papers Indicate Coverup: Documents from '80s Show Accounting Irregularities Were Hidden from Pentagon"
- "Revolving Door Leads to Jail: Former Acquisition Official Convicted of Steering Business to Boeing for Personal Gain"
- "Contractor 'Knew How to Grease the Wheels': ADCS Founder Spent Years Cultivating Political Contacts"
- "Graft Lurks Within Pentagon's 'Black Budget': Top-Secret Items Escape Oversight"
- "Contractor Pleads Guilty to Corruption: Probe Extends Beyond Bribes to Congressman"
- "From Cash to Yachts: Congressman's Bribe Menu; Court Documents Show Randall 'Duke' Cunningham Set Bribery Rates"
- "Defense Contractor Guilty in Bribe Case"
- "There's No Watchdog for Secret Budgets"
- "5 Americans Indicted in Iraq Bid Probe: 3 Officers Among Those Accused of Taking Cash, Gifts Tied to Projects"
- "Feinstein Quits Committee Under War-Profiteer Cloud; Report Documents Military Contracts for Firms Owned by Senator's Husband"

Anyone who cares to accumulate all such news articles may look forward to full employment for the rest of his life.

Notwithstanding the many culprits who are caught in the act, one must realistically assume that a far greater number gets away scot-free. As Ernest Fitzgerald, an extraordinarily knowledgeable authority with almost fifty years of relevant personal experience, has observed, the entire system of military procurement is pervaded by dishonesty: "Government officials, from the majestic office of the president to the lowest, sleaziest procurement office, lie routinely and with impunity in defense of the system," and "the combination of loose procurement rules and government acquiescence in rip-offs leaves many a crook untouched."[9]

Among the instructive cases that made their way through the justice system in recent years are several related to convicted congressman Randall "Duke" Cunningham, a war hero and former titan of the MICC sent to a federal penitentiary. Chief among the persons of interest in an FBI investigation was Brent Wilkes, a D.C. highflier who was alleged to have been involved tangentially in events leading to the sacking of former congressman and director of Central Intelligence Porter Goss. According to a May 7, 2006, report in the *New York Daily News,* ongoing FBI and CIA investigations of Kyle (Dusty) Foggo, formerly the third-ranking official at the CIA, who resigned in May 2006 amid a variety of allegations,

> have focused on the Watergate poker parties thrown by defense contractor Brent Wilkes, a high-school buddy of Foggo's, that were attended by disgraced former Rep. Randy (Duke) Cunningham and other lawmakers.
>
> Foggo has claimed he went to the parties "just for poker" amid allegations that Wilkes, a top GOP fund-raiser and a member of the $100,000 "Pioneers" of Bush's 2004 reelection campaign, provided prostitutes, limos and hotel suites to Cunningham.
>
> Cunningham is serving an eight-year sentence after pleading to taking $2.4 million in bribes to steer defense contracts to cronies.
>
> Wilkes hosted regular parties for 15 years at the Watergate and Westin Grand Hotels for lawmakers and lobbyists. Intelligence sources said Goss has denied attending the parties as CIA director, but that left open whether he may have attended as a Republican congressman from Florida who was head of the House Intelligence Committee.[10]

In your mind, multiply this squalid little scenario by one thousand, and you will begin to gain a vision of what goes on in the MICC's higher reaches.

---

9. Fitzgerald, *The Pentagonists,* 312, 290.
10. Richard Sisk, "Behind the Goss Toss," *New York Daily News,* May 7, 2006.

The daily routine there is evidently not all wailing and gnashing of teeth over how to defend the country against murderous Islamic maniacs—our country's leaders require frequent periods of rest and recreation.

Legal Corruption of Government Officials

The truly big bucks, of course, need not be compromised in the least by this sweaty species of fraud and workaday corruption.[11] Just as someone who kills one person is a murderer, whereas someone who kills a million persons is a statesman, so the government officials who steer hundreds of billions of dollars, perhaps without violating any law or regulation, to the Star Wars contractors and the producers of other big-ticket weapon systems account for the bulk of the swag laundered through the Department of Defense and the Department of Homeland Security. (Lest the latter organization be overlooked, see James Bennett's enormously revealing account of scams there.)[12] By "without violating any law," I am not stating that this huge component of the MICC is squeaky clean—far from it—but only that the corruption in this area, in dollar terms, falls mainly under the heading of legal theft or at least in the gray area.[13] As a Lockheed employee once wrote to Fitzgerald, "[T]he government doesn't really need this stuff. It's just the best way to get rich quick. If they really needed all these nuclear bombs and killer satellites, they wouldn't run this place the way they do."[14] I personally recall Fitzgerald's saying to me more than twenty years ago at Lafayette College, "A defense contract is just a license to steal."

Absence of Proper Accounting Invites Theft

Fitzgerald aptly appeared as a witness at Senator Chuck Grassley's September 1998 hearings titled "License to Steal: Administrative Oversight of Financial

---

11. Kovacic, "Blue Ribbon Defense Commissions," 89–90, 103 n. 197; and Kovacic, "The Sorcerer's Apprentice," 118, 130 nn. 94–101.

12. James T. Bennett, *Homeland Security Scams* (New Brunswick, N.J.: Transaction, 2006).

13. Stubbing, *The Defense Game,* 407.

14. Quoted in Fitzgerald, *The Pentagonists,* 313. See also Carlton Meyer, "Editorial: The Submarine Mafia," *G2mil: The Magazine of Future Warfare* (August 2002), at http://www.g2mil.com/Aug2002.htm.

Control Failures at the Department of Defense." At those hearings, Grassley released two new audit reports prepared by the General Accounting Office and another report prepared by his staff in cooperation with the Air Force Office of Financial Management. According to Grassley's September 21, 1998, press release, "These reports consistently show that sloppy accounting procedures and ineffective or nonexistent internal controls leave DoD's [Department of Defense] accounts vulnerable to theft and abuse. Failure by the DoD to exercise proper accounting procedures has resulted in fraud and mismanagement of the taxpayers' money."[15]

Although this sort of complaint has become an annual ritual dutifully reported in the press, the Pentagon has never managed to put its accounts into a form that can even be audited. Like Dick Cheney, who chose not to fight in the Vietnam War, the military brass seems to have had "other priorities," even though for almost two decades the Defense Department has invariably stood in violation of the Government Management Reform Act of 1994, which requires government departments to make an annual financial audit.[16]

Testifying before a congressional committee on August 3, 2006, Thomas F. Gimble, the Defense Department's acting inspector general, emphasized "financial management problems that are long standing, pervasive, and deeply rooted in virtually all operations." Expanding on this general observation with specific reference to the fiscal year 2005 agencywide principal financial statements, he stated: "We issued a disclaimer of opinion for the statements because numerous deficiencies continue to exist related to the quality of data, adequacy of reporting systems, and reliability of internal controls." Of the nine organizational components "required by the Office of Management and Budget (OMB) to prepare and obtain an audit opinion on their FY 2005 financial statements," only one received an unqualified opinion and one a qualified opinion. "All the others," stated Gimble, "including the agency-wide financial statements, received a disclaimer of opinion, *as they have every year in the past. . . .* The weaknesses

---

15. Chuck Grassley, "Grassley Seeks Expert Testimony from Government Accountants, Watchdogs; Hearing Set to Examine Financial Control Failures at Defense Department," press release, September 1998, at http://grassley.senate.gov/releases/1998/p8r09-21.htm.
16. Robert Higgs, *Resurgence of the Warfare State: The Crisis since 9/11* (Oakland, Calif.: The Independent Institute, 2005), 55–61. See also Government Management Reform Act of 1994, Public Law No. 103-356, October 13, 1994.

that affect the auditability of the financial statements also impact other DoD programs and operations and contribute to waste, mismanagement, and inefficient use of DoD resources. These weaknesses affect the safeguarding of assets and proper use of funds and impair the prevention and identification of fraud, waste, and abuse."[17]

In Iraq since the U.S. invasion in 2003, billions of dollars have simply disappeared without leaving a trace.[18] Surely they did not evaporate in the hot desert sun. The accounts at Homeland Security are in equally horrible condition.[19] No one knows how much money or specific property is missing from these two departments or where the missing assets have gone. If a public corporation kept its accounts this atrociously, the Securities and Exchange Commission would shut it down overnight. Government officials, however, need not worry about obedience to the laws they make to assure their credulous subjects that everything is hunky-dory inside the walls. When they are of a mind, they simply flout those laws with impunity.

Contributions by Political Action Committees to Politicians and Their Parties Are Bribes

Political action committees (PACs) evolved and eventually obtained legal validation as vehicles for making lawful bribes to candidates for federal offices and to their political parties. Candidates now count on them for a large share

---

17. U.S. Department of Defense, Office of the Inspector General, "Statement of Thomas F. Gimble, Acting Inspector General, Office of the Inspector General, Department of Defense, Before the Subcommittee on Federal Financial Management, Government Information and International Security, Senate Committee on Homeland Security and Governmental Affairs, on 'Financial Management at the Department of Defense,'" August 3, 2006, 1–2, at http://www.dodig.mil/fo/DODIG-HrngStatement080306.pdf, emphasis added. See also Matt Kelly, "Defense Official Says Pentagon Hid Unspent Funds in Accounts," *USA Today*, January 17, 2007.

18. "Audit: U.S. Lost Track of $9 Billion in Iraq Funds," *CNN.com News Report*, January 30, 2005, at http://edition.cnn.com/2005/WORLD/meast/01/30/iraq.audit. See also Jim Krane, "Audit: U.S.-Led Occupation Squandered Aid," *Global Policy Forum*, January 29, 2006, at http://www.globalpolicy.org/security/issues/iraq/dfi/2006/0129squandered .htm; and Hope Yen, "Auditors: Billions Squandered in Iraq," *Dallas Morning News*, February 16, 2007, at http://www.dallasnews.com/forums/viewtopic.php?t=3647.

19. Bennett, *Homeland Security Scams*, 110–11.

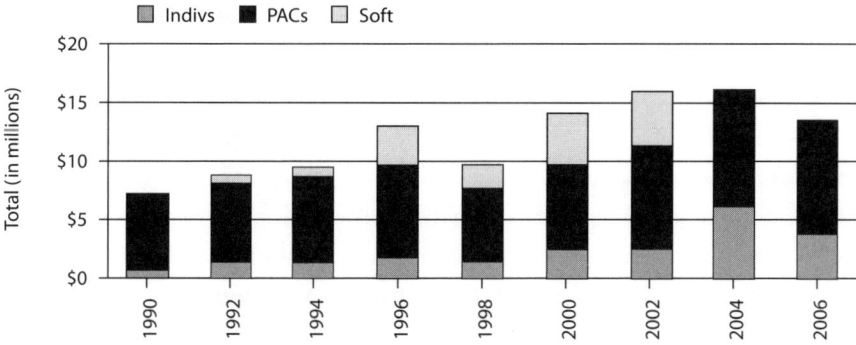

Figure 19.1 Contributions by "Defense" Interests in Federal Elections, 1990–2006

Note: Soft money contributions (defined as those that do not explicitly urge voters to cast their ballots for specific candidates) were banned by the Bipartisan Campaign Finance Reform Act after the 2002 elections.

Methodology: The numbers are based on contributions of $200 or more from PACs and individuals to federal candidates and from PAC, soft money and individual donors to political parties, as reported to the Federal Election Commission. Although election cycles are shown in the chart as 1996, 1998, 2000, etc., they actually represent two-year periods. For example, the 2002 election cycle runs from January 1, 2001, to December 31, 2002.

Source: Center for Responsive Politics, data displayed at http://www.opensecrets.org /industries/indus.asp?Ind=D.

of their campaign funds, and everyone older than eleven with an IQ higher than seventy knows that these contributions are made with an understanding that they will elicit a quid pro quo from the recipients who win the elections.

Military-economic interests have not been timid about forming PACs and transferring huge sums of money through them to the candidates. According to the Center for Responsive Politics, "defense" PACs transferred more than $70 million to candidates and parties in the election cycles from 1990 to 2006. Individuals and soft-money contributors (before soft-money contributions were outlawed after the 2002 elections) in the "defense" sector added more than $37 million, bringing the total to nearly $108 million.[20] No one knows how many dollars military interests added by means of illegal and hence unrecorded contributions, but the addition is most likely substantial if we may judge by the many accounts of individual instances of such contributions brought to light

---

20. These figures are available at http://www.opensecrets.org/industries/indus.asp?Ind=D.

over the years. Figure 19.1 shows the amounts transferred during the past nine election cycles.

One may deny, of course, that PAC contributions constitute a form of corruption, inasmuch as they are legal within the statutorily specified limits, but such a denial would elevate form over substance. Both the givers and the receivers understand these payments in exactly the same way that they understand illegal forms of bribery, even though they never admit this understanding in public—political decorum must be served, if only to protect the children.

How Government Corrupts Business

A brief review of the history of U.S. military contracting helps to clarify my claim that military-economic transactions tend to corrupt business. The most important historical fact is that before 1940, except during wartime, such dealings amounted to very little. The United States had only a tiny standing army and no standing munitions industry worthy of the name. When wars occurred, the government supplemented the products of its own arsenals and navy yards with goods and services purchased from private contractors, but most such items were off-the-shelf civilian goods, such as boots, clothing, food, and transportation services. To be sure, plenty of occasions arose for garden-variety corruption in these dealings, including bribes, kickbacks, provision of shoddy goods, and so forth,[21] but such malfeasances were usually one-shot or fleeting transgressions because the demobilization that followed the conclusion of each war removed the opportunity for such corruption to become institutionalized to a significant degree in law, persistent organizations, or ongoing practice. Like gaudy fireworks, these sporadic outbursts of corruption flared brightly and then turned to dead cinders. No substantial peacetime contracting existed to fuel enduring corruption of the military's private suppliers, and much of the contracting that did take place occurred within the constraints of rigid solicitations and sealed-bid offers, which made cozy deals between a military buyer and a private seller difficult to arrange. At late as fiscal year 1940,

---

21. Stuart D. Brandes, *Warhogs: A History of War Profits in America* (Lexington: University Press of Kentucky, 1997).

the War Department made 87 percent of its purchases through advertising and invitations to bid.[22]

These conditions changed abruptly and forever in 1940: the challenges the government faced during the two years before the United States became a declared belligerent in World War II and the manner in which it responded to them had an enduring effect in shaping the contours of the MICC and hence in establishing the MICC's characteristic corruption of business.

The Franklin D. Roosevelt administration, desperate to build up the nation's capacity for war after the breathtaking German triumphs in the spring of 1940, made an abrupt about-face, abandoning its relentless flagellation of businessmen and investors and instead courting their favor as prime movers in the buildup of the munitions industries. Most of the relevant businessmen, however, having been anathematized and legislatively pummeled for the previous six years, were reluctant to enter into such deals for a variety of reasons, chief among them being their fear and distrust of the federal government.[23]

To placate the leery businessmen by shifting the risks from them onto the taxpayers, the government adopted several important changes in its procurement laws and regulations. These changes included negotiated cost-plus-fixed-fee contracts instead of contracts arrived at within the solicitation-and-sealed-bid system; various forms of tax breaks; government loan guarantees; direct government funding of plants, equipment, and raw materials; and provision of advance and progress payments, sparing the contractors the need to obtain and pay interest on bank loans. All of these arrangements, with greater or lesser variations in their details from time to time, became permanent features of the MICC.[24]

Even more important, as the new system operated on a vast scale during World War II, dealings between military purchasers and private suppliers

22. Robert Higgs, *Depression, War, and Cold War: Studies in Political Economy* (New York: Oxford University Press, 2006), 39.

23. Higgs, *Depression, War, and Cold War,* 36–38.

24. U.S. Senate, Committee on Armed Services, *Defense Organization: The Need for Change,* Staff Report to the Committee on Armed Services, U.S. Senate, 99th Cong., 1st sess., Committee Print, S. Prt. 99-86 (Washington, D.C.: U.S. Government Printing Office, 1985), 32, 42, 553–67.

assumed a fundamentally new form. As described by Elberton Smith, the official historian of the U.S. Army's economic mobilization during the war,

> [t]he relationship between the government and its contractors was gradually transformed from an "arm's length" relationship between two more or less equal parties in a business transaction into *an undefined but intimate relationship*—partly business, partly fiduciary, and partly unilateral—in which the financial, contractual, statutory, and other instruments and assumptions of economic activity were reshaped to meet the ultimate requirements of victory in war. Under the new conditions, *contracts ceased to be completely binding;* fixed prices in contracts often became only tentative and provisional prices; excessive profits received by contractors were recoverable by the government; and potential losses resulting from many causes—including errors, poor judgments, and performance failures on the part of contractors—were averted by modification and amendment of contracts, with or without legal "consideration," whenever required by the exigencies of the war effort.[25]

Although Smith was describing the system as it came to operate during World War II, almost everything he described fits the postwar MICC as well,[26] especially his depiction of the buyer-seller dealings as constituting "an undefined but intimate relationship" and his recognition that "contracts ceased to be completely binding." Thus, the institutional changes made in 1940–41 and the wartime operation of the military-industrial complex in the context of these new rules put permanently in place the essential features of the modern procurement system, which has repeatedly demonstrated its imperviousness to reform for the past sixty-five years. It was too good a deal to give up even after the demise of the USSR and the end of the Cold War, and with breathtaking chutzpah the system's kingpins parlayed the box-cutter attacks of September 11, 2001, into an excuse to pour hundreds of billions of additional dollars into purchases of Cold War weaponry.[27]

---

25. Elberton R. Smith, *The Army and Economic Mobilization* (Washington, D.C.: U.S. Army, 1959), 312, emphasis added.
26. See Higgs, *Depression, War, and Cold War,* 31–33.
27. See Harvey M. Sapolsky and Eugene Hgolz, "The Defense Industry's New Cycle," *Regulation* (Winter 2001): 44–49; David Isenberg and Ivan Eland, *Empty Promises: Why*

Under the old, pre-1940 system, a private business rarely had anything to gain by wining and dining military buyers or congressmen. Unless a firm made the lowest-priced sealed-bid offer to supply a carefully specified good, it would not get the contract. Military buyers knew what they needed, and they had a tightly limited budget with which to get it. After 1940, however, the newly established "intimate relationship" opened up a whole new world for wheeling and dealing on both sides of the transaction—it was often difficult to say whether the government official was shaking down the businessman or the businessman was bribing the government official. In fact, until the military purchasing agency certified a company as qualified, the firm could not make a valid offer, even in the context of competitive bidding. In the post-1940 era, only a small fraction of all contracts emerged from formally advertised, sealed-bid competition, and most contracts were negotiated without any kind of price competition.[28]

Before the 2003 U.S. attack on Iraq, for example, "SAIC [Science Applications International] was awarded seven contracts, together worth more than $100 million, without competitive bidding," for nation-building work in Iraq. "The Defense Department's justification for the no-bid contracts: 'We need the immediate services of a fully qualified contractor who has the unqualified support and confidence of the Pentagon leadership.'" Deputy Secretary of Defense Paul Wolfowitz certainly had good reason to hold SAIC in complete confidence: besides all of the other hookups typical of such deals, one of SAIC's "subject matter experts" for the contracted work was Shaha Riza, who happened to be Wolfowitz's girlfriend.[29] As history marched on, the Wolfowitz-Riza connection became, as they say, even curiouser and curiouser.[30]

Deals came to turn not on price, but on a firm's technical and scientific capabilities, size, experience, and established reputation as a military supplier—

the Bush Administration's Half-Hearted Attempts at Defense Reform Have Failed, Cato Institute Policy Analysis no. 442 (Washington, D.C.: Cato Institute, June 11, 2002); Higgs, "The Cold War Is Over"; and Larry Makinson, *Outsourcing the Pentagon: Who Benefits from the Politics and Economics of National Security?* (Washington, D.C.: Center for Public Integrity, September 29, 2004), at http://www.publicintegrity.org/pns/report.aspx?aid=385.

28. Higgs, *Depression, War, and the Cold War,* 39; and Stubbing, *The Defense Game,* 226, 411.

29. Barlett and Steel, "Washington's $8 Billion Shadow."

30. See "Shaha Riza," *Wikipedia,* at http://en.wikipedia.org/wiki/Shaha_Riza.

vague attributes that are easier to fudge for one's friends. From time to time, deals also turned on the perceived need to keep a big firm from going under. For example, Fen Hampson observes that in the early 1970s "[t]he bidding [for production of the C-4 (Trident I) missile] was not opened to other companies because Lockheed was encountering financial difficulties at the time and desperately needed the business."[31] Indeed, scholars have identified an extensive pattern of rotating major contracts and dubbed it a "follow-on imperative" or a "bailout imperative," a virtual guarantee against bankruptcy regardless of mismanagement or other corporate ineptitude.[32] Subcontracts might also be used to prop up failing firms, and in nearly every large-scale project they served as the principal means of spreading the political patronage across many congressional districts.[33]

In truth, military contract deals, especially the many important changes introduced into them after their initial formulation ("contract nourishment"), permitting contractors to "buy in now, get well later,"[34] came to turn in substantial part on "who you know." In Richard Stubbing's words, "Often it is raw politics, not military considerations, which ultimately determines the winner."[35] All the successful major prime contractors—such as Lockheed Martin,[36]

---

31. Fen Osler Hampson, *Unguided Missiles: How America Buys Its Weapons* (New York: W. W. Norton, 1989), 92.

32. See the following works by scholars who take this position: H. L. Nieburg, *In the Name of Science* (Chicago: Quadrangle Book, 1966); James R. Kurth, "Aerospace Production Lines and American Defense Spending," in *Testing the Theory of the Military-Industrial Complex,* edited by Steven Rosen (Lexington, Mass.: Lexington Books, 1973), 142–44; Richard F. Kaufman, "MIRVing the Boondoggle: Contracts, Subsidy, and Welfare in the Aerospace Industry," *American Economic Review* 62 (1972), 289; Lloyd J. Dumas, "Payment Functions and the Productive Efficiency of the Military Industrial Firms," *Journal of Economic Issues* 10 (June 1976), 458; Jacques S. Gansler, *The Defense Industry* (Cambridge, Mass.: MIT Press, 1980), 49, 172, 227; and Stubbing, *The Defense Game,* 185–89, 200–4.

33. Kotz, *Wild Blue Yonder,* 128–29; and Kenneth R. Mayer, "Patterns of Congressional Influence in Defense Contracting," in Higgs, ed., *Arms, Politics, and the Economy,* 218–31.

34. Stubbing, *The Defense Game,* 179–84.

35. Stubbing, *The Defense Game,* 165.

36. See Richard Cummings, "Lockheed Stock and Two Smoking Barrels," *Playboy* (February 2007), at http://www.playboy.com/magazine/features/lockheed/index.html.

General Dynamics,[37] Rockwell,[38] Bechtel,[39] Halliburton,[40] and SAIC,[41] for ex-ample—demonstrated beyond any doubt that cultivating friends in high places yields a high rate of return in the MICC. Without such friends, a firm may be hard pressed to survive in this sector at all.

The tight budget constraints of the pre-1940 peacetime periods became vastly looser afterward as trillions of dollars poured out of the congressional appropria-tions process during the endless national emergency of the Cold War and its sequel, the so-called war on terror. As Nick Kotz observes, "Now that the stakes in profits and jobs were far higher than those of any government program in history, dividing the spoils ensured that the game of politics would be played on a grand scale."[42] (Of course, the game of politics in reality, as distinct from the high school civics idealization, is essentially the game of corruption.) In fiscal year 2007, for example, the Department of Defense anticipated outlays of approximately $90 billion for procurement; $162 billion for operations and maintenance; $72 billion for research, development, test, and evaluation; and $8 billion for military construction—components that sum to $332 billion.[43] Nearly all of this loot would end up in the pockets of private contractors; military per-sonnel costs are separate from these accounts.

With plenty of money to go around, all that a would-be contractor needs is an old buddy in the upper reaches of a military bureaucracy or a friend on the House military appropriations subcommittee or in the Senate. (Nowadays, more than ever before, a single member of Congress can create magnificent

---

37. See Roger Franklin, *The Defender: The Story of General Dynamics* (New York: Harper and Row, 1986).

38. See Kotz, *Wild Blue Yonder*.

39. See Laton McCartney, *Friends in High Places: The Bechtel Story: The Most Secret Corpo-ration and How It Engineered the World* (New York: Simon and Schuster, 1988).

40. See Dan Briody, *The Halliburton Agenda: The Politics of Oil and Money* (Hoboken, N.J.: Wiley, 2004).

41. See Barlett and Steele, "Washington's $8 Billion Shadow."

42. Kotz, *Wild Blue Yonder*, 50.

43. U.S. Department of Defense, Office of the Under Secretary of Defense (Comptrol-ler), *National Defense Budget Estimates for FY 2007* (Washington, D.C.: U.S. Department of Defense, March 2006), 15, at http://www.dod.mil/comptroller/defbudget/fy2007/fy 2007_greenbook.pdf.

gifts for his friends by making "earmarks," or furtive amendments to an appropriations bill that everyone understands to be nothing but an individual legislator's pound of flesh taken out of the taxpayer's unfortunate corpus.) If one does not have such a friend in high places, one can acquire him (or her, as the infamous Darleen Druyun illustrates) by ponying up the various forms of bribes to which many Pentagon officials and members of Congress have shown themselves to be highly receptive.[44] After all, the bureaucrat or the member of Congress is not giving away his own money.

To keep this gravy train on the track, contractors and their trade associations as well as the armed forces themselves devote great efforts to increasing the amount of money Congress appropriates for "defense" and now also for "homeland security." Their campaign contributions and other favors go predominantly to the incumbent barons—congressional leaders and committee chairpersons—and to the "hawks" who have never met a defense budget big enough to satisfy them. As Fitzgerald notes, "In Washington you can get away with anything as long as you have the high moguls of Congress as accessories before and after the fact."[45]

Furthermore, as Kotz observes, "There is a multiplier effect as the different military services, members of Congress, presidential administrations, and defense industries trade support for each other's projects."[46] In other words, the defense budget is not simply the biggest logroll in Congress; it is the biggest logroll in Washington, D.C., and its environs.[47] Hampson remarks: "[B]ureaucratic and political interests approach weapons acquisition and defense budget issues as non-zero-sum games; that is, as games where there are rewards and payoffs to all parties from cooperation or collusion."[48] Only the taxpayers lose, but their interests do not count: they are not "players" in this game, only victims of its depredations.

To give the public a seeming interest in the whole wretched racket, the contractors also spend substantial amounts of money cultivating the public's yearning to have the military dish out death and destruction to designated

---

44. See Colarusso, "Revolving Door Leads to Jail."
45. Fitzgerald, *The Pentagonists,* 91.
46. Kotz, *Wild Blue Yonder,* 325.
47. Stubbing, *The Defense Game,* 98.
48. Hampson, *Unguided Missiles,* 282.

human quarry around the world—Commies, gooks, ragheads, Islamofascists, narcoterrorists, and so forth—who are said to threaten the precious American way of life. For example, Rockwell, a military contractor whose massive secret contributions helped to reelect Richard Nixon in 1972,[49] once mounted "a secret grass-roots campaign code-named Operation Common Sense" that included "a massive letter-writing campaign . . . [soliciting] support from national organizations . . . and [the] production of films and advertisements as well as prepared articles, columns, and editorials that willing editors could print in newspapers and magazines"—all the news that's fit to print, so to speak.[50] Much money goes into producing glorification of the armed forces—"the few, the proud, the Marines," blah, blah, blah—and reports of those forces' stupidities and brutalities in exotic climes are dismissed as nothing but the fabrications of leftists and appeasers or, if they cannot plausibly be denied, are alleged to be nothing more than the isolated misbehavior of a few "bad apples."[51]

Lest the armed forces themselves prove insufficiently imaginative in conceiving of new and even more expensive projects for their fortunate suppliers to carry out, the contractors hire battalions of mad geniuses to design the superweapons of the future and buy regiments of former generals and admirals to market these magnificent creations to their old friends and subordinates currently holding down desks at the Pentagon. Thus, as General James P. Mullins, former commander of the Air Force Logistics Command, has written, "[T]he prime contractors are where the babies really come from." He explains: "[T]he contractor has already often determined what it wants to produce before the formal acquisition process begins. . . . The contractor validates the design through the process of marketing it to one of the services. If successful, the contractor gets a contract. Thus, to a substantial degree, the weapon capabilities devised by contractors create military requirements."[52]

---

49. Kotz, *Wild Blue Yonder,* 103–4; Fitzgerald, *The Pentagonists,* 84.

50. Kotz, *Wild Blue Yonder,* 134–35.

51. Higgs, *Resurgence of the Warfare State,* 153–96. See also Robert Higgs, "No Moral Excuse" and "The President Seems out of Touch with Events on the Ground in Iraq," *LewRockwell.com,* May 31, 2006, at http://www.lewrockwell.com/higgs/higgs43.html.

52. James P. Mullins, *The Defense Matrix: National Preparedness and the Military-Industrial Complex* (San Diego, Calif.: Avant Books, 1986), 91. See also Stubbing, *The Defense Game,* 174, and Barlett and Steele, "Washington's $8 Billion Shadow."

Consider, for example, the multifaceted activities of SAIC, a bulwark of the national-security state and the virtual epitome of a contemporary MICC contractor: "SAIC executives have been involved at every stage of the life cycle of the war in Iraq. SAIC personnel were instrumental in pressing the case that weapons of mass destruction existed in Iraq in the first place, and that war was the only way to get rid of them. Then, as war became inevitable, SAIC secured contracts for a broad range of operations in soon-to-be-occupied Iraq. When no weapons of mass destruction were found, SAIC personnel staffed the commission that was set up to investigate how American intelligence could have been so disastrously wrong."[53] Although one might condemn SAIC for a variety of crimes—indeed, the company already sports a "record of lawsuits, charges brought by whistle-blowers, allegations of profiteering, fines assessed by federal judges, and repeated investigations and government audits"[54]—no one can accuse the firm's managers of lacking cheek.

In sum, the military-supply firms exemplify a fundamentally corrupt type of organization. Their income ends up in their bank accounts only after it has first been extorted from the taxpayers at gunpoint—hence, their compensation essentially amounts to receiving stolen property. They are hardly unwitting or unwilling recipients, however, because they are not drafted to do what they do. No wallflowers at this dance of death, they eagerly devote strenuous efforts to encouraging government officials to wring ever greater amounts from the taxpayers and to distribute the loot in ways that enrich the contractors, their suppliers, and their employees. These efforts include both the licit and the illicit measures I have described, spanning the full range from making a legal campaign contribution to providing prostitutes to serve the congressman or the Pentagon bigwig after he has become bored with playing poker in the contractor's suite at a plush D.C. hotel.[55]

---

53. Barlett and Steele, "Washington's $8 Billion Shadow."
54. Barlett and Steele, "Washington's $8 Billion Shadow."
55. Note well: such "entertainment" expenses are likely to be accounted "allowable costs" by the defense contractor who bears them, and with only routine audacity he may add to them an "overhead" charge—the entire sum to be reimbursed ultimately by the taxpayers. In general, "overhead proves to be a huge moneymaker for defense firms" (Stubbing, *The Defense Game,* 205). Kotz describes Rockwell's billing for entertainment, public relations, and lobbying in connection with its contract to build the B-1 bomber (*Wild*

Can Anything Be Done?

The short answer is probably not. The MICC is deeply entrenched in the U.S. political economy, which itself has been gravitating toward complete economic fascism for more than a century.[56] Decades of studies, investigations, blue-ribbon commission reports, congressional hearings and staff studies, and news media exposés detailing the MICC's workings from A to Z have scarcely put a dent in it.[57] For the most part, the official scrutiny is just for show, and the unofficial scrutiny is easily dismissed as the work of outsiders and "America haters" who don't know what they are talking about.

Official evaluations, at their frankest, conclude that "[p]ast mistakes—whether in the procurement of a weapon system or in the employment of forces during a crisis—do not receive the critical review that would prevent them from recurring. . . . The lessons go unlearned, and the mistakes are repeated."[58] Such evaluations, though seemingly forthright and penetrating, strike me as far-fetched. Of course, people sometimes makes mistakes, but if people with the power to change an arrangement refrain from doing so for decades on end, the most reasonable conclusion is that they prefer things as they are—that is, as a rule, there are no long-lasting "failed policies," properly speaking. To apply here what I wrote previously in regard to several other kinds of policies: "Government policies succeed in doing exactly what they are supposed to do: channeling resources bilked from the general public to politically organized and influential interest groups."[59] Therefore, one must conclude that the MICC serves its intended purposes well, however much its chronic crimes and intrinsic

---

Blue Yonder, 137.) Fitzgerald describes similar charges by General Dynamics—as well as boarding expenses for an executive's dog—and by Pratt and Whitney, including $7,085 for hors d'oeuvres at a Palm Beach golf resort and $2,735 for strolling musicians at another bash (*The Pentagonists,* 197, 198–99). The contractors sometimes billed the government twice for the same outrageous expenses. In 1992, a former SAIC executive stated under oath in a deposition that "mischarging" had become "institutionalized within the company" (Barlett and Steele, "Washington's $8 Billion Shadow").

56. See Higgs, *Crisis and Leviathan,* and Robert Higgs, *Neither Liberty nor Safety: Fear, Ideology, and the Growth of Government* (Oakland, Calif.: The Independent Institute, 2007).

57. Higgs, "The Cold War Is Over."

58. U.S. Senate, Committee on Armed Services, *Defense Organization,* 8.

59. Robert Higgs, "The Myth of 'Failed' Policies," *The Free Market* 13, no. 6 (June 1995), 1. See also Kotz, *Wild Blue Yonder,* 242–45.

corruption sully its self-proclaimed nobility. What you and I call corruption is, after all, precisely what the military-economic movers and shakers call the good life. As Paul Light remarked recently about the government contracting system, "All the players with any power like it."[60]

The most significant factor in this scenario is that the post–World War II U.S. foreign policy of global hegemony and recurrent military intervention ultimately places a strong floor beneath the MICC and serves as an all-purpose excuse for its many malfeasances.[61] As Ludwig von Mises observed, "The root of the evil is not the construction of new, more dreadful weapons. It is the spirit of conquest. . . . The main thing is to discard the ideology that generates war."[62] Until the scope of the U.S. government's geopolitical aspirations and hence the scale of its military activities are drastically reduced, not much opportunity will exist for making its system of military-economic fascism less rapacious and corrupt.

60. Quoted in Scott Shane and Ron Nixon, "In Washington, Contractors Take on Biggest Role Ever," *New York Times,* February 4, 2007.

61. See Ivan Eland, *The Empire Has No Clothes: U.S. Foreign Policy Exposed* (Oakland, Calif.: The Independent Institute, 2004). See also Chalmers Johnson, *The Sorrows of Empire: Militarism, Secrecy, and the End of the Republic* (New York: Metropolitan Books, 2004).

62. Ludwig von Mises, *Human Action: A Treatise on Economics*, 3rd rev. ed. (Chicago: Contemporary Books, 1966), 832. See also Robert Higgs and Carl Close, eds., *Opposing the Crusader State: Alternatives to Global Interventionism* (Oakland, Calif.: The Independent Institute, 2007).

20

Caging the Dogs of War

How Major U.S. Neoimperialist Wars End

> Power concedes nothing without a demand. It never did and
> it never will. Find out just what any people will quietly sub-
> mit to and you have found out the exact measure of injustice
> and wrong which will be imposed upon them, and these will
> continue till they are resisted with either words or blows, or
> with both. The limits of tyrants are prescribed by the endur-
> ance of those whom they oppress.
> —Frederick Douglass, August 3, 1857

ALL WARS END, but someone must bring them to an end: some-
one in authority must order the men to stop fighting, or the fighters themselves
must decide to stop fighting even if doing so requires that they disobey standing
orders. Someone makes a decision either way to bring the war to an end, and
we may presume (in conformity to the precepts of methodological individualism) that the actor makes the decision only because he believes that it serves his
interest, however he may conceive of that interest. In general in our day, nations
do not go to war spontaneously, nor do they lay down their arms spontaneously.
National leaders make those decisions, and they make them in their own interest.

Any other view is romantic and obscurantist, notwithstanding the torrents
of propaganda by which leaders and their court intellectuals attempt to represent themselves as "servants" of the nation, embodiments of "the national will,"
or executors of "the public interest." Even if political and military leaders were
inclined to put the public's interest ahead of their own, they would have no
way to identify such a foggy and multifaceted entity. Each individual has many
interests, and different individuals have different sets of interests, but nobody

225

has discovered a defensible method of aggregating all these interests into a single "social interest." Although we may feel confident that the great multitude prefers peace to war, other things being equal, even this claim is contestable. Anyone who circulates in American society knows full well that many Americans love war and killing, and, other things being equal, they would be delighted to have the U.S. military constantly engaged in slaughtering people around the world. Fortunately, such individuals count no more heavily than their peace-loving neighbors so long as they do not hold positions of high political authority. "The people" do not decide questions of war and peace directly, and even their indirect effect on the decision process is usually tenuous and variable. As a first approximation, the realistic political scientist may take for granted that in this country "the masses don't count." In most cases, they can be brought to acquiesce in anything the movers and shakers dictate that they do, notwithstanding a modicum of grumbling and disobedience at the margins.

Although some people recognize that specific, self-interested leaders make the decisions that plunge a nation or another large social group into war, many fewer people employ this insight systematically in seeking to understand why wars end. People too often simply presume that one side unequivocally "defeats" the other, and therefore the other capitulates because it has no capacity for further fighting. Rarely, however, is this depiction accurate. Even in horribly damaged and occupied societies, individuals may continue to fight in some fashion, if only as loosely organized civilian insurgents or guerillas combating an occupation force. In 1945, for example, the Germans and the Japanese might have continued to fight in various ways, and, indeed, the U.S. authorities were surprised when they did not do so.[1]

In Iraq during the U.S. occupation of the past nine years, resistance has been stout, if temporally fluctuating and spatially shifting. Given the circum-

---

1. In Germany, U.S. officials expected "'werewolves,' or cells of fanatical, violent Nazis who would harass the occupation army in suicide attacks and sabotage," but "[n]othing of the sort happened" (James L. Payne, "Did the United States Create Democracy in Germany?" *The Independent Review* 11, no. 2 (fall 2006), 215). And although Japanese soldiers had fought fanatically during the war and rarely surrendered even when defeated in battle, "for the most part the Japanese populace acquiesced to the directives of the occupying forces" (Christopher J. Coyne, *After War: The Political Economy of Exporting Democracy* [Stanford, Calif.: Stanford University Press, 2008], 123).

stances there, it seems unlikely that the resistance fighters will give up completely until U.S. and other foreign forces leave the country. Therefore, if the war is to end—rather than to continue indefinitely, as presidential candidate Senator John McCain was pleased to contemplate—that end will come only when U.S. leaders determine that its continuation no longer serves their interest. (I am setting aside the possibility of a general mutiny in which the U.S. armed forces refuse to continue fighting. Although this event is conceivable, I cannot foresee its occurrence in the prevailing circumstances.) Therefore, the question becomes: What events might bring the U.S. authorities to conclude that stopping the war serves their interest?

We have two important precedents for the ending of a major U.S. neoimperialist war—the Korean War and the Vietnam War, especially the latter. Although neither case provides a perfect analogy, comparisons may still be worthwhile as we try to identify the events and influences that bring U.S. political leaders to perceive that continuation of such a war no longer serves their interest.

The Iraq War: A Catastrophic Success

> For where your treasure is, there will your heart be also.
> —Matthew 6:21

On the campaign trail in October 2004, Vice President Dick Cheney created a small stir when, speaking of the Iraq War, he declared: "I think it has been a remarkable success story to date when you look at what has been accomplished overall."[2] In view of the rampant violence raging in Iraq, the widespread devastation of the country's human and material resources, and the dim prospects for its future peace and prosperity, Cheney's statement seemed bizarre, and the Democrats seized on it as still another example of the disconnect between the George W. Bush administration and reality. Yet, on closer inspection, we can see that the war had indeed been a huge success, though not in the way that the vice president intended to claim.

---

2. "Vice President and Mrs. Cheney's Remarks in Wilmington, Ohio," Roberts Convention Center, Wilmington, Ohio, October 25, 2004, at http://www.whitehouse.gov/news/releases/2004/10/20041026-7.html.

In a characteristically unwitting way, President Bush himself stumbled upon a resolution of the seeming paradox when he told *Time* magazine's interviewers in the summer of 2004 that the war had proved to be a "catastrophic success." By that oxymoron, he sought to convey the idea that in the invasion the U.S. military forces had overcome the enemy unexpectedly quickly, "being so successful so fast that an enemy that should have surrendered or been done in escaped and lived to fight another day."[3] Although this hypothesis seems far-fetched as an explanation of the nature and extent of the ongoing resistance waged against the U.S. occupation forces and their collaborators in Iraq, the term *catastrophic success* does precisely express the character of the war. We need only bear in mind that the catastrophe afflicts one set of people, whereas the success accrues to an entirely different set.

Moreover, to appreciate the war's success, we must keep in the forefront of our thinking the instrumental rationality of its perpetrators. We must ask: Who bears the responsibility for launching and continuing the war? What are these individuals trying to achieve? And have they in fact achieved these objectives? Having answered these questions correctly, we shall be obliged to conclude that the war has been a huge success for those who brought it about, however disastrous it has been for many others, especially for the unfortunate people of Iraq.

A short list of the war's perpetrators must include the president and his close advisers; the neoconservative intriguers who stirred up and continue to stoke elite and popular opinion in support of the war; the members of Congress who abdicated their exclusive constitutional responsibility to declare war, authorized the president to take the nation to war if he pleased, and then financed the war by a series of enormous appropriations from the Treasury; certain politically well-placed persons in the munitions, petrochemical, and financial industries; and members of other interest groups who have chosen to support a war that they perceive as promoting Israel's interests or as bringing about the fulfillment of biblical prophecy. Each of these responsible parties has gained greatly from the war.

---

3. Quoted in Nancy Gibbs and John F. Dickerson, "Inside the Mind of George W. Bush," *Time,* August 29, 2004, at http://www.time.com/time/magazine/article/0,9171,689400-1,00.html.

President Bush sought above all to be reelected. In his 2004 campaign, he made no apologies for the war; indeed, he sought to take credit for launching it and for waging it relentlessly since the invasion. Vice President Cheney also campaigned actively on the same basis. Bush and Cheney's efforts yielded them the prize they sought.

In reshuffling his cabinet for a second term, the president retained the belligerent Donald Rumsfeld as secretary of defense. Paul Wolfowitz, Douglas Feith, and other key warmongers remained in their top positions at the Pentagon, and other neocon desk warriors, such as Lewis "Scooter" Libby, Cheney's chief of staff, and Elliott Abrams, a special assistant to the president at the National Security Council, retained their important offices elsewhere in the government—continued success for one and all. Even George "Slam Dunk" Tenet, who resigned as director of Central Intelligence of his own accord, but not because the president held him accountable for what were called the manifest failures of U.S. intelligence efforts during his tenure, later emerged from the darkness to accept the Presidential Medal of Freedom in recognition of what the president described as Tenet's "tireless efforts" in service to the nation.[4]

Members of Congress had no regrets about authorizing Bush to attack Iraq or about continuing to fund the war lavishly. These career politicians crave nothing more than reelection to office, and nearly all the incumbents who sought reelection in the 2004 elections gained this supreme objective: all but one (Tom Daschle) of the 26 incumbent senators who ran and all but 6 of the 402 incumbent representatives who ran succeeded—outcomes that imply a reelection rate greater than 98 percent for incumbents who ran in both houses combined.[5] Backing the war obviously proved to be entirely compatible with, if not absolutely essential to, the legislators' quest for continued tenure in office. If as a consequence of their political actions in the service of their personal ambitions, thousands of Iraqi children had to lose their eyesight or their legs or even their lives, well, *c'est la guerre*. Politics is no place for sissies.

---

4. "President Presents Medal of Freedom," December 14, 2004, at http://www.whitehouse .gov/news/releases/2004/12/20041214-3.html.
5. Election results and related data are available from the University of Michigan Documents Center at http://www.lib.umich.edu/govdocs/elec2004.html#results.

While authorizing enormous increases in military spending during the past ten years, members of Congress have helped themselves to generous servings of pork from the defense-appropriations bills they have passed. According to Winslow T. Wheeler of the Center for Defense Information in Washington, D.C., "by the time Congress had finished with the [fiscal year 2005 appropriations bill for the defense department] in July [2004], House and Senate members had added more than 2,000 of these 'earmarks'" for home-district projects, thereby dishing out to themselves a record-setting "$8.9 billion in pork" to use in buying votes from their constituents.[6] Nor did they stop at that point; each succeeding year has offered a new opportunity for more of the same. In this workaday plundering of the taxpayers for wholly self-serving reasons, congressional doves as well as hawks, Democrats as well as Republicans relish the opportunity to act as pork hawks.[7]

Between fiscal years 2001 and 2007, national defense outlays, defined narrowly as in the government's official reports, rose by nearly 88 percent (50 percent after official adjustment for inflation). This still-continuing upsurge ranks with the great military buildups of the 1960s and the 1980s.[8] The beauty of this increased spending, of course, is that every dollar of it lands in somebody's pocket. Those to whom the pockets belong make a practice of lobbying hard for increased military spending, and they are prepared to compensate in various ways, some legal and some not, the politicians and bureaucrats who steer the money their way.[9]

---

6. Winslow T. Wheeler, "Don't Mind If I Do: Congress Says It's Going All Out for the Troops. Here's $8.9 Billion in Pork That Says It's Not," *Washington Post,* August 22, 2004, at http://www.washingtonpost.com/wp-dyn/articles/A20380-2004Aug20.html.

7. Robert Higgs, "Beware the Pork Hawk: In Pursuit of Reelection, Congress Sells Out the Nation's Defense," in *Against Leviathan: Government Power and a Free Society,* 235–45 (Oakland, Calif.: The Independent Institute, 2004).

8. A convenient source of official data on military spending, sliced and diced in various ways, is the so-called Green Book published annually by the Department of Defense. My calculations here rely on data in U.S. Department of Defense, Office of the Under Secretary of Defense (Comptroller), *National Defense Budget Estimates for FY 2008* (Washington, D.C.: U.S. Department of Defense, 2007), at http://www.defenselink.mil/comptroller /defbudget/fy2008/fy2008_greenbook.pdf.

9. Robert Higgs, "Military-Economic Fascism: How Business Corrupts Government and Vice Versa," *The Independent Review* 12, no. 2 (Fall): 299–316 (Chapter 19 in this volume).

Procurement of goods and services from private contractors has been a major item in the increased military spending of recent years. In fiscal year 2000,
the top ten contractors together received prime contract awards of $50.6 billion;
just six years later, in fiscal year 2006, they got $107.8 billion—an increase of 113
percent (70 percent even after a generous adjustment for inflation).[10]

A useful gauge of how greatly the run-up in the volume of military contracting enriched the owners of these companies, who include many members of
Congress, is the Philadelphia Stock Exchange Defense Sector Index (DFX.X).
This measure tracks the stock prices of sixteen leading aerospace and defense
companies—including Lockheed Martin, Boeing, Northrop Grumman, General Dynamics, and Raytheon, which are the biggest boys on this block nowadays. At the time of the U.S. attack on Iraq in March 2003, this index began
to rise steadily, and it continued to rise with only brief and slight setbacks until
the general market downturn late in 2007, by which time it had increased by
approximately 185 percent.[11] During the same period, the Dow Jones Indus-
trials and the Standard and Poor's 500 indexes had advanced less than half as
much, and the NASDAQ Composite Index only about two-thirds as much. In
short, recent years have brought a bonanza to the merchants of death.

Lest anyone think that an aspiring smaller fellow cannot play in this major
league, let Halliburton serve as an inspiring counterexample. Back in fiscal
year 2002, this company ranked thirty-seventh among the Defense Department's prime contractors. Owing to the war and Halliburton's foot in the door

---

Members of Congress also hold many millions of dollars worth of personal investments
in companies that do substantial business with the Pentagon. For estimates, see Lindsay
Renick Mayer, "Strategic Assets," *Capital Eye,* April 3, 2008, at http://www.capitaleye
.org/capital_eye/inside.php?ID=342.

10. For fiscal year 2000 data, see U.S. Department of Defense, *100 Companies Receiving the Largest Dollar Volume of Prime Contract Awards—Fiscal Year 2000* (Washington,
D.C.: U.S. Department of Defense, 2001); for fiscal year 2006 data, see Ana Marte, "The
U.S. Military: By the Numbers," *The Defense Monitor* 36, no. 6 (November–December
2007), 6.

11. For a chart of this index's movements since its inception in November 2001, go
to http://www.marketwatch.com/tools/quotes/intchart.asp?symb=DFX.X&time=20
&freq=1&comp=&compidx=aaaaa%7Eo&compind=&uf=o&ma=&maval=&lf=1&lf2
=&lf3=&type=2&size=1&txtstyle=&style=&submitted=true&intflavor=basic&origurl
=%2Ftools%2Fquotes%2Fintchart.asp.

as oil field–service expert and caterer to the troops in Iraq and its environs, the company leaped to seventh place in the rankings in fiscal year 2003, with prime contracts in that year valued at $3.9 billion.[12] Furthermore, even this outstanding corporate success seems to have been but a springboard to greater accomplishments. By the end of 2004, Halliburton's contracts for Iraq work had accumulated to approximately $10.8 billion, with more in the pipeline. During the three fiscal years from 2004 through 2006, the company received prime contract awards from the Department of Defense valued at approximately $20 billion, and in fiscal year 2006 it ranked sixth on the Pentagon's list of top contractors.[13] Perhaps it helps to have friends in high places.

Notwithstanding the success that Halliburton, Bechtel, Dyncorp, and other "old boy" service contractors have achieved in connection with the Iraq War, the really big military money still goes to the suppliers of whiz-bang weapons platforms and related products: aircraft, rockets, ships, tanks and other combat vehicles, satellites, as well as communications and other electronic equipment, along with software, maintenance, training, and upgrades for these products. In this arena of institutionalized cronyism, the living dead rise from the Cold War graveyard to haunt the halls of Congress whenever the defense-appropriations subcommittees are in session. You might wonder how the military will employ, say, an F/A-22 fighter, a B-2 bomber, or an SSN-774 attack submarine to protect you from a small nuke or a vial of anthrax slipped into the country along with the many shipments of contraband goods that enter unseen by government agents. But never mind. Just keep repeating to yourself: there is a connection between the war on terror and the hundreds of billions being spent on useless Cold War weaponry. It is important to Congress, the Pentagon, and the big contractors that you make this connection.

As for the Christian (dispensationalist) soldiers marching onward as to war—in this case, it's more than a metaphor—in order to ease the worries of God's chosen people about Israel's hostile neighbors or to hasten the glorious mayhem of the prophesied end times, suffice it to say that these fundamentalists

---

12. U.S. Department of Defense, *100 Companies Receiving the Largest Dollar Volume of Prime Contract Awards—Fiscal Year 2003* (Washington, D.C.: U.S. Department of Defense, 2004).
13. Marte, "The U.S. Military," 6.

worked hard to elect their favorite man to the presidency, and they succeeded in doing so. Indeed, one can scarcely imagine a viable national politician who would come closer to satisfying this interest group than George W. "Faith-Based" Bush.

In sum, when we ask ourselves who took the United States to war in Iraq (and keeps it engaged there) and what those individuals hoped to gain by doing so, we quickly come to appreciate what a roaring success this venture has been and continues to be for all of them. In view of the endless death and destruction being visited upon the hapless people of Iraq, however, not to mention the great and growing number of deaths, injuries, and mental disorders being suffered by U.S. troops in the Mesopotamian killing fields, we might well describe this adventure as a catastrophic success.

War Weariness

> Governments that violate peace must be treated as robbers
> and murderers are treated within each state.
> —Ludwig von Mises, c. 1940[14]

War weariness is the prevailing public sentiment in the third stage of a major U.S. neoimperialist war. In this prolonged stage, most people have grown tired of the war. They have surrendered their prior illusions about the glorious outcomes it was supposed to bring. They have come to understand that for them it is worse than pointless, that its costs have been real and its benefits a chimera, and that it seems likely to damage them further as it continues. Yet the war goes on and on, with no end in sight. We are now well into this stage of the present wars in Iraq and Afghanistan.

I recall all too well the war weariness of the late 1960s and early 1970s. By 1968, most Americans had come to understand that no good outcome lay in store for them in Vietnam. The war was unwinnable in any meaningful sense. Yet its daily horrors continued with no prospect of stopping: more bombing, more shelling, more close-contact combat in the jungles and rice paddies. Each

---

14. Quoted in Jörg Guido Hülsmann, *Mises: The Last Knight of Liberalism* (Auburn, Ala.: Ludwig von Mises Institute, 2007), 741–42.

year tens of thousands of young Americans were wounded, killed, or taken prisoner, many of them draftees sucked into the maelstrom as de facto military slaves, and hundreds of thousands of Vietnamese and other Asians were slaughtered. Each horrible day was followed by another horrible day, each horrible month by another horrible month, each horrible year by another horrible year until, weighted down by despair, one wondered whether the madness would ever end. The wars in Iraq and Afghanistan now elicit the same hopeless feeling.

By "major U.S. neoimperialist wars," I mean those in Korea, Vietnam, and Iraq. Long before them, in the Philippines from 1899 to 1902 the American people had a foretaste of neoimperialist wars to come, but the Philippine war never reached a great enough magnitude or affected the general public deeply enough to become a large factor in its outlook on national affairs. Then, as now, some people actually approved of the war from start to finish. In those days, racism was more flagrant and redder in tooth and claw than it is now, which helps to explain why so many Americans supported a totally inexcusable imperialist venture.

In Korea, Vietnam, and Iraq, the U.S. experience presented a similar course of events. In each case (except in Iraq, where the conflict has not yet run its full course), the war moved through four stages: I, upper-echelon plotting; II, initiation and early combat; III, sustained combat and strategic stalemate; and IV, cessation of combat and workable resolution.

The stages may vary in length and form. Stage I, in which U.S. leaders and their official and unofficial advisers concoct their war plans, may go on for years, as it did for the present Iraq war, or it may go on for only a short while, as it did for the Korean War, when U.S. diplomatic blunders and unanticipated events provoked the North Korean invasion and triggered U.S. engagement in the fighting. Stage II may occupy weeks or months, whereas Stage III always drags on for years. Stage IV may take different forms. The tense, heavily armed truce in Korea bore no resemblance to the hasty, unceremonious, and humiliating U.S. exodus from Vietnam, yet each outcome served the same purpose—to silence the guns.

Each stage elicits or corresponds to a particular public mood. Stage I takes place with blissful public ignorance. Few people appreciate that their national leaders and wannabe leaders, secreted in their inner sanctums, are up to no good. The onset of Stage II invariably ignites great public enthusiasm as the people rally around their national leaders, "support the troops," and reflexively accept the tales they are told about the enemy's wickedness and their own nation's blamelessness and its well-grounded justification for sending its armed forces into combat abroad. Note well: in neoimperialist wars, by definition, the fighting always occurs "over there," where it remains conveniently out of sight of the American public, which relies heavily on what its leaders say about relevant events and conditions on the ground—declarations that are at best biased and distorted accounts and at worst brazen and calculated lies.

In Stage III, as the war drags on, the casualties and financial costs accumulate, the "cake walks" fail to eventuate, and so the initial enthusiasm for the war fades. When military reversals, gross leadership mistakes, and embarrassing U.S. atrocities come to light, the public shifts even more quickly from support to disapproval.

However disillusioned and embittered the public may become, though, it cannot—or perhaps it simply will not—do anything effective to change the government's course. Even if the war-making president is chased from office, as Lyndon B. Johnson was in effect in 1968, his successor may simply continue the U.S. engagement, as Richard M. Nixon did for many years, widening the war in the process. Once the U.S. government goes to war, the public is simply stuck with it because in this country the public will not actually rebel against the government, and nothing short of rebellion can ensure an affirmative government response to the public's preferences.

No president will admit that his decision to undertake the war was a mistake from the get-go. Notice, for example, George W. Bush's complete, intractable dismissal of every sort of public disapproval of his war in Iraq, despite polls that showed huge drops in support for the war and in approval of his leadership and despite the Democratic takeover of the House and Senate in the midterm elections of 2006. He continued to order the armed forces to fight, and they continued to obey. In our system of government, no one can stop the hell-bent Caesar. People could only hope that when Bush's term expired, he would actually step down and that his successor would set a new course, as Dwight D. Eisenhower did in 1953. We now know, of course, that those hopes were in vain: the Barack Obama administration brought about no genuine disengagement in Iraq, substantially increased the U.S. forces in Afghanistan, and widened the war by staging many more attacks on alleged terrorists or their sympathizers within Pakistan.

In general, however (to repeat my earlier point), only when the ruling political elites conclude that *their personal interests*—and, of course, the interests of the special-interest coalition that props them up financially—will suffer if the war is continued will they act decisively to end it on the best terms available. Thus does Stage IV finally arrive, bringing the general public a sense of relief, although in the higher political circles, leaders and strategists always launch into finger pointing and blame casting with regard to who "lost China" this time around.

These characteristic stages of U.S. neoimperialist war are not merely descriptive; they also reflect the political logic of the U.S. system of government. Most important, they arise from the Reality of Rule, which is to say from the government's effectively having gone to war permanently against the bulk of the American people as well as episodically against unfortunate groups of foreigners in the Third World, where the U.S. government seeks to establish or maintain its hegemony. By saying that the government has placed itself in a state of war against most of the people—namely, all those outside its own supportive coalition—I mean no more and no less than what John Locke meant when he wrote about this condition in his *Second Treatise of Government:*

> [W]henever the Legislators endeavour to take away, and destroy the Property of the People [that is, their lives, liberties, and estates], or to reduce them to Slavery under Arbitrary Power [as done most recently by enactment of the Military Commissions Act of 2006], they put themselves into a state of War with the People, who are thereupon absolved from any farther Obedience. . . . [The same] holds true also concerning the supreame Executor, who having a double trust put in him, both to have a part in the Legislative, and the supreme Execution of the Law, Acts against both, when he goes about to set up his own Arbitrary Will [now termed the "inherent powers of the presidency"], as the Law of the Society.[15]

As Locke argued, people cannot be presumed to have consented to the exercise of government powers that do not protect but rather destroy their natural rights

---

15. John Locke, *Two Treatises of Government,* edited by Peter Laslett (Cambridge, U.K.: Cambridge University Press, [1690] 1988), §222, p. 412.

to life, liberty, and property, and therefore when the government takes such destructive actions, it acts as a mere robber or murderer; that is, it places itself in a state of war against them. Can anyone seriously deny that the U.S. government from its very inception has chronically violated the people's natural rights to life, liberty, and property and that its audacity in this regard has recently risen to heights that the absolute monarchs of old would have envied?

Because the government is always in a state of war against most of the people, whom it exploits and torments for the profit or pleasure of its supporting coalition, it invariably finds that as the immediate fear and knee-jerk nationalism of Stage II wear away, the people come to see more and more plainly that they are being sacrificed on the altar of their rulers' ambition, folly, and corruption. They understand increasingly that they are being made to play the patsy for the reptilian creatures who control the government. In short, they begin to see, as F. A. Hayek warned in *The Road to Serfdom*,[16] that under a system of unchecked government powers the worst really have got on top and that the masses, down on the bottom, are in danger of suffocation under the crushing weight of gross, impudent oppression.

Yet, notwithstanding this growing awareness, the people have been so deeply conditioned and so callously propagandized to equate loyalty to the country and loyalty to the government that they hesitate to act vigorously in their own self-defense. Many fall for cheap tricks that divert their attention or shift the blame for their troubles onto socially marginalized or unpopular groups such as immigrants and Muslims. They are also bombarded ceaselessly with official disinformation, which the cooperative mainstream news media dish out in ample servings each hour of each day. The government, we are told, has never made any serious mistakes, and if it ever should err, it will do so only with the best of intentions. Holding actions of this sort help the government to retard the growth of public resentment against its crimes as Stage III drags on.

So in the wake of the 2006 elections, in which one faction of the War Party displaced the other in control of Congress, we had scant grounds for expecting a great change of course in the conduct of the wars in Iraq and Afghanistan. The Democrats had announced grand plans to fleece and bully the public in the greater service of the leading special-interest groups that helped to elect

---

16. F. A. Hayek, *The Road to Serfdom* (Chicago: University of Chicago Press, 1944).

them (a promise they ultimately kept, soon after Barack Obama took office, by enacting their so-called "stimulus bill" in February 2009), and the Republicans, eminently pleased to serve as the loyal, not-much-opposed opposition, looked forward to bipartisan cooperation in logrolling the splendid 2,000-page statutes in which every species of outrage and robbery is declared to be the law of the land. The wars were certain to continue, at least for another two years and perhaps for another five or ten. And why not? Only the people at large—those beyond the precincts of the ruling figures and their major supporters—stood to lose. And what member of the power elite really gives a damn about them?

Perhaps these exploited outsiders, given their slow-witted willingness to tolerate their own oppression, don't really care much about themselves. They have their creature comforts and their amusements, so the sacrifice of their rights to life, liberty, and property does not strike them as an especially big deal. In any event, they imagine that when the government's hammer comes down hard, it will strike their Muslim neighbor or the Mexican immigrant on the other side of town, not themselves.

More and more, however, like everyone except the political schemers who brought the present wars to pass, they cannot help but feel the growing weight of war weariness.

What Might Induce U.S. Leaders to End the War?

> Guns on an empty stomach
> Are not to every people's taste.
> Merely swallowing gas
> They say, does not quench thirst
> And without woollen pants
> A soldier, it could be, is brave only in summer.
> —Bertolt Brecht, "Guns Before Butter," 1939

What might cause our government's leaders to reach a new conclusion about what serves their personal interest? Several developments might turn the trick. Nearly all of them work by heightening the public's anger regarding their leaders' decision to continue the war.

The decisive development in similar situations has historically been the cumulation of public costs, especially the costs in life and limb. In both the Korean

War and the Vietnam War, the public's disfavor with the engagement closely tracked the cumulation of casualties. As political scientist John Mueller showed in his book *War, Presidents, and Public Opinion,* "[E]very time American casualties increased by a factor of 10, support for the war dropped by about 15 percentage points" in the polls.[17] Support for the present wars has also dropped dramatically since their beginning. Indeed, as Mueller has noted recently, "Casualty for casualty, support has declined far more quickly than it did during either the Korean War or the Vietnam War."[18] Yet it seems to me that the *intensity* of the public's abhorrence of the present wars is much less than it was in the revulsion against the Vietnam War.

One reason the public has continued to tolerate the leaders' continued prosecution of the wars in Iraq and Afghanistan is that the casualties have not been nearly so great, by an order of magnitude, as they were in Korea and Vietnam. Approximately 6,000 U.S. military personnel have died in Iraq and Afghanistan so far. That amounts to only one death for every 50,000 persons living in the United States, and therefore the loss of life has not cut deeply into the public psyche—most Americans have not been personally acquainted with anyone killed in the war. (The vastly greater loss of Iraqi lives seems to have made even less impression on Americans.) As Mueller notes, "[T]he military has worked enterprisingly to keep Americans from seeing pictures of body bags or flag-draped coffins in the hope that this will somehow arrest the decline in enthusiasm for the war effort."[19] Sad to say, the public may not turn decisively—which is to say, intensely and angrily—against the leaders' continued prosecution of these wars until many more American soldiers have died.

Economic costs have also mounted, and they have loomed relatively much larger in the present wars than in the earlier wars in Korea and Vietnam. Who says the military leaders never learn? They've certainly learned how to increase hugely the financial costs of fighting a war. Estimates of the costs to date vary widely, depending on how one accounts for various joint, indirect, and entailed costs, but a total cost in the neighborhood of a trillion dollars is not implausible,

17. John E. Mueller, *War, Presidents, and Public Opinion* (New York: Wiley, 1973), 60–61.
18. John E. Mueller, "The Iraq Syndrome," *Foreign Affairs* (November–December 2005), at http://www.foreignaffairs.org/20051101faessay84605/john-mueller/the-iraq-syndrome .html.
19. Mueller, "The Iraq Syndrome."

and delayed costs, including those associated with decades of care for the legions of physically and mentally disabled, will add enormously to the total.[20]

In earlier wars, even though the costs were relatively greater in blood than in dollars, the public eventually wearied of the economic sacrifices entailed by the financial expenses of continued fighting. Economist Hugh Mosley concludes that the Johnson administration "was reluctant to resort to increased taxes to finance the war for fear of losing public support for its policy of military escalation."[21] Historian Stephen Ambrose writes that President Richard Nixon "realized that for economic reasons (the war was simply costing too much) and for the sake of domestic peace and tranquility he had to cut back on the American commitment to Vietnam"; the retrenchment was "forced on [him] by public opinion."[22]

As the current economic difficulties persist, the public may well object more strenuously to the government's squandering of such vast amounts of tax money on a senseless continuation of the wars in Iraq and Afghanistan. When people's purses are not so full, they may resent every additional dollar spent on these wars more than they did previously. They ultimately may become so angry that they will take actions to punish severely the political leaders who continue to support the war. Serious political challengers might attract a mass following by embracing the example of Dwight D. Eisenhower, who promised in the 1952 campaign to end the enormously unpopular war in Korea and, after he took office, kept his promise expeditiously. This prospect appears extremely unlikely so far, however. The incoming Obama administration signaled only a desire to shift military effort from Iraq to Afghanistan—scarcely a propitious move—and this promise is unfortunately one of the few the president has kept.

When substantial negative feedback begins to jeopardize the incumbents' personal job security, not to speak of the respect and fawning the electorate lavishes on them, the incumbents will begin to take notice and to discount more

---

20. See, for example, the $3 trillion estimate of the wars' total costs in Joseph Stiglitz and Linda J. Bilmes, *The Three Trillion Dollar War: The True Cost of the Iraq Conflict* (New York: Norton, 2008).

21. Hugh G. Moseley, *The Arms Race: Economic and Social Consequences* (Lexington, Mass.: D. C. Heath, 1985), 153.

22. Stephen E. Ambrose, *Rise to Globalism: American Foreign Policy Since 1938,* 4th ed. (New York: Penguin, 1985), 242–43.

heavily the contributions from big defense contractors, big financial establish-ments, petrochemical companies, and other high rollers who have encouraged them to stay the hopeless course—though not hopeless for these special inter-ests, of course; as I have noted, the war has been a bonanza for them. George W. Bush parlayed a campaign of fear mongering into his reelection in 2004, but unless another major terrorist attack occurs in the United States, the public will grow increasingly resistant to such appeals and more eager to throw the rascals out as the war's costs continue to mount.

It is terribly unfortunate that escalating costs in blood and money are the only proven means of bringing the general public to resist strongly political leaders who are committed to continuation of unnecessary, unwise, and immoral wars. Some of us wish that rational argument, cogent evidence, and humane sentiment would persuade a preponderance of the public to demand an end to these wars. History suggests, however, that only personal grief and economic pain will induce the American public to act against their perfidious leaders. Needless to say, if the public remains as passive and as easily bamboozled as it has been during the past ten years, the wars will continue, maybe even for the hundred years that presidential candidate Senator McCain declared would be "fine with me."[23]

---

23. Quoted in Kate Phillips, "McCain Said '100'; Opponents Latch On," *New York Times,* March 27, 2008, at http://www.nytimes.com/2008/03/27/us/politics/27check.html.

21

Cumulating Policy Consequences, Frightened Overreactions, and the Current Surge of Government's Size, Scope, and Power

THE FINANCIAL AND economic crisis that came to a head in the late summer of 2008 has brought forth a huge government response, many elements of which are without precedent. The crisis, however, did not appear out of nowhere. In important regards, its roots lie, first, in government policies to promote more widespread homeownership than would occur in a free market and, second, in the Federal Reserve System's mismanagement of interest rates and the money stock. Although the crisis is far from over as I write, it appears already that the surge of extraordinary government actions and new policies it has provoked will give rise to important, permanent increases in the government's size, scope, and power. In this way, it mimics the national emergencies of the past century.

Dimensions of the Crisis and the Government's Responses to It

Although the National Bureau of Economic Research places the recent peak of economic activity in the fourth quarter of 2007,[1] real gross domestic product (GDP) did not reach its peak until the second quarter of 2008. By the second quarter of 2009, real GDP had fallen by 4 percent.[2] Likewise, financial

---

1. National Bureau of Economic Research, Business Cycle Dating Committee, "Determination of the December 2007 Peak in Economic Activity," available at http://www.nber.org/cycles/dec2008.html.
2. Official estimates of real GDP, produced by the U.S. Department of Commerce, Bureau of Economic Analysis, are available at http://research.stlouisfed.org/fred2/data/GDPC1.txt.

stringencies in the certain credit markets began to appear in 2007, but they did not become widely noticed until September 2008, when, toward the end of the month, a full-fledged financial panic developed, and commentary in the news media and the statements of public officials took on a frightened tone. The civilian unemployment rate began to rise after March 2007, when it stood at 4.4 percent, and by October 2009, it had reached 10.2 percent.[3]

In response to the growing economic troubles, especially the perceived "credit crunch" of September 2008, policymakers in the George W. Bush administration (most notably Treasury Secretary Henry Paulson), in Congress, and at the Federal Reserve System (the Fed) responded by initiating a series of unprecedented actions to rescue tottering banks and other financial institutions and to inject credit into the financial system.[4] On October 3, Congress passed and the president signed the Emergency Economic Stabilization Act of 2008 (Public Law 110-343). Title 1 of this statute authorized the Treasury secretary to create the Troubled Assets Relief Program (TARP) and authorized as much as $700 billion for the purchase of so-called troubled assets, primarily mortgage-related securities, held by banks and other financial institutions. Unable to implement the planned acquisition of troubled assets, the Treasury instead used the TARP mainly to inject funds into the banks by purchasing preferred shares and warrants to purchase common stock from them. Also in September, the Fed took control of the insurance giant American International Group (AIG),[5] and the Federal Housing Finance Authority took over the huge government-sponsored enterprises (GSEs) Fannie Mae and Freddie Mac, secondary lending institutions that held or insured more than half of the total value of U.S. residential mortgages.[6]

---

3. Official estimates of the civilian unemployment rate, produced by the U.S. Department of Labor, Bureau of Labor Statistics, are available at http://research.stlouisfed.org/fred2/data/UNRATE.txt.

4. For a useful annotated compilation of the series of events making up the crisis and the government's responses to it, see "Credit Crisis—the Essentials," *New York Times,* n.d., available at http://topics.nytimes.com/top/reference/timestopics/subjects/c/credit_crisis/index.html.

5. In addition to other aid, the Fed agreed to lend AIG $60 billion and acquired control of nearly 80 percent of the company.

6. The government did not nationalize Fannie Mae and Freddie Mac outright but placed them into conservatorship, taking an ownership interest in the form of senior preferred

By the end of 2008, the Fed had also made large, unprecedented types of loans and had given other forms of assistance, including loan guarantees, asset swaps, and lines of credit to securities dealers; commercial-paper sellers; money-market mutual funds; Fannie Mae, Freddie Mac, and the Federal Home Loan Banks; buyers of certain asset-backed securities based on consumer and small-business loans; Citigroup (related to losses resulting from a federal government guarantee of a specified pool of assets); and fourteen foreign central banks.[7]

The Treasury and the Federal Deposit Insurance Corporation also took a variety of other large-scale actions to prop up credit and housing markets during the final quarter of 2008.[8]

After Barack Obama became president, his administration and Democratic leaders in Congress concentrated on gaining passage of a new "economic stimulus" bill, and these efforts ultimately resulted in enactment of the American Recovery and Reinvestment Act of 2009 (Public Law 111-5), which the president signed into law on February 17. This statute authorizes a great variety of spending increases as well as some tax reductions over the period from 2009 to 2019. According to initial estimates prepared by the Congressional Budget Office (CBO), the combined amount of these spending increases and tax cuts comes to $787 billion over these ten years.[9] More recent estimates of the stimulus bill's cost, which the CBO updates periodically, have been substantially greater.[10]

The Obama administration also proceeded at the end of April 2009 with two complex "restructuring" arrangements that essentially amounted to government takeovers of General Motors (GM) and Chrysler, both of which were

---

shares and receiving warrants that would permit the government to acquire 79.9 percent of the common shares of each company. Authority for these actions came from the Housing and Economic Recovery Act of 2008 (Public Law 110-289).

7. Brief descriptions of these Fed programs and the amounts of money or other assistance involved in each of them appear in Congressional Budget Office, *The Budget and Economic Outlook: Fiscal Years 2009 to 2019* (Washington, D.C.: U.S. Government Printing Office, 2009), appendix table A-1, 35–38.

8. For brief descriptions, see Congressional Budget Office, *The Budget and Economic Outlook,* appendix table A-2, 39–41.

9. "Getting to $787 Billion," *Wall Street Journal,* February 17, 2009, at http://online.wsj .com/public/resources/documents/STIMULUS_FINAL_0217.html.

10. Stephen Dinan, "CBO Raises Its Stimulus Cost Estimate, Again," *Washington Times,* February 23, 2011.

teetering on the brink of bankruptcy. Commentator Carl Horowitz calls this action "one of the most radical moves in the history of American industry," noting that it came not long after the federal government had made huge emergency loans to the companies. The government had also forced the resignations of the chief executive officers of the two companies, Rick Wagoner of GM and Robert Nardelli of Chrysler.[11] By the end of July 2009, total government aid to the two firms had cumulated to $65 billion.[12]

Writing in the *Wall Street Journal* on June 15, 2009, Bob Davis and Jon Hilsenrath summarized the extraordinary recent surge of government actions: "Since the onset of the financial crisis nine months ago, the government has become the nation's biggest mortgage lender, guaranteed nearly $3 trillion in money-market mutual-fund assets, commandeered and restructured two car companies, taken equity stakes in nearly 600 banks, lent more than $300 billion to blue-chip companies, supported the life-insurance industry and become a credit source for buyers of cars, tractors and even weapons for hunting."[13] Although this statement falls far short of giving a comprehensive account of the government's responses to the crisis, it suffices to justify the conclusion that within less than a year the perceived emergency had provoked a huge surge in the federal government's size, scope, and power.

This surge also entailed major fiscal eruptions, including tremendous increases in federal expenditures and an even greater percentage run-up of federal debt. According to the August 2009 update prepared by the CBO, federal outlays for fiscal year 2009 would total $3,688 billion, an increase of 24 percent over the total for the previous year. This increase, which is wholly without peacetime precedent in U.S. history, would raise federal outlays from 21.0 percent of GDP to 26.1 percent. Moreover, because federal receipts were forecast to contract by almost 17 percent in 2009, the annual federal budget deficit was expected to

---

11. Carl Horowitz, *Obama Arranges Takeover of GM and Chrysler; Auto Workers Union Gets Huge Stake* (Falls Church, Va.: National Legal and Policy Center, 2009), at http://www .nlpc.org/stories/2009/05/01/obama-administration-arranges-takeover-gm-and-chrysler -auto-workers-union-gets-hu.

12. "US Govt to Sell GM and Chrysler Stock," BNET, available at http://www.bnet.com /2407-13071_23-325401.html.

13. Bob Davis and Jon Hilsenrath, "Federal Intervention Pits 'Gets' vs. 'Get-Nots,'" *Wall Street Journal,* June 15, 2009.

increase from $459 billion in 2008 to $1,587 billion in 2009, an increase of 246 percent. The CBO forecast that the 2009 deficit would be equal to 11.2 percent of GDP, up from 3.2 percent in the previous year. The borrowing required to finance this gargantuan deficit in the federal budget was forecast to increase the U.S. debt held by the public from $5,803 billion at the end of fiscal year 2008 to $7,612 billion at the end of 2009, an increase of $1,809 billion, or 31 percent in a single year.[14]

Although these figures for the U.S. Treasury are mind-boggling for an economist or financial historian, the Fed's recent actions have been even more astonishing. Figure 21.1 shows the most important of these actions, the abrupt increase in the monetary base, which must be seen to be believed.[15] As the figure shows, the monetary base—currency in circulation plus commercial bank reserves at the Fed—historically increased smoothly at a fairly modest rate of growth. Between August 2008 and January 2009, however, the Fed took a variety of actions, as described earlier, that caused the country's monetary base to double in only five months. After January 2009, the monetary base remained in this extraordinarily elevated range. In September and October 2009, it increased even further, reaching all-time highs.

This monetary-policy action places the purchasing power of the U.S. dollar in grave jeopardy because the monetary base, as its name indicates, is the foundation on which the U.S. money stock rests. Other things being equal, the Fed's more than doubling of the monetary base will ultimately result in a more than doubling of the money stock and hence in a tremendous reduction of the dollar's purchasing power, with a variety of negative effects on the economy.

---

14. All data cited in this paragraph are drawn from U.S. Congressional Budget Office (CBO), *The Budget & Economic Outlook: An Update* (Washington, D.C.: U.S. Government Printing Office, August 2009), summary table 1, p. 2, at http://cboblog.cbo.gov/?p =346. The CBO's estimates of spending and the deficit turned out to err on the high side. After the end of the fiscal year , the actual spending total was reported as $3.52 trillion (equal to about 25 percent of GDP) and the deficit as $1.42 trillion (equal to about 10 percent of GDP). See "US Deficit Surges to All-Time Record," *Daily Finance,* October 16, 2009, at http://www.dailyfinance.com/2009/10/16/us-deficit-surges-to-all-time-record.
15. The graph and the underlying data it depicts are from the publicly accessible database maintained by the Federal Reserve Bank of St. Louis, at http://research.stlouisfed.org/fred2/series/BOGUMBNS?cid=124.

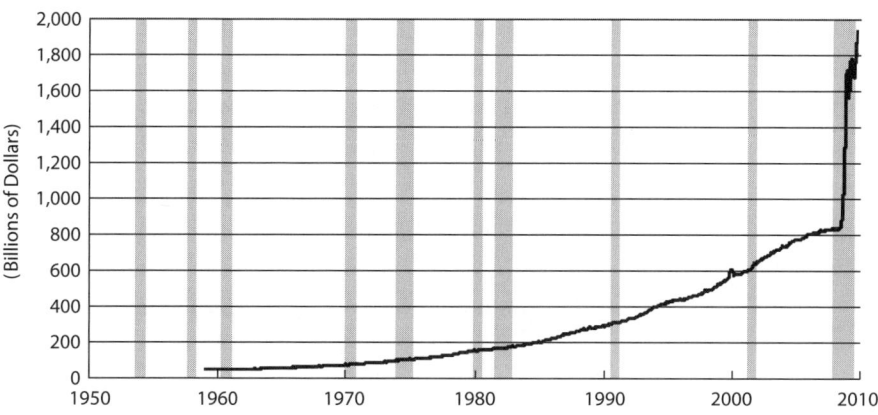

Note: Shaded areas indicate U.S. recessions
Source: Board of Governors of the Federal Reserve System

Figure 21.1 Board of Governors Monetary Base, Not Adjusted for Changes in Reserve Requirements (BOGUMBNS)

As of this writing, the banks as a whole have simply absorbed the additional reserves rather than using them as the basis for increasing the volume of their loans and investments and thereby setting in motion the process by which, in a fractional-reserve commercial banking system, the money stock is increased, mainly by the commercial banks' creation of new checking-account balances. Between August 2008 and January 2009, legally excess commercial-bank reserves at the Fed increased from less than $2 billion to nearly $800 billion, and in October 2009 they amounted to $995 billion, an all-time high.[16] Should the banks begin to employ these excess reserves to make new loans and investments, however, the Fed will face a dilemma: either do nothing to mop up the excess reserves, allowing them to become the fuel for rapid price inflation, or mop them up, most likely either by traditional open-market operations or by offering the banks a much higher rate of interest on their reserve balances at the Fed. Either choice entails increasing the rate of interest, and political pressures are certain to be brought to bear against the Fed's taking such an action, especially

---

16. Data on excess reserves are available at http://research.stlouisfed.org/fred2/data /EXCRESNS.txt.

if the recession has not ended and the rate of unemployment remains high. Fed chairman Ben Bernanke has expressed the opinion that the Fed possesses "the tools" to deal with this problem, but others (I include myself here) remain skeptical that he will do so successfully.[17] In any event, the Fed's emergency actions since August 2008 have created serious economic risks, which make private planning much more difficult and thereby impede the market economy's successful functioning. In such circumstances, much "smart money" simply sits idle or goes into safe, low-yielding investments, such as Treasury bills.[18]

Cumulating Policy Consequences

The current crisis, like every major economic emergency, occurs in the context of predisposing conditions, institutions, and policies that took shape over a long period. Although many people are inclined on each such occasion to conclude that "capitalism has failed," a pure market system does not just spontaneously break down. Such a system automatically produces feedback information that guides and motivates producers, investors, and consumers to make constant adjustments to changing conditions. Profits and losses, with the corresponding growth, decline, and disappearance of firms that they bring forth, give market participants reliable indications of whose plans have succeeded and whose plans have failed in meeting consumer demands at prices that permit costs to be covered. No one knows the future, and therefore entrepreneurs in a pure market system may make mistakes in appraising the profitability of the various alternatives they perceive as open to them. But sustained, large-scale mistakes are unlikely to occur because the constant flow of price and profit information, combined with the knowledge that one's own wealth is at stake, gives market participants the necessary information and the personal

---

17. See, for example, "Bernanke's Exit Dilemma," *Economist Online,* August 4, 2009, at http://economistonline.blogspot.com/2009/08/bernankes-exit-dilemma.html; and Jeannine Aversa, "Bernanke's Tough Task: Withdrawing Emergency Aid," *ABC News,* August 21, 2009, at http://abcnews.go.com/Business/WireStory?id=8379185&page=1.
18. Tom McGinty and Cari Tuna, "Jittery Companies Stash Cash," *Wall Street Journal,* November 3, 2009.

incentive to make appropriate forward-looking adjustments long before overall economic conditions have become severely distorted on a wide scale.

When governments intervene, however, the effect is to "falsify" the market's signals. Subsidies permit firms that would go bankrupt to continue in business, even though they are failing to cover their full costs in the market and therefore are in effect transforming valuable inputs into less-valuable outputs—which is to say, generating economic waste. Government price fixing (including the Fed's manipulation of interest rates) distorts the pattern of resource allocation and misleads investors into making commitments ill suited to future economic conditions. Government regulations and taxes penalize firms that are successfully satisfying consumer demands: they diminish the firms' net returns and cause them to produce less or drive them out of business, notwithstanding their actual contribution to overall economic efficiency. When market participants are subject to a welter of such government interventions, they may commit resources in a way that allows distortions and imbalances to cumulate until the burdens these mistakes entail can no longer be sustained, and a sudden crash reveals the unsoundness of the overall economic structure.

The current crisis has arisen in large part from the way in which governments, especially the federal government, have intervened in the housing and housing-finance markets over a long period that stretches back to the 1930s. During the early 1930s, the contraction of economic activity and the unevenly falling prices brought about severe distress in housing and financial markets. As businesses failed, incomes fell, and unemployment rose, many homeowners could not make their scheduled mortgage or tax payments and therefore lost their homes to foreclosure or tax sale.

The Franklin D. Roosevelt administration responded to this dire situation by, among other things, obtaining congressional approval for creation of the Home Owners' Loan Corporation (HOLC) in 1933. This government institution restructured approximately one million mortgages on nonfarm, owner-occupied homes, changing the obligations from short-term (usually three to five years), interest-only loans with balloon repayments of the entire principal to long-term (initially fifteen years, later extended in some cases by up to ten years), fully amortized loans, and thereby prevented many foreclosures that otherwise would have occurred. Of course, these arrangements also amounted to a bailout for the banks and other lending institutions that held the refinanced mortgages, and therefore they foreshadowed the similar bailouts the government has undertaken in 2008 and later years. The HOLC was terminated in 1951.[19]

In 1934, the National Housing Act (Public Law 73-479) created the Federal Housing Administration (FHA) to insure private lenders against default on conventional, long-term, amortized mortgage loans and the Federal Savings and Loan Insurance Corporation to insure deposits in savings institutions that specialized in recycling their deposits into mortgage loans. These actions caused more money to flow into mortgage loans than would have flowed in their absence. Thus, the government, in effect, undertook to divert loanable funds into housing purchases and hence to divert labor and capital into house construction and related activities.

A more portentous New Deal action occurred in 1938, when the FHA administrator exercised his statutory authority to charter the Federal National Mortgage Association (generally called "Fannie Mae"). "The primary purpose of Fannie Mae was to purchase, hold, or sell FHA-insured mortgage loans that had been originated by private lenders. After World War II, Fannie Mae's authority was expanded to include VA [Veterans Administration]–guaranteed home mortgages."[20] At this time, Fannie Mae was simply part of the U.S. government. In 1968, the institution was split into two parts: the Government National Mortgage Association (generally called "Ginnie Mae") and a reconstituted, privatized Fannie Mae.

Ginnie Mae was initially and remains today a wholly government-owned corporation that guarantees the payment of interest and principal on mortgage-backed securities backed by federally insured or guaranteed loans. This guarantee is an explicit U.S. government commitment. Ginnie Mae debt therefore has the same credit rating as U.S. Treasury debt. The institution's Web site explains: "[T]he Ginnie Mae guaranty allows mortgage lenders to obtain a better price for their mortgage loans in the secondary market. The lenders can

19. Lowell Harriss, *History and Policies of the Home Owners' Loan Corporation* (New York: National Bureau of Economic Research, 1951), 1–6.
20. Fannie Mae, "About Fannie Mae," at http://www.fanniemae.com/aboutfm/charter.jhtml.

then use the proceeds to make new mortgage loans available."[21] Thus, like all of the other government institutions engaged in this sector, from the HOLC to the presently existing ones, Ginnie Mae seeks to make homeownership less costly and therefore more widespread than it would be in a freely functioning, private-property market without government intervention.

Between 1968 and 1970, the reconfigured Fannie Mae became a private, government-sponsored enterprise (GSE) engaged as a purchaser in the secondary market for residential mortgages. An anomalous institution, Fannie Mae was made subject to regulatory oversight by the Department of Housing and Urban Development, exempted from oversight by the Securities and Exchange Commission, not required to hold as much capital as competing private financial institutions, freed from the obligation to pay state and local income taxes, and provided with a $2.25 billion line of credit from the U.S. Treasury. Five of the eighteen members of the board of directors could be named by the president of the United States.[22] Although the institution's debt no longer enjoyed an explicit Treasury guarantee, many market participants believed that the government would back it, if need be, and therefore Fannie Mae was able to borrow at interest rates only slightly higher than those on U.S. government debt.[23] The general understanding was that the institution would be considered "too big to fail," and, indeed, it ultimately was so considered.

Ostensibly to provide a competitor for Fannie Mae, the government created in 1970 the Federal Home Loan Mortgage Corporation (generally called "Freddie Mac") and authorized this government-sponsored enterprise to purchase mortgages in the same fashion as Fannie Mae. Freddie Mac was seemingly a private, shareholder-owned corporation, yet it enjoyed the same statutorily stipulated advantages as Fannie Mae in the secondary mortgage market and

21. Ginnie Mae, "About Ginnie Mae," at http://www.ginniemae.gov/about/about.asp?Section=About.

22. Lawrence J. White, "Fannie Mae, Freddie Mac, and Housing: Good Intentions Gone Awry," in *Housing America: Building out of a Crisis,* edited by Randall G. Holcombe and Benjamin Powell (New Brunswick, N.J.: Transactions, 2009), 265–68.

23. White, "Fannie Mae, Freddie Mac, and Housing," 266–67; Alan Reynolds, "Fannie Mae and Freddie Mac Should Be Cut Down and Cut Loose," *U.S. News and World Report,* July 21, 2008.

the same widespread perception of an implicit government guarantee of its own debt, as shown by the low interest rate it paid when selling its own securities.[24] Freddie Mac's Web site proclaims: "[W]e reduce the costs of housing finance and expand housing opportunities for all families, including low-income and minority families. It is a unique mortgage finance system that makes homeownership a reality for more of America's families."[25] To be sure, this GSE, like its giant competitor, did make homeownership more widespread than it would have been in a pure, private-property, free-market system absent interventions such as the creation of privileged GSEs. Many observers would eventually come to appreciate, however, that homeownership was made too easy and too widespread for the good of the country at large.[26] Too many homeowners holding title to "too much home" but possessing little or no equity in it contributed to the creation of a fragile, excessively leveraged, overall economic structure.

By 2008, Fannie Mae and Freddie Mac owned or guaranteed approximately half of the $12 trillion in residential mortgage loans outstanding in the United States.[27] According to a staff report of the House Committee on Oversight and Government Reform, "Fannie Mae and Freddie Mac were in fact leaders in risky mortgage lending."

> According to an analysis presented to the Committee, between 2002 and 2007, Fannie and Freddie purchased $1.9 trillion of mortgages made to borrowers with credit scores below 660, one of the definitions of "subprime" used by federal banking regulators. This represents over 54% of all such mortgages purchased during those years. If one factors in Alt-A and adjustable-rate mortgages, this analysis found that, at the end of 2008, Fannie and Freddie were still exposed to $1.6 trillion of risky default-prone loans. Thus, at year-end 2008, Fannie Mae and Freddie Mac were responsible for 34 percent of all outstanding subprime mortgages and

---

24. Fannie Mae, "About Fannie Mae." See also Freddie Mac, "Our Mission," at http://www.freddiemac.com/corporate/company_profile/our_mission/.
25. Freddie Mac, "Company Profile," at http://www.freddiemac.com/corporate/company_profile/.
26. White, "Fannie Mae, Freddie Mac, and Housing," 272–73, 278–79.
27. Charles Duhigg, "Loan-Agency Woes Swell from a Trickle to a Torrent," *New York Times,* July 11, 2008.

60 percent of all outstanding Alt-A mortgages in the United States. . . . [N]onprime loans, which accounted for only 34% of the GSEs' risk exposure at the end of 2008, were suffering a 6% delinquency rate, accounting for 90% of the GSEs' losses. . . . The continuing losses caused by Fannie and Freddie's binge on junk mortgages have already cost the taxpayers dearly. . . . The sum of these federal aid packages brings the total current taxpayer exposure to GSE liabilities to over $700 billion.[28]

This report also adduces substantial evidence that these GSEs did not simply make bad decisions about lending standards on their own. For decades, especially during the past decade, they sustained strong political pressure from members of Congress beholden to an "affordable housing" coalition of special-interest groups who sought greater and greater relaxation of conventional underwriting standards for mortgage loans, even though many loans were eventually being made to borrowers with low credit ratings and no documentation of their income or assets.[29] Noting that "Fannie and Freddie used high leverage to borrow money and gamble on low-down payment affordable and speculative mortgages," the report concludes that "[u]nlike Wall Street, however, the GSEs did this with the mandate and the blessing of Congress and successive Administrations, which encouraged them to use their government-granted competitive advantages to engage in a race to the bottom, boosting the national homeownership rate for political gain." Most important, "[t]he consequences of these policies have also brought the entire global financial system to the brink of collapse, destroying trillions in equity and untold numbers of lives."[30]

To sum up the GSEs' role in establishing important preconditions for the financial crisis that came to a head in September 2008, one can scarcely do better than to quote the conclusions reached in this House staff report:

---

28. U.S. House of Representatives, Committee on Oversight and Government Reform, *The Role of Government Affordable Housing Policy in Creating the Global Financial Crisis of 2008*, staff report (Washington, D.C.: U.S. Government Printing Office, July 7, 2009), 24–25.

29. U.S. House of Representatives, *The Role of Government Affordable Housing Policy*, 5–8, 12–17, 20–23.

30. U.S. House of Representatives, *The Role of Government Affordable Housing Policy*, 25, 26.

The housing bubble that burst in 2007 and led to a financial crisis can be traced back to federal government intervention in the U.S. housing market intended to help provide homeownership opportunities for more Americans. This intervention began with two government-backed corporations, Fannie Mae and Freddie Mac, which privatized their profits but socialized their risks, creating powerful incentives for them to act recklessly and exposing taxpayers to tremendous losses. Government intervention also created "affordable" but dangerous lending policies which encouraged lower down payments, looser underwriting standards and higher leverage. Finally, government intervention created a nexus of vested interests—politicians, lenders and lobbyists—who profited from the "affordable" housing market and acted to kill reforms. . . . While government intervention was not the sole cause of the financial crisis, its role was significant and has received too little attention.[31]

In a careful, independent analysis, Stan J. Liebowitz concurs, documenting that "mortgage underwriting standards had been under attack by virtually every branch of the government [including the Fed] since the early 1990s."[32]

Another factor that has not received its due attention, although it may have been the most critical one, is the Fed's policy from 2001 to 2005. During these years, the Fed, in an attempt to reverse the 2001 recession and to restore economic growth, pushed the interest rates it controls to extraordinarily low levels. The effective Federal Funds rate, which is the Fed's principal target rate in its efforts to control the overall credit markets, was quickly pushed from 6.5 percent in 2000 to a low of 1 percent by mid-2003 and kept there for the next year. Although the Fed began to increase the effective Federal Funds rate in mid-2004, this rate did not exceed 2 percent until December 2004, and it reached 3 percent only in May 2005.[33] Thus, given that the contemporary rate of inflation was roughly 2–3 percent per year, the Fed was actually holding the effective real Federal Funds rate in the negative range for about three years.

---

31. U.S. House of Representatives, *The Role of Government Affordable Housing Policy*, 2.
32. Stan J. Liebowitz, "Anatomy of a Train Wreck: Causes of the Mortgage Meltdown," in Holcombe and Powell, eds., *Housing America*, 288.
33. Data on the effective Federal Funds rate are available at http://research.stlouisfed.org /fred2/data/FEDFUNDS.txt.

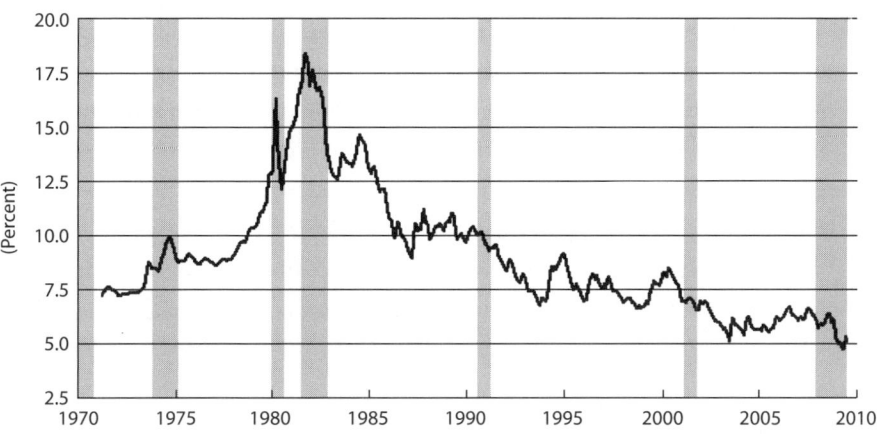

Note: Shaded areas indicate US recessions. 2009 research.stlouisfed.org
Source: Board of Governors of the Federal Reserve System

Figure 21.2 Thirty-Year Conventional Mortgage rate (MORTG)

Small wonder, then, that related interest rates also remained unusually low during this period. Perhaps most important, the interest rate on conventional thirty-year home mortgages fell from 8.5 percent in May 2000 to less than 6 percent by January 2003, and it rarely exceeded 6 percent afterward, rising above that level consistently only after October 2005 and even then never exceeding 6.8 percent as a monthly average (see figure 21.2).[34] Thus, allowing for price inflation of 2–3 percent per year, the real rate on conventional, long-term, mortgage loans remained at roughly 3–4 percent for several years after 2002. In short, during that period, the Fed made bank credit, including loans for house purchases, very cheap. By doing so, the Fed fueled the housing bubble. After all, no matter how easy the terms may be in a mortgage-loan market backed up by reckless GSEs, transactions still require that funds be available to the financial institutions that originate the loans. Absent this ample supply of monetary fuel, the development of the housing bubble would have been much less likely, if not impossible.

Further evidence of this Fed action may be seen in the brisk rate of growth of the money stock. Between December 2000 and December 2006, the money stock as measured by the M2 concept increased from $4,948 billion to $7,061

---

34. Data on the thirty-year conventional mortgage rate are available at http://research .stlouisfed.org/fred2/series/MORTG?cid=114. My graph comes from the same source.

billion, or by 42.7 percent in just six years (which implies an average annual rate of growth of 6.1 percent).[35] To put this monetary growth into perspective, one may consider that from the fourth quarter of 2000 to the fourth quarter of 2006, real GDP increased by only 15.2 percent (which implies an average annual rate of growth of 2.4 percent).[36] Thus, in this period the money stock was growing at roughly 2.5 times the rate at which real output was growing.

My view of the Fed's primary responsibility for fueling the housing boom and hence for causing the many unfortunate consequences that ensued when this boom ultimately went bust accords with the view expressed by Stanford University economist John B. Taylor:

> Monetary excesses were the main cause of the boom. The Fed held its target interest rate, especially in 2003–2005, well below known monetary guidelines that say what good policy should be based on historical experience. Keeping interest rates on the track that worked well in the past two decades, rather than keeping rates so low, would have prevented the boom and the bust. Researchers at the Organization for Economic Cooperation and Development have provided corroborating evidence from other countries: The greater the degree of monetary excess in a country, the larger was the housing boom.[37]

Frightened Overreactions

Since the onset of the current economic troubles, U.S. policymakers have acted as if (1) they are frightened (or seek to frighten others)—insisting that the impending dangers are so ominous that unless extraordinary measure are

---

35. Data on the monthly M2 money stock are available at http://research.stlouisfed.org/fred2/data/M2NS.txt.

36. Data on quarterly real GDP are available at http://research.stlouisfed.org/fred2/data/GDPC1.txt.

37. John B. Taylor, "How Government Created the Financial Crisis," *Wall Street Journal,* February 9, 2009. Among other economists who have reached the same conclusion about the fundamental cause of the housing boom, see especially Mark Thornton, "The Economics of Housing Bubbles," in Holcombe and Powell, eds., *Housing America,* 237–62; and Gerald P. O'Driscoll Jr., "The Financial Crisis: Origins and Consequences," *Intercollegiate Review* 44 (Fall 2009): 4–12.

taken immediately, a catastrophe may occur—and (2) they do not know what they are doing—devising one new measure after another, seemingly in ad hoc responses to a sequence of perceived problems, especially in the various credit markets, and frequently reversing course, even abandoning major initiatives altogether and replacing them with a new bailout du jour.

Moreover, while constantly proclaiming that by their efforts they seek to remedy economywide or even worldwide problems, they have undertaken an unprecedented degree of tailoring in deciding which institutions to help and which to forsake. In this regard, they have given the distinct impression that, rather than implementing broad-gauge monetary or fiscal policy, they are engaging in financial and economic "industrial policy," picking winners with little or no apparent economic logic to support their decisions. Bear Stearns must be saved; Lehman Brothers can be allowed to sink. Citigroup must be saved; CIT Group can be allowed to fall into bankruptcy. GM and Chrysler must be saved; countless smaller firms scattered across the economy can be allowed to go down. In these circumstances, a firm's survival might well turn on having friends at the Treasury, at the Fed, or in Congress.

Small wonder that the pace of lobbying has quickened perceptibly.[38] The *Wall Street Journal* reports: "Government spending as a share of the economy has climbed to levels not seen since World War II. The geyser of money has turned Washington into an essential destination for more and more businesses. Spending on lobbying is up, as are luxury hotel bookings in the capital."[39] Thus, the existing policies amount to a recipe for political (i.e., economically irrational) allocation of resources, which is scarcely reassuring for those seeking to divine the economy's future.

Writing in mid-November 2008, Edmund L. Andrews observed: "White House and Treasury officials have been devising policy on the fly for months now, as what began as a panic over losses on subprime mortgages broadened into a crisis that wreaked havoc on Wall Street, at major commercial banks

---

38. Mark Landler and David D. Kirkpatrick, "Lobbyists Swarm the Treasury for Piece of Bailout Pie," *New York Times,* November 12, 2008; David Cho, Steven Mufson, and Tomoeh Murakami, "In Shift, Wall Street Goes to Washington," *Washington Post,* September 13, 2009.

39. Davis and Hilsenrath, "Federal Intervention Pits 'Gets' vs. 'Get-Nots.'"

and in the broader economy itself."⁴⁰ In a December 18, 2009, speech at the American Enterprise Institute, President Bush explained rather defensively why he had approved the big financial bailout bill ultimately enacted on October 3: "I was in the Roosevelt Room and Chairman Bernanke and Secretary Paulson, after a month of every weekend where they're calling, saying, we got to do this for AIG, or this for Fannie and Freddie, came in and said, the financial markets are completely frozen and if we don't do something about it, it is conceivable we will see a depression greater than the Great Depression. So I analyzed that and decided I didn't want to be the President during a depression greater than the Great Depression, or the beginning of a depression greater than the Great Depression. So we moved, and moved hard."⁴¹ Taylor notes that "[t]he realization by the public that the government's [TARP] intervention plan had not been fully thought through, and the official story that the economy was tanking, likely led to the panic seen in the next few weeks." Moreover, "this [panic] was likely amplified by the ad hoc decisions to support some financial institutions and not others and [by the] unclear, seemingly fear-based explanations of programs to address the crisis."⁴²

Further evidence that policymakers were flying by the seat of their pants comes from the sheer number and variety of significant policy actions taken in the brief period from early September to mid-November 2008 and somewhat less frantically in the months afterward. Kathleen Pender lists the following government actions:

> Sept. 7: The Treasury takes over mortgage giants Fannie Mae and Freddie Mac, putting them into a conservatorship and pledging up to $200 billion to back their assets.
>
> Sept. 16: The Fed injects $85 billion into the failing American International Group [AIG], one of the world's largest insurance companies.

---

40. Edmund L. Andrews, "U.S. Shifts Focus in Credit Bailout to the Consumer," *New York Times,* November 13, 2008.

41. Quoted in Karen Tumulty, "President Bush Uses the D-Word," *Swampland: A Blog About Politics,* December 18, 2009, at http://swampland.blogs.time.com/2008/12/18/president-bush-uses-the-d-word/.

42. Taylor, "How Government Created the Financial Crisis."

Sept. 16: The Fed pumps $70 billion more into the nation's financial system to help ease credit stresses.

Sept. 19: The Treasury temporarily guarantees money market funds against losses up to $50 billion.

Oct. 3: President Bush signs the $700 billion economic bailout package.

Oct. 6: The Fed increases a short-term loan program, saying it is boosting short-term lending to banks to $150 billion.

Oct. 7: The Fed says it will start buying unsecured short-term debt from companies, and says that up to $1.3 trillion of the debt may qualify for the program.

Oct. 8: The Fed agrees to lend AIG $37.8 billion more, bringing the total to about $123 billion.

Oct. 14: The Treasury says it will use $250 billion of the $700 billion bailout to inject capital into the banks, with $125 billion provided to nine of the largest.

Oct. 14: The FDIC [Federal Deposit Insurance Corporation] says it will temporarily guarantee up to a total of $1.4 trillion in loans between banks.

Oct. 21: The Fed says it will provide up to $540 billion in financing to provide liquidity for money market mutual funds.

Nov. 10: The Treasury and Fed replace the two loans provided to AIG with a $150 billion aid package that includes an infusion of $40 billion from the government's bailout fund.[43]

Not since the explosion of government intervention into economic affairs at the outset of the New Deal has such a rapid-fire succession of significant measures been taken in such short order. Any one of these measures ordinarily might have been studied, debated, and refined for months before its implementation. This time, however, scarcely any of them received more than perfunctory consideration, and many of them were adopted so hastily that it is difficult to

---

43. Kathleen Pender, "Government Bailout Hits $8.5 Trillion," *San Francisco Chronicle,* November 26, 2008.

believe that they received more than a few hours of serious thought by more than a handful of people. Never in U.S. history have so many measures of such great importance come forth from so few decision makers in so little time.

Even when Congress as a whole voted, as it did on the bailout bill enacted on October 3, 2008, few members had much genuine grasp of the legislation they were being urged to approve. Most were stampeded into going along by the exhortations of frightened leaders in the executive and legislative branches and by Fed chairman Ben Bernanke. Four days after Congress approved and the president signed the Emergency Economic Stabilization Act of 2008, Congressman Ron Paul wrote: "The rallying cry heard all over the Hill the past two weeks was that Congress must act. Our economy is facing a meltdown. Would this bill fix it? Nobody could really explain how it would. In fact, few demonstrated any real understanding of credit markets, of derivatives, of credit default swaps or mortgage-backed securities. If they did, they would have known better than to vote for this bill. All they knew was that this administration was saying some frightening things, and asking for a lot of money."[44]

We conceivably might survey all of the extraordinary actions the government took in the late summer and autumn of 2008 and conclude only that, given the conditions at that time, the authorities had little choice and acted only as the situation clearly required if catastrophe were to be averted. "There is no playbook for responding to turmoil we have never faced," Secretary Paulson declared in mid-November. "We have done what was *necessary* as facts and conditions in the market and economy have changed, adjusting our strategy to most effectively address the crisis."[45] Although this account is conceivable, it is highly implausible. Much more plausible, in my view, is the interpretation that if indeed the government's objective were simply to avert catastrophe, then it clearly overreacted. It perceived a serious potential for disaster where the actual potential was much smaller or in many specific areas virtually nonexistent. It consistently failed to consider how if the government did nothing, private parties might meet the existing challenges by means of their own devising because

---

44. Ron Paul, "The Do-Something Congress," *LewRockwell.com,* October 7, 2008, at http://www.lewrockwell.com/paul/paul483.html.

45. Henry M. Paulson, "Fighting the Financial Crisis, One Challenge at a Time," *New York Times,* November 17, 2008, emphasis added.

they have such a great incentive to do so. In short, the government overreacted in part because the handful of government decision makers who wielded the greatest power at the time assumed that central government action ought to be the *first resort* in a perceived crisis.

Consider the crisis atmosphere that the government and the news media created in late September and early October 2008 and to a somewhat lesser extent in the four or five subsequent months. As Brian Gilmore, executive vice president of a Massachusetts trade association, stated in November 2008, "The whole psychology is that the sky is falling, even though it's not."[46] The media and government story line, repeated again and again, as if mere repetition made it true, was that the credit markets were "locked up," "clogged," "melted down," "frozen," or, in other metaphors, effectively inoperative. One financial dealer after another told news reporters that "nobody is lending" or used words to the same effect.

Yet when I examined the Fed's comprehensive data for the volume of lending in various credit markets at the time, I found nothing to warrant these hysterical views.[47] Financial analysts who looked into the matter more extensively than I did had no more success in finding evidence that would justify the panic. Finally, in January 2009 *Global Finance* reported that "[a] chorus of dissenting voices has emerged that is challenging the widely held belief that interbank lending markets have dried up, commercial lending is being curtailed, and non-financial commercial paper markets have virtually ground to a halt." The article cited the analysis of researchers at the Federal Reserve Bank of Minneapolis and a report by Octavio Marenzi, head of the research firm Celent, who stated: "While there is no denying that we are mired in a very serious financial crisis, this does not yet appear to have transformed into a general credit crisis. In aggregate, credit and lending markets appear to be functioning well and in many cases are actually operating at historically high levels." Marenzi concluded that unless

---

46. Quoted in Ross Kerber, "Small-Business Loans Still Flowing; Many in Mass. Find No Barrier," *Boston Globe,* November 21, 2008.

47. See, for example, my blog posts "Credit Is Flowing, Sky Is Not Falling, Don't Panic," *The Beacon,* September 23, 2008, at http://www.independent.org/blog/?p=201; "The Data Don't Justify Financial-Market Panic," *The Beacon,* October 8, 2008, at http://www.independent.org/blog/?p=255; and "My Credit Is Not Frozen (nor Are Most Others')," *The Beacon,* October 11, 2008, at http://www.independent.org/blog/?p=289.

policymakers had undisclosed data to support their actions, it appeared that they were "making generalizations based on the situation of a particular set of businesses or banks."[48]

Throughout the recent crisis, policymakers seem to have operated on the basis of two unspoken assumptions: (1) the volume of outstanding credit should never decline; and (2) if the volume of outstanding credit does decline, the government should act to reverse that decline. Neither assumption makes good economic sense. Past increases in the volume of credit may have been excessive; indeed, in the mortgage-lending market, one would have been hard pressed to deny such excesses after so many subprime and (slightly higher quality) Alt-A loans became delinquent.[49] One cannot easily justify the idea that foolhardy loans made in the past, now being wiped off the accounts in foreclosure proceedings, ought to be propped up or quickly replaced by loans that under present conditions can scarcely be any less foolhardy. Yet many of the government's emergency policies seemed designed to achieve precisely this nonsensical objective.[50] If credit retrenchment is occurring for good reasons, then the government's actions to offset it are unnecessary, and they will most likely be mischievous as well. Government loans or loan guarantees will prop up borrowers who ought never to have received the loans in the first place. Such measures diminish the economy's overall efficiency and lay the foundation for a recurrence of similar troubles at a later stage.

Many of the government's crisis actions seemed to be aimed, however, not at doing what makes economic sense, but at saving selected incumbent firms that got into trouble by making bad bets. Apart from anything that might be said about taking money from responsible parties and giving it to irresponsible parties, such policies in effect maintain an economic condition in which profits

---

48. Quoted in "United States: Credit Crunch May Be a Myth," *Global Finance* 23 (January 2009), 4.

49. "Subprime, Alt-A Mortgage Delinquencies Rising: S&P," Reuters, May 22, 2008, at http://www.reuters.com/article/gco3/idUSN2249493920080522; Paul Jackson, "Alt-A Mortgage Loan Delinquencies Nearly as Bad as Subprime," *NuWire Investor,* May 1, 2009, at http://www.nuwireinvestor.com/articles/alt-a-mortgage-loan-delinquencies-nearly-as-bad-as-subprime-52903.aspx.

50. Patrice Hill, "Easy-Money Mortgages Still Provided, by the Feds," *Washington Times,* October 19, 2009.

remain private, but losses are socialized. The moral hazard thus promoted may be the worst consequence of the government's crisis policies in the long run. "This crisis," declared Charles I. Plosser, president of the Federal Reserve Bank of Philadelphia, "whether it's because of the Fed or the Treasury or Congress, has created a lot of new moral hazard. Once you have done this once, even though it was in a severe crisis, the temptation will be for people to figure that in the next crisis you'll do it again."[51] What major firm's managers in the future will fear having to bear the full consequences of imprudent actions? Will not all such actors appreciate that the government stands ready to bail out their firms on the grounds that they are "too big to (be allowed to) fail" or that permitting them to fail poses too great a "systemic risk"?

The latter claim was advanced repeatedly when officials at the Treasury and the Fed explained their actions. Thus, on October 14, 2008, Secretary Paulson issued a statement that declared: "[O]ur actions are extensive, powerful and transformative. They demonstrate that the government will do what is necessary to restore the flow of funds on which our economy depends and *will act to avoid, where possible, the failure of any systemically important institution*."[52] The notion of systemic risk denotes the potential for an institution's failure to set in motion a cascade of other failures, ultimately bringing down the entire economic system or at least a large part of it. It is a frightening prospect, and members of Congress generally defer to Fed or Treasury officials who explain that the powers they possess or seek will be used to avert it. (Deference is not always forthcoming, however. At a hearing on July 15, 2008, Senator Jim Bunning told Bernanke: "Now the Fed wants to be a systemic risk regulator. But the Fed is a systemic risk."[53]) Despite the centrality of systemic risk in the rhetoric employed by

---

51. Quoted in Edmund L. Andrews and David E. Sanger, "U.S. Is Finding Its Role in Business Hard to Unwind," *New York Times,* September 14, 2009.

52. "Statement by Secretary Henry M. Paulson, Jr. on Actions to Protect the U.S. Economy," *Wall Street Journal,* October 14, 2008, emphasis added. See also "Oral Statement by Secretary Henry M. Paulson, Jr. on Regulatory Reform Before House Committee on Financial Services," U.S. Department of the Treasury press release, July 10, 2008, at http://www.treas.gov/press/releases/hp1074.htm.

53. Quoted in John Carney, "Bunning to Bernanke: You Are a Systemic Risk," *Dealbreaker,* July 15, 2008, at http://dealbreaker.com/2008/07/bunning-to-bernanke-you-are -a.php.

policymakers, it has not been well established as a serious threat. In a substantial econometric study published recently in the *Journal of Financial Economics,* the investigators conclude that "systemic risk is limited even during major financial crises."[54] Regardless of its actual likelihood of wreaking major harm, however, systemic risk is an idea that lends itself splendidly to fear mongering.

The Ratchet Effect

During the past century, whenever the government abruptly expanded its size, scope, and power during a national emergency, it never returned completely to its precrisis dimensions or even to the dimensions that it would have attained had precrisis trends continued. I call this phenomenon the "ratchet effect."[55] In view of the political logic of this phenomenon and the particular facts of the current crisis and the government's responses to it, we are likely to see the same pattern of events in the present case that we have seen in the past.

The government's size, as measured by its fiscal dimensions, almost certainly will remain at a greater level for many years after the current emergency has passed. According to the baseline-projection update published by the CBO in August 2009, federal outlays were projected to jump from 21.0 percent of GDP in fiscal year 2008 to 26.1 percent in 2009 and then fall back to lower ratios in subsequent years. However, the retrenchment is currently forecast to return the outlay percentage only to 22.6 percent in fiscal year 2013, after which it will increase slowly until 2019, when it will be 23.4 percent, or 2.4 percentage points greater than it was in 2008. We would be fools to take such projections seriously for more than the very short term. Long before the ten-year projection period

54. Sohnke B. Bartram, John Hund, and Gregory W. Brown, "Estimating Systemic Risk in the International Financial System," *Journal of Financial Economics* 86 (December 2007): 835–69.

55. For more on this effect, see especially Robert Higgs, *Crisis and Leviathan: Critical Episodes in the Growth of Government* (New York: Oxford University Press, 1987); Robert Higgs, *Against Leviathan: Government Power and a Free Society* (Oakland, Calif.: The Independent Institute, 2004); and Robert Higgs, *Neither Liberty nor Safety: Fear, Ideological Change, and the Growth of Government* (Oakland, Calif.: The Independent Institute, 2007).

has run its course, unanticipated changes in economic conditions and government fiscal activities will almost certainly have occurred, displacing the government's spending ratio from its currently projected path. Nevertheless, the current projections do tell us that unless the government's future spending and taxing levels are altered substantially from those implied by currently existing laws or the economy performs substantially better than forecast, the upshot of the present surge in outlays will be a permanently higher level of federal outlays relative to GDP—a fiscal ratchet effect.

The CBO's projections also indicate that federal taxes as a percentage of GDP will recover from their relatively low levels of 2009 and 2010, and after 2012 they will lodge in the relatively high range (by the standard of the past forty years) of 19–20 percent. Federal debt held by the public is projected to rise every year, ascending from $5,803 billion (or 40.8 percent of GDP) at the end of fiscal year 2008 to $14,324 billion (or 67.8 percent of GDP) at the end of fiscal year 2019. The CBO report concludes: "Over the long term (beyond the 10-year baseline projection period), the budget remains on an unsustainable path. Unless changes are made to current policies, the nation will face a growing demand for budgetary resources caused by rising health care costs and the aging of the population. Continued large deficits and the resulting increases in federal debt over time would reduce long-term economic growth by lowering national saving and investment relative to what would otherwise occur, causing productivity and wage growth to gradually slow."[56]

It also seems likely that the government's responses to the crisis of 2008–2009 will permanently enlarge the scope of its intervention in the economy. The government has acquired major ownership stakes in hundreds of commercial banks as well as in AIG, GM, and Chrysler. It may retain a portion of this ownership and control for a long time. Fannie Mae and Freddie Mac are now effectively government-owned and operated enterprises, and they, along with the recently bloated FHA,[57] remain the overwhelmingly dominant players in the secondary mortgage market, exerting a huge effect on mortgage financing and hence on the markets for residential housing and all the goods and services associated

---

56. CBO, *The Budget and Economic Outlook,* 4–5.
57. Hill, "Easy-Money Mortgages."

with it—altogether a substantial part of the economy and a sector that plays an especially important role in generating macroeconomic booms and busts.

In addition, the Fed has vastly expanded the scope of its lending and other operations, and it now effectively implements a financial industrial policy by its decisions to aid selected firms and industries rather than others—if the Fed is not "picking winners," it is certainly deciding who will be spared a market-determined fate as a loser.[58] How the Fed will exercise these new powers in the long run remains unclear at present, and Fed officials insist that they intend to withdraw from many of the new areas they have recently entered once the crisis has passed, but it would be surprising if none of the recent "emergency" policies remained in the Fed's arsenal to bulk up its powers. According to the *Washington Post,* "Wall Street executives say the legacy could be enduring."[59] A *New York Times* report adds, "Obama administration officials bristle at even the hint that their rescue measures have ushered in a new era of 'big government.' But supporters and critics alike worry that it will be difficult to shrink the government to anything like its former role."[60] Many of the recently created vested interests in these new interventionist measures are sure to press for their perpetuation.

Moreover, owing to the Fed's recent success in its quest for authority to act as a super-regulator of all firms (nonbanks as well as banks) whose failure might pose a systemic risk to the economy,[61] embodied in the provisions of the Dodd-Frank financial-reform bill,[62] the current crisis has produced another highly sig-

---

58. On how the Fed's unprecedented expansion of its portfolio has transformed it into the conductor of a de facto industrial policy, see Randall G. Holcombe, "Transforming America: The Bush–Obama Stimulus Programs," *The Freeman* 59 (September 2009), 34–35; and Jeffrey Rogers Hummel, "Ben Bernanke versus Milton Friedman: The Federal Reserve's Emergence as the U.S. Economy's Central Planner," *The Independent Review* 15, no. 4 (Spring 2011), 485–518.

59. Cho, Mufson, and Murakami, "In Shift, Wall Street Goes to Washington."

60. Andrews and Sanger, "U.S. Is Finding Its Role in Business Hard to Unwind."

61. Alison Vekshin, "Obama's Fed Risk Regulator Plan Fades as Lawmakers Back Council," *Bloomberg,* July 23, 2009, at http://www.bloomberg.com/apps/news?pid=20601070&sod =a_H7XBO4IEB8; Alan S. Blinder, "An Early-Warning System, Run by the Fed," *New York Times,* July 25, 2009.

62. Dodd-Frank Wall Street Reform and Consumer Protection Act, Public Law 111-203, July 21, 2010.

nificant ratchet effect on the scope of government. In particular, the Dodd-Frank statute creates and empowers a Financial Stability Oversight Council—almost certain to be dominated in practice by the Fed—to mitigate systemic risk and maintain systemic financial stability.[63] This council possesses "a complete menu of choices available in terms of what they can require banks to do in order to reduce risks to the system (up to and including preemptively breaking up big troubled banks)."[64] This development amounts to a major increase in the government's supervisory and regulatory power.

The government's engagement as a systemic-risk regulator unfortunately serves as a perfect example of what F. A. Hayek called the pretense of knowledge.[65] After all, this arrangement is tantamount to hiring the selfsame fox that has been devouring the chickens as the security guard for the henhouse. Moreover, it is difficult to envision how the government can conceivably attempt to regulate the firms it takes to be posing a systemic risk without wreaking major economic mischief. In a passage that remains as apt today as it was in 1776, Adam Smith warned: "The statesman, who should attempt to direct private people in what manner they ought to employ their capitals, would not only load himself with a most unnecessary attention, but assume an authority which could safely be trusted, not only to no single person, but to no council or senate whatever, and which would nowhere be so dangerous as in the hands of a man who had folly and presumption enough to fancy himself fit to exercise it."[66] Smith was warning against what he had earlier called the presumptuous "man of system,"

---

63. William Sweet, "Dodd-Frank Act Becomes Law," Harvard Law School Forum on Corporate Governance and Financial Regulation, July 21, 2010, at http://blogs.law.harvard .edu/corpgov/2010/07/21/dodd-frank-act-becomes-law/.
64. Simon Johnson, "An Early Stress Test for the Financial Stability Oversight Council," The Baseline Scenario, October 21, 2010, at http://baselinescenario.com/2010/10/21/an -early-stress-test-for-the-financial-stability-oversight-council/.
65. Friedrich August von Hayek, "The Pretence of Knowledge," Nobel Prize Lecture, December 11, 1974, at http://nobelprize.org/nobel_prizes/economics/laureates/1974/hayek -lecture.html. For specific application of Hayek's concept to Bernanke's actions in 2008, see Doug French, "Ben Bernanke's Pretense of Knowledge," *Mises Institute Daily Article*, December 6, 2008, at http://mises.org/story/3247.
66. Adam Smith, *An Inquiry into the Nature and Causes of the Wealth of Nations* (New York: Modern Library, 1937), 423.

who "is apt to be very wise in his own conceit."[67] Today, we may include in that general class the presumptuous "man of systemic risk regulation." In view of the seemingly limitless scope of this species of regulation and the likelihood of its being exercised in a very harmful manner, it poses an especially great risk to the economy's successful functioning.

---

67. Adam Smith, *The Theory of Moral Sentiments*, edited by D. D. Raphael and A. L. Macfie (Indianapolis, Ind.: Liberty Fund, 1982), 233.

PART IV

Review of the Troops

22

Review of

War, Revenue, and State Building: Financing the Development of the American State

by Sheldon D. Pollack

HISTORIAN CHARLES TILLY famously reduced several centuries of modern European history to the formula "war made the state, and the state made war." The maxim has proved enduring not because of its novelty—after all, many others had already said essentially the same thing—but because of its concision and punch. Sheldon D. Pollack, in his new book *War, Revenue, and State Building: Financing the Development of the American State* (Ithaca, N.Y.: Cornell University Press, 2009), expands Tilly's formulation, as it were, to make it read: war made the state, and when, primarily during a succession of wars, rulers successfully devised effective means of garnering many more resources from society, the state first made wars and later established a welfare state. This version is not so punchy, but it is surely undeniable. Pollack also seeks to determine whether recent interpretations of revenue capture and state building by political scientists and historians, who have focused on European history, also apply to the rise of the U.S. state. In particular, his "objective in this book is to elucidate the linkages between the sources of public revenue available to the American state at specific junctures of its history, the revenue strategies pursued by its political leaders in response to these factors, and the consequential impact of their revenue strategies on the development of the American state" (p. 6).

Rulers are not free to take as much as they like from society or to take what they do get in any manner whatsoever. "In democratic states," Pollack observes, "rulers must enter into 'revenue coalitions' with powerful groups and interests in society, providing benefits (e.g., protection, subsidies, or favored status) in return for their revenue contributions. . . . Taxation is but one of countless methods used to raise revenue; however, it has proven to be the most efficient and effective for extracting great quantities of revenue from prosperous economies" (p. 9). Pollack recognizes that rulers possess substantial autonomy, and the "central argument of this book is that state autonomy ultimately depends on the state's fiscal powers—its capacity to extract revenue from society" (p. 20). A state that has run out of money has not only run out of luck but also exhausted its ability to survive.

Pollack premises his historical survey on a remarkably clear-eyed view of the nature of the state and its operations. States originated in the activities of mounted raiders ("roving bandits") who preyed on the settled populations that proliferated during the Agricultural Revolution. These raiders plundered their victims, hauling away portable valuables and sometimes the people themselves as slaves. However, the raiders gradually saw greater advantage in settling among their victims (becoming "stationary bandits"), ruling their communities and insisting on a continuing stream of tribute. Thus, the state assumed its classic form as essentially a protection racket, albeit one that sought legitimacy via priestly endorsement and other measures. States that succeeded in establishing a system for garnering regular revenues from their subjects thereby transformed themselves from "plunder states" to "tax states." In their final stage, they devoted increasing proportions of their expenditures not simply to making war, but also to the maintenance of a "welfare state." After 1945, the United States achieved unique status as a great warfare state combined with a great welfare state.

Thus, in Pollack's characterization, the current U.S. state "is a 'tax state' that operates a benign form of a 'protection racket'—collecting 'tribute' in the form of income taxation and in return providing such public goods as protection from criminals and foreign invaders, free markets, a stable currency, and the 'rule of law' (e.g., recourse to law courts to enforce contracts)" (p. 22). Some observers ardently dispute this system's benignity, not to mention the extent to which contemporary markets are truly free and the currency stable, but one cannot deny that an ostensible "exchange" occurs between the state and its subjects at large. The oft-encountered claim that a "social contract" underlies this essentially coercive arrangement surely deserves to be considered a convenient myth that serves to prop up the legitimacy of those who exercise its supreme power (pp. 46–48). In any event, Pollack's chapter titled "The State: Coercion and Tribute" raises many of the essential issues related to the nature of the state, and it will prove instructive to readers who take the state, its powers, and its panoply of activities for granted, as if all of these things were as natural as rain and snow.

Pollack devotes two chapters to the emergence and development of European states during the past five or six centuries. These states arose when changes in military technology gave a more decisive advantage to rulers who could operate on a large financial scale and therefore pay for well-trained and well-equipped professional troops, muskets and cannon, stronger fortifications, well-armed navies, and other elements of the new techniques of waging war. Princes who devised more effective ways to raise revenue systematically, by "laying imposts on wealthy individuals, land, and commercial activities" (p. 69), could equip themselves with superior armed forces and defeat the forces of other principalities, plundering those areas and incorporating them into their own realms. In this way, the stronger states gained territory and subject population, and the weaker states tended to disappear. "In 1500, there were some five hundred principalities, independent city states, and uncontested territories in Europe; by 1900, the number of European states had fallen to approximately twenty-five" (p. 67).

During the nineteenth century, as democratic political institutions gained ground, the European states found it necessary to make increasing concessions, which eventually culminated in a "transformation of the raison d'être of the state. . . . The rulers needed to forge durable relations with a wider range of social classes, providing a quid pro quo to the newly enfranchised classes to preserve what was left of the old order" (p. 88). Bismarck's Germany led the way in the 1880s, instituting compulsory sickness and accident insurance for workers and old-age and disability pensions. Other western European nations adopted similar programs soon thereafter. Although labor unions and social-democratic political parties generally supported these programs, the major impetus for them came from the top, not from the downtrodden. As Pollack observes, "[M]uch of the initiative behind these programs came from state actors, rather than unions or political parties on the left." He quotes Peter Swenson's conclusion that "'private interests were simply overwhelmed by state officials and policy experts with their autonomous problems, ideals, ambitions, and powers'" (p. 94). When the United States adopted such programs, first at the state level and later, especially in the 1930s, at the national level, Progressive intellectuals, well-placed do-gooders, and state functionaries played a similar leadership role.

Pollack maintains that "the high cost of operating social welfare programs coupled with the great expenses associated with maintaining a modern military force is driving even the most prosperous democratic states of Western Europe and North America toward long-term financial insolvency" (p. 85). He does not say, though, how he believes this situation will be resolved, and, indeed, it is probably impossible at present for anyone to venture more than a guess. All we know for certain is that the system built between the late nineteenth century and the late twentieth century contains the seeds of its own destruction. Nonetheless, political forces intent on its perpetuation remain strong, and a great deal of political fury surely awaits us as modern states adapt, as they must, to the hard realities of having promised much more than they can deliver.

On page 100, Pollack finally comes to his main subject, the development of the American state, by which he means the national state (he deals with the U.S. "states" [Alabama, Connecticut, etc.] only in passing and in relation to the national or "federal" government). Although he devotes the remaining 200 pages to this subject, his discussion is curiously unbalanced in that he discusses the earlier periods, when the national state was weaker and more limited, at greater length than he discusses the periods, especially World War II and its aftermath, when this state gained and exercised its greatest powers and, as Pollack's theme alerts us, systematically seized its greatest revenues.

If the national government was initially weak in the United States relative to the great European states, it was so because most political leaders wanted it that way. The United States of America was created by revolutionaries from thirteen independent states that, having seceded from the British Empire, saw the advantage of joining forces for the purpose of loose cooperation in the fight to sustain their separation from Britain. Most of the revolutionary troops were state militiamen, and the states bore much of the war's financial cost directly. Cooperation with the Continental Congress was vacillating and half-hearted. The national government during the early years of the war and later under the Articles of Confederation (ratified March 1781) had no power to tax, and its assessments on the states generally brought forth scant returns. Hence, the Continental Congress resorted to issuing more than $240,000 in paper money, which quickly became worthless, and to borrowing from foreigners, especially the French and the Dutch.

When the government under the Constitution was established, a few powerful figures, most notably Alexander Hamilton, wished to adopt the institutions common to the powerful mercantilist states of Europe, but most Americans preferred to keep nearly all the power at the state level, expressing "an unrelenting hostility toward centralized government that can be traced to an indigenous strain of political thought that first emerged in British North America in the 1750s and 1760s" (p. 106). Although Hamilton succeeded during his term as the first secretary of the Treasury in establishing many of the national institutions he desired—especially the collection of taxes (mainly tariffs), the maintenance of a standing army, the establishment of a national bank, and the assumption and payment of remaining war debts, including those of the states—these institutions for a long time had only a limited reach. "For decades, the triumph of the nationalists was more potential than actual," says Pollack (p. 184). Seven decades later the War Between the States, which brought an explosion of taxation and government expenditure, helped to give new vitality to some of the nationalists' schemes, producing "the belated fulfillment of Alexander Hamilton's vision of an American fiscal-military state modeled on eighteenth-century England" (p. 211).

Nevertheless, the bloated wartime apparatus was soon largely dismantled, and for the remainder of the nineteenth century American government reverted for the most part to its prewar structure, with both revenue raising and power wielding concentrated at the state and local levels. Even the lower-level governments, with notable exceptions, left people largely free to pursue happiness as they thought best. On the eve of World War I, "[n]otwithstanding the efforts of Progressive reformers, the American state remained a fragmented political organization dominated by patronage politics and political parties, lacking the 'universal' professional bureaucracy, professional standing army, and revenue-extraction capacity possessed by the strong nation-states of nineteenth-century Europe" (p. 242).

Then, in the twentieth century, wars—above all, World War II—became the occasions for finally transcending the old system of limited, relatively weak national government and authentic dual federalism. The costs of major wars increased manyfold: the War Between the States cost the Union more than the national government had spent in its entire previous history; World War I cost roughly ten times more than the War Between the States; and World War II cost roughly ten times more than World War I.

After ratification of the Sixteenth Amendment in 1913, the world wars brought dramatic increases in income-tax rates, and World War II in particular pulled the bulk of the working population into the income-tax-paying group. Pollack gives good capsule accounts of these wartime tax surges, emphasizing that their permanent incorporation into the federal government's financial operations consigned to the dust bin of history the central state's longstanding reliance on revenues from tariffs and internal excises. Now the government had made itself a partner in the private economy's prosperity: when people flourished there, the government had the means in place to rake off a substantial share of their gains. (Should people realize losses, however, they were generally on their own.) Adoption of income-tax withholding in 1943 made the government's seizure of much of this revenue virtually automatic, even when taxpayers heartily wished to evade payment. The government also used the wars, which were financed primarily by borrowing, as propitious occasions for injecting its operations more firmly into the markets for financial securities, thereby giving Hamilton's goal in this regard a realization beyond even his wildest dreams.

Space here does not permit mention of all of the interesting facts and judicious interpretations Pollack has packed into his book. He writes very well, and he draws on a plethora of recent scholarly studies. The book is not pathbreaking in the historian's sense, however: virtually all of the author's sources, except for statutes, are secondary works; in a sense, the book tells us nothing we did not already know if we had taken the time to read as widely as Pollack has read. Yet even this well-read author has strangely neglected the relevant works by economists and economic historians in favor of works by historians and political scientists, and here and there his conclusions go awry as a result—for example, when he maintains that the War Between the States promoted a "prosperous market economy" during the war (p. 229), that the Great Depression began with the stock-market crash of October 1929 (p. 254), and that only 5.5 percent of the population served in the armed forces during World War II (p. 259). He might have profited from, among other sources, Larry Neal's massive three-volume collection of studies titled *War Finance* (Aldershot, U.K.: Edward Elgar, 1994). Had he perused this collection, he probably would not have written that "we know remarkably little about the relationship between state development and public revenue" (p. 25). Economists have been writing actively on this topic at least since Adam Smith's time.

Pollack's exposition also evinces at least two unresolved tensions. First, he recognizes that modern central governments function as protection rackets, yet he often writes as though their triumph was for the better and concludes that even if they are protection rackets, they are "benign" ones (p. 22; see also pp. 86–87, 281–83, 293–94). Second, he speaks repeatedly of how "efficiently" the modern state extracts revenue from society, yet he also acknowledges that the present welfare states of the economically advanced countries are unsustainable. One way to resolve these tensions is to conclude that although these states have always been and remain today highly objectionable protection rackets—cunningly operated ones in the more recent ("democratic") era—their revenue extraction cannot continue much longer to keep pace with the rulers' short-sighted promises; hence, the welfare state as currently fashioned cannot persist because before long its financial requirements will exceed the number of golden eggs the government can squeeze out without killing the goose (the private economy) that lays them.

23

Review of

New Deal or Raw Deal? How FDR's Economic Legacy Has Damaged America

by Burton Folsom Jr.

NOT EVERYONE LOVED President Franklin D. Roosevelt. Even in 1936, when he enjoyed his most lopsided electoral victory, almost 17 million voters cast their ballots for Alf Landon. During Roosevelt's long presidency, he attracted vigorous literary critics, such as H. L. Mencken, John T. Flynn, and Garet Garrett. But the winners write the history, and for many years the bulk of the writing about Roosevelt and the New Deal amounted to little more than hagiography.

As the original Roosevelt idolaters aged and died, however, more balanced appraisals gradually began to appear, and several good iconoclastic books have appeared recently, including Thomas Fleming's *The New Dealers' War* (2001), Gene Smiley's *Rethinking the Great Depression* (2002), Jim Powell's *FDR's Folly* (2003), and Amity Shlaes's *The Forgotten Man* (2007). Burton Folsom's new book, *New Deal or Raw Deal? How FDR's Economic Legacy Has Damaged America* (New York: Simon & Schuster, 2008), belongs to this genre.

Folsom builds his discussion around what he calls "the Roosevelt legend," the handiwork of historians who idolize FDR and applaud the New Deal—if they cavil, they do so only by lamenting that the New Deal did not go far enough to create a socialist paradise. If Folsom does not give this legend a knockout blow, he certainly thrashes it severely, and no honest reader can come away from this well-documented book with a positive view of FDR or his economic nostrums.

Folsom presents a colorful overview of the economic events of the 1930s, drawing on the latest revisionist literature to strengthen his critique of the New Deal, but readers who want a strictly economic appraisal will probably do better by going directly to the new interpretive sources he employs. Where

Folsom shines brightest is, first, in his appraisal of Roosevelt as a person and as a politician and, second, in his demonstration of the great extent to which the vaunted New Deal was little more than a partisan political endeavor, albeit an exceptionally successful one.

Roosevelt has always been renowned for his charm and charisma, and there is no gainsaying that many people were taken in by his glibness and ebullient self-confidence. Underneath this appealing surface, however, the real Roosevelt was anything but attractive. Instead, he was callous, self-centered, devious, manipulative, and chronically dishonest. Having been an indifferent student, he was "no intellectual" (p. 17). In particular, he knew little about economics and made scant effort to learn. Nevertheless, he pushed through his hugely unsettling economic policies largely to serve political ends, justifying his actions with the foolish idea that merely "trying something" made sense even though he had no well-founded idea of the economic effects this blind flailing would produce.

Folsom presents a valuable discussion of the great extent to which taxes were increased during the 1930s, especially excise taxes—on alcoholic beverages, gasoline, cigarettes, radios, movie tickets, and many other goods—that bore relatively heavily on lower-income people. From 1933 through 1936, federal excise taxes exceeded federal individual and corporate income taxes combined, and during the following four years excises always brought in at least 40 percent of federal revenue. After 1935, Social Security payroll taxes diminished poor people's wages disproportionately.

Especially from 1935 onward, Roosevelt plunged into class warfare. He sought a variety of soak-the-rich taxes and got Congress to approve several of them in 1935, 1936, and 1937, including an economically damaging tax on corporate retained earnings, a prime source of funding for new firms. He sent the IRS on punitive expeditions against political opponents Huey Long and Hamilton Fish, newspaper publishers William Randolph Hearst and Moses Annenberg, and former Treasury secretary Andrew Mellon, among others. At the same time, he instructed the IRS to back away from investigations of political favorites, such as Texas congressman Lyndon B. Johnson. The president also directed the FBI to investigate people he disliked.

Folsom gives an eye-opening account of various ways in which the Roosevelt administration used the billions of dollars of relief funds at its disposal for partisan political purposes. "If we probe deeply into Roosevelt's popularity," he writes, "we almost always discover the presence of patronage—the creating and the manipulating of federal jobs to strengthen his political support" (p. 169). FDR did not invent patronage, of course, but he increased its scale by an order of magnitude.

After Roosevelt tried to pack the Supreme Court in 1937, the New Deal began to sputter, and new programs and taxes became more difficult to push through Congress. His attempt to "purge" uncooperative legislators in the 1938 elections failed, angering many senators and representatives in the process. "The president became resented more than adored," writes Folsom, "and soon Congress was altering his legislation and overriding his vetoes" (p. 206). The 1937–38 "depression within a depression" cost the president even more support.

Nonetheless, the bulk of the New Deal persisted. Indeed, many of the programs it instituted remain in effect today. Folsom concludes: "The myth that these programs were once valuable, that they helped end the Great Depression, and that they restored prosperity to the United States has been enough to keep them going" (p. 264). Moreover, with or without the myth, in general once a government program has been created, "bureaucrats within the program flock to defend it; [and] those receiving benefits from the program strive to retain it" (p. 264).

24

Review of

Churchill, Hitler, and "the Unnecessary War": How Britain Lost Its Empire and the West Lost the World

by Patrick J. Buchanan

WINSTON LEONARD SPENCER CHURCHILL (1874–1965) was an extraordinary man. As a soldier, politician, and writer, he made a deep imprint on world history for more than half a century. He is best known as the prime minister who rallied his countrymen during the fateful Battle of Britain and thereby, many people believe, stemmed the flood that was sweeping Adolf Hitler to world conquest. Small wonder that *Time* magazine named him its Man of the Century, a designation that many other admirers have embraced.

Churchill, however, never waited idly for the world to construct his legend. From the 1890s onward, he strove to put himself in the places, especially the wars, where he would be best situated to advance his fame and realize his ambitions, and as he made his way through a series of adventures, he promptly wrote articles and books about each of them, thereby shaping in large degree how others would view his actions. Moreover, he was an excellent writer: his articles and books sold very well, and in 1953 he was awarded the Nobel Prize in Literature. His sharp wit and dazzling rhetoric enhanced his reputation.

In *Churchill, Hitler, and "the Unnecessary War"* (New York: Crown Books, 2008), Patrick J. Buchanan seeks to demolish the Churchill myth along with several related ones, and he is surprisingly successful in doing so. I say "surprisingly" not because the myth itself was ever unassailable—excellent historians, including the great Ralph Raico, long ago pounded Churchill's feet of clay into dust—but because Buchanan is known primarily as an ideological polemicist, yet in this book he presents respectably balanced and well-documented arguments for his theses. If he is not himself a professional historian, he has absorbed the works of scores of well-reputed historians, and he carefully assesses a number of counterarguments against his position. Although he presents no previously unreported facts, he offers abundant evidence expressed in clear, forceful prose. All in all, he makes a persuasive case.

Buchanan correctly views the two world wars as "two phases of a Thirty Years' War." He argues that both phases were unnecessary and that Great Britain "turned both European wars into world wars" (pp. *x*, *xvii*).

For World War I, he maintains: "Had Britain not declared war on Germany in 1914, Canada, Australia, South Africa, New Zealand, and India would not have followed the Mother Country in. Nor would Britain's ally Japan. Nor would Italy, which London lured in with secret bribes of territory from the Habsburg and Ottoman empires. Nor would America have gone to war had Britain stayed out. Germany would have been victorious, perhaps in months. There would have been no Lenin, no Stalin, no Versailles, no Hitler, no Holocaust" (p. *xvii*).

For World War II, he maintains: "Had Britain not given a war guarantee to Poland in March 1939, then declared war on September 3, bringing in South Africa, Canada, Australia, India, New Zealand, and the United States, a German-Polish war might never have become a six-year war in which fifty million would perish" (pp. *xvii–xviii*).

He argues that the decisive event in the run-up to World War II was not the infamous 1938 appeasement at Munich, because the Germans had good reason to reabsorb the Sudetenland from Czechoslovakia, but the 1939 guarantee, which was foolish of the British to make and foolish of the Poles to rely on because Britain had no means of defending Poland when Hitler attacked after Polish leaders refused to return Danzig to Germany and allow a German passageway through the Polish Corridor.

Buchanan begins his narrative at the end of the nineteenth century and ends it at the conclusion of World War II. Churchill occupies center stage in this extended drama because he "was the most bellicose champion of British entry into the European war of 1914 and the German-Polish war of 1939" (p. *xx*). Along the way, Buchanan adduces evidence that Kaiser Wilhelm II, a grandson of Queen Victoria and nephew of King Edward VII, did not seek war with Great Britain (in 1910 he "marched in Edward's funeral—in the uniform of a British field marshal" [p. 11]). Likewise, thirty years later Hitler wished to avoid war with Great Britain, whose people and empire he admired: "His dream was of an alliance with the British Empire, not its ruin" (p. 319).

The *Lebensraum* he sought lay to the east of Germany, not to the west. The Germans did not seek to "conquer the world," despite frequent claims to that effect, and in any event they lacked the means to achieve such a conquest.

No short review can depict the breadth, the depth, and the many fascinating details of Buchanan's book. Read it and see for yourself. It may well challenge your most cherished beliefs about Winston Churchill and the world-shattering Thirty Years' War of 1914–45.

25

Review of

The Pearl Harbor Myth: Rethinking the Unthinkable

by George Victor

ALMOST FROM THE moment the Japanese bombs began falling on the U.S. fleet at Pearl Harbor, the prime question has been, "What did President Franklin D. Roosevelt and his subordinates know about the impending attack, and when did they know it?" A series of official investigations during and immediately after the war failed to silence the president's critics or to satisfy those who were skeptical about the official explanations. Even now the debate continues. George Victor's *The Pearl Harbor Myth* (Dulles, Va.: Potomac Books, 2007) is the latest substantial contribution to this controversy.

Although Victor, a retired psychologist, might seem an unlikely candidate to make an important contribution to this subject, and although he presents no new evidence, he adroitly exploits the relevant official reports and the historical literature. He expresses his account in clear, fact-filled prose, highlighting the inconsistencies in various testimonies.

He finds that the Roosevelt administration deliberately provoked the attack, knew it was coming, and did not attempt to stop it, yet he describes himself as an admirer of Roosevelt and declares that "moral and legal judgments are outside the purpose here" (p. 61). If the president and his lieutenants conspired to bring the United States into the war in Europe through the Pacific "back door," he concludes, they did only what all governments sometimes do—conspire, blame scapegoats, and then cover up their conspiracies by destroying evidence, coercing witnesses, and lying—and they did it for an excellent reason: to save the world from conquest by Hitler.

The government conducted this Machiavellian maneuvering because the great majority of the populace opposed entry into the war unless the United States were attacked. Hence, Roosevelt, who ardently desired (and worked relentlessly) to take the country into the war, needed to incite such an attack to unify the people in support of U.S. entry. "Establishing a record in which the enemy fired the first shot was a theme that ran through Roosevelt's tactics" (p. 184). Despite hostile but clandestine U.S. naval actions against German ships and submarines in the North Atlantic in 1941, the Germans refused to take the bait.

On the other side of the world, more than two years of U.S. economic warfare against Japan had placed the Japanese economy in a tightening stranglehold. War was almost inevitable, yet for Roosevelt's political purposes it remained imperative "that Japan commit the first overt [military] act" (p. 104), as a dispatch from Washington cautioned General Walter Short, the U.S. Army commander in Hawaii. Short and the navy commander, Admiral Husband Kimmel, were set up as the fall guys to be blamed for lack of preparation when the U.S. forces at Pearl Harbor were caught "by surprise" in a "sneak attack"—such surprise and sneakiness being key elements of the enduring myth that Victor aims to explode.

As Secretary of War Henry L. Stimson wrote two weeks before the Japanese attack, "[T]he question was how we should maneuver them into the position of firing the first shot without allowing too much danger to ourselves" (quoted on p. 257). The attack, Victor writes, "was expected to get Congress to declare war on Japan. The crucial needs were to save the Soviet Union [from a Japanese invasion] and have Japan attack in circumstances that would move Congress to declare war on Germany" (p. 257).

Why didn't the president instead make a frank, straightforward request that Congress declare war, explaining why he considered U.S. entry into the war to be desirable? Because he thought that approach would fail.

On December 2, 1941, the president "told a subordinate that he expected to be at war with Japan within a few days. On December 4 [Secretary of the Navy Frank] Knox told a subordinate the same [thing]" (p. 267). Yet Short and Kimmel were not alerted to the attack that high officials in Washington expected to occur shortly. Midlevel army and navy officers had urgently recommended that the commanders in Hawaii be warned, but their superiors had rejected those pleas.

After news of the attack reached Washington, Roosevelt convened his War Council. According to Harry Hopkins, "[T]he conference met in not too tense an atmosphere because . . . all of us believed that . . . the enemy was Hitler and that he could never be defeated without force of arms; that sooner or later we were bound to be in the war and that Japan had given us an opportunity" (quoted on p. 290).

Although Victor's apology for the Roosevelt administration's aggressive, devious actions during the years preceding the attack on Pearl Harbor strikes me as highly problematical, I recommend *The Pearl Harbor Myth* as a thorough, clearly written, and generally even-handed account of the events that led to U.S. engagement in World War II. For the typical American who still clings to the myth, the book will be a revelation.

26

Review of
Unwarranted Influence: Dwight D. Eisenhower and the Military-Industrial Complex
by James Ledbetter

ON JANUARY 17, 1961, President Dwight D. Eisenhower gave his final presidential speech, which turned out to be his most memorable by virtue of this warning: "In the councils of government, we must guard against the acquisition of unwarranted influence, whether sought or unsought, by the military-industrial complex. The potential for the disastrous rise of misplaced power exists and will persist." James Ledbetter makes this speech the fulcrum for his brief but carefully researched and smoothly written book on the military-industrial complex (MIC), *Unwarranted Influence: Dwight D. Eisenhower and the Military-Industrial Complex* (New Haven, Conn.: Yale University Press, 2011). He looks into Eisenhower's past to discover how a five-star general arrived at this seemingly incongruous warning and traces how the idea of the MIC evolved after 1961 as it became grist for a variety of mills.

Ledbetter recognizes the MIC's fuzzy meaning, but for purposes of his analysis he supposes that "we can approximately define MIC as a network of public and private forces that combine a profit motive with the planning and implementation of strategic policy" (p. 6). For virtually all scholars, the MIC comprises the armed forces and the civilian military leadership, the relevant committees and leadership of Congress, and the private contractors who supply goods and services to the military. Many analysts also include lesser players, such as the leading universities, certain scientists and think tanks, veterans' groups, certain labor unions, and local politicians whose jurisdictions include military bases or contractors' facilities.

Although the MIC obviously has powerful and widespread supporters, it has always attracted critics, who indict it on several counts, including wasteful military spending, diversion of government spending from social programs, economic distortions, enlargement of military influence in American society, promotion of a culture of state secrecy, and suppression of individual liberties. Rather than extensively evaluating these criticisms, Ledbetter focuses on the changing *idea* of the MIC, assessing contemporary arguments about it in the light of criteria suggested in Eisenhower's speech.

Ledbetter finds antecedents in several notions advanced previously, including the merchants-of-death thesis, the war-economy thesis, the garrison-state thesis, and the technocratic-elite thesis. These theses retain some pertinence within the MIC thesis.

Ledbetter traces Eisenhower's concern about military-economic relations back at least to 1930–31, when Ike participated in army planning for industrial mobilization. Having studied industrial agreements, possible takeovers, and price controls, he was uneasy about such military involvement in the economy. Ledbetter concludes that the "importance of keeping a peacetime separation between business and the military would stay with him for the rest of his life" (p. 51). As president, Eisenhower continued to emphasize "the need for restrained military spending to *preserve* American economic liberty" (p. 61).

Soon after becoming president, Eisenhower gave his second-most-memorable speech, the "Chance for Peace" address, on April 16, 1953. Stalin had just died, and the president sought to move the United States toward a less menacing relationship with the USSR by proposing measures to promote greater cooperation and trust between the Cold War adversaries. He highlighted the great opportunity costs of ongoing large-scale military preparedness. "Every gun that is made, every warship launched, every rocket fired signifies, in the final sense, a theft from those who hunger and are not fed, those who are cold and are not clothed" (p. 68). Although the "Chance for Peace" initiative bore no fruit and the Cold War assumed even more menacing dimensions after 1953, Eisenhower's concern about its costly distortion of the U.S. economy clearly prefigured the concerns he expressed in his farewell address almost eight years later.

Ledbetter's attempts to tie down exactly who coined the term *military-industrial complex* proved unsuccessful. Eisenhower's chief speechwriter, Malcomb Moos, has often been credited, but even though he seemed to have been happy to let people think he had come up with the term, he never bluntly claimed to have done so. Ledbetter's examination of successive drafts of the speech revealed no unambiguous evidence of who introduced it.

In any event, the term resonated with diverse political groups in the 1960s, including the New Leftists inspired by C. Wright Mills's analysis of the power elite; critics of wasteful military spending, such as Senator William Proxmire; and various antiwar groups. The idea of the MIC eventually merged into references to the "warfare state" and the "national-security state."

Over the years, many congressional investigations and other studies have been undertaken of Pentagon contracting and other aspects of military-economic relations in the United States. Serious problems—cost overruns, late deliveries, official and corporate corruption, crony-capitalist bailouts, de facto industrial policymaking, and many others—have been documented again and again. Despite repeated attempts ostensibly to root out these misfeasances and malfeasances, nothing fundamental ever changes in the MIC's operation. Even now, more than twenty years after the USSR imploded and the Cold War ended, the United States spends more than ever on the military and does so as wastefully and nonchalantly as it did before, with no serious repercussions. Despite a long-standing statutory requirement that the Defense Department be audited annually, it never has been and cannot be owing to the sorry state of its financial records.

Ledbetter astutely concludes that "it is difficult to see how the United States would be sufficiently motivated to eliminate the MIC, let alone replace it with something superior. . . . [I]t is nearly impervious to democratic reform" (pp. 202–3). As he notes, the root problem is not so much the wretched performance of contractors and the self-interested actions of implicated parties in Congress and the military as it is the stupendously wide scope of U.S. geopolitical ambitions. As long as the U.S. government continues to perceive a "vital" interest in nearly every place and nearly every dispute in the wide world, any hope of realizing Eisenhower's dream of cutting the MIC down to size and moving toward genuine disarmament and peace is doomed to disappointment.

27

Review of

Is War Necessary for Economic Growth? Military Procurement and Technology Development

by Vernon W. Ruttan

VERNON W. RUTTAN, Regents Professor Emeritus in the Department of Applied Economics and adjunct professor in the Hubert H. Humphrey Institute of Public Affairs at the University of Minnesota, is a well-known contributor to the literature on the economics of technological change. In his latest book, *Is War Necessary for Economic Growth?* (New York: Oxford University Press, 2006), he ostensibly seeks to establish the relationship, if any, between the U.S. government's preparation for or engagement in warfare and the creation of new general-purpose technologies that contribute to increasing the rate of economic growth.

I would like to think that the publisher's marketing department, not the author, bears responsibility for the book's foolish title. If we know anything at all about economic growth, we know that peace is among its essential conditions. No nation can expect to improve its economic well-being in the midst of a maelstrom of death and destruction. In fact, what Ruttan examines is not war at all, but government subsidies to and direct engagement in technological development and government purchases of technically advanced goods and services. That these subsidies, engagements, and purchases occur under the rubric of "war" or "defense" is almost incidental. The military aspect matters only in the political sense that historically the U.S. government has marshaled the greatest amounts of resources for research and development in connection with military endeavors.

Seeking "[t]o demonstrate that military and defense-related procurement has been a major source of technology development across a broad spectrum of industries that account for an important share of U.S. industrial production" (p. vii), Ruttan presents in successive chapters capsule economic histories of technological development in six areas: interchangeable parts and mass production; aircraft; electrical power generation and nuclear energy; computers; the Internet; and space-related goods, such as missiles, satellites, and related communications systems. In each chapter, he draws on a wide selection of secondary sources to describe how the government's involvement affected the course of technological change. Although these descriptive chapters are informative and clearly written, they present no new evidence or analysis. Economic historians will be familiar with the broad outlines of much of the information offered, if not with all of the details.

Ruttan does not claim that the six areas he discusses constitute a random sample of all industries or even of industries in which the government has actively engaged in stimulating technological development. Indeed, he appears to have chosen these six areas because he knew beforehand that the government played an especially important role in each of them. Given this aspect of the evidence Ruttan considers, the reader must hesitate to place great weight on the book's findings. Yes, interchangeable parts, aircraft, computers, and so forth have been important areas in which the government contributed to hastening certain technological developments, but these areas are far from composing the whole economy. Areas such as nuclear power generation and space-related activities have even less significance for the overall economy.

Ruttan's discussions in this book are strictly tertiary. Indeed, in several regards the book resembles a textbook. Various topics are discussed in boxes set apart from the main text (for example, "postal subsidies for airline development," "the national energy laboratories," and "origins of the global positioning system"). All of the tables and figures are borrowed from secondary sources or from well-known published collections of data. Each chapter includes an extensive set of references. The indexes occupy about 10 percent of the book's total pages.

In the final chapter, Ruttan draws some more general conclusions, in the form of informed personal judgments, about the government's engagement in the various areas considered in the descriptive chapters. These conclusions take the following approach: "In the absence of military support for R&D during World War II and military procurement during the Korean War, the transition to jet commercial aircraft propulsion would have occurred much more slowly" (p. 164). Well, yes, of course. Such conclusions say little more than that the government generated *some* spillover effect on the rate and direction of technological change in commercial areas related to the military projects for which the government spent lavishly. When Ruttan tries to go further, however—when he opines, for example, that between 1900 and 1950 "productivity growth in the electric power industry was the major driver of productivity growth in the entire U.S. economy" and that "[d]uring the last several decades of the twentieth century the computer and microprocessor emerged as the major drivers of productivity growth in the U.S. economy" (p. 166)—his judgments may well be questioned. What he means by "major driver" is neither obvious nor explicated.

In a box called "Military R&D: The Productivity Puzzle" (pp. 169–71), Ruttan raises critical questions for his analysis that he does not answer adequately. He again gives only his considered judgment. At one point, however, that judgment seems damaging for his own ultimate conclusions, when he states: "My own view is that we do not yet have, and perhaps cannot have, a body of rigorous econometric evidence against which to evaluate the economic impact of defense and defense-related R&D and procurement" (p. 170). He avers that "careful narrative analysis of individual cases is at present a more effective method of capturing the effects of complementarity than econometric analysis" (p. 170). This judgment is problematic because although careful narratives may reveal many things that econometric analysis does not, they nevertheless cannot answer the ultimately crucial, intrinsically quantitative question: What was the overall net payoff to the government's expenditures, considering military and commercial results together? Moreover, because the military aspects of the matter take place within an essentially nonmarket context, as Ruttan explicitly recognizes at one point (pp. 169–70), only the commercial (that is, private-market) part of the return on the government's subsidies, direct engagement, and procurement can be computed in a meaningful way, and computation of even that part of the net return raises difficult analytical challenges.

Ruttan accepts too readily the conclusion derived from neoclassical blackboard economics that private actions give rise to "market failure" because of "suboptimal" amounts of investment in technological change. He laments that " [t]he United States has not yet designed a coherent set of institutional arrangements for public support of R&D for civil purposes" (p. 182). Here one is tempted to remark, "Thank God." If the government were to get even more deeply involved in making big financial bets (with the taxpayers' money) about technological development, the most probable result would be a massive waste of resources arising from the inherently political nature of any likely government program. If you want a template, just think of ethanol.

Finally, Ruttan anticipates that because of changes in the nature of military technology and the diminished prospects for a great military mobilization such as World War II or the Cold War, the government will not make efforts comparable to those it made in the past, and hence the rate of economic growth will be diminished. He asks: "Will it take a major war or threat of war to induce the mobilization of the scientific, technical, and financial resources necessary to develop major new general-purpose technologies? My answer to this question, based on historical experience, is that it may" (p. 185). Although this flaccid conclusion leaves Ruttan looking forward to "incremental rather than . . . revolutionary changes in both military and commercial technology" during the next half century (p. 185), we need not fret. In truth, Ruttan does not know what the technological future holds in store; indeed, no one does.

Ruttan seems excessively focused on technological change per se; he does not give adequate attention to the economics of the matter. The general population does not benefit from faster technological progress unless the rate of return on that development is supernormal. As Ruttan recognizes at one point, "[T]he advances in scientific and technical knowledge and commercial technology induced by demand for defense and defense-related technology in the past imposed very heavy opportunity costs on the U.S. economy" (p. 185). The government has obviously specialized in pouring money into military projects decades in advance of the advent of opportunities for significant commercial applications. Moreover, the wastes associated with military R&D and military procurement of goods and services are themselves legendary, as amply documented by the contributors to a book I edited, *Arms, Politics, and the Economy: Historical and Contemporary Perspectives* (New York: Holmes & Meier, 1990). In contrast, motivated by sufficiently free markets, clever scientists, inventors, and engineers are never likely to run out of promising ideas to develop—ideas that contribute directly to human well-being rather than to the enlarged potential for wreaking death and destruction that military technological development seeks.

28

Review of

After War: The Political Economy of Exporting Democracy

by Christopher J. Coyne

CAN U.S. OR OTHER Western military forces establish self-sustaining liberal democracy in a country with a different type of politico-economic order? U.S. government leaders believe they can do so, or so it appears if we may judge by the dozens of attempts they have made since the late nineteenth century. From the Spanish-American War to the present wars in Afghanistan and Iraq, U.S., British, and other Western leaders, relying on military force, have undertaken to remake defeated, subjugated, occupied, or colonized societies into market-oriented, democratically governed, rule-of-law systems. In the great majority of cases, these attempts have failed. In *After War: The Political Economy of Exporting Democracy* (Stanford, Calif.: Stanford University Press, 2008), Christopher J. Coyne brings economic analysis to bear in explaining why this quest so often fails. He also points the way toward a policy stance more likely to meet with success.

• • •

Coyne defines his terms early on. He focuses his analysis on national *reconstruction,* by which he means "the rebuilding of both formal and informal institutions. . . . [This] involves the restoration of physical infrastructure and facilities; minimal social services; and structural reform in the political, economic, social, and security sectors" (p. 9). He distinguishes reconstruction from the related terms *state building, nation building,* and *peacekeeping,* which he treats as subsets of reconstruction. Success in national reconstruction implies "the achievement of a self-sustaining liberal democratic, economic, and social order that does not rely on external monetary or military support" (p. 10). He intends his analysis to be purely positive, neither requiring nor entailing any normative assumptions or conclusions.

Coyne's specific contribution is the application of economic tools to the analysis of reconstruction and related matters. He proceeds not by specifying a formal mathematical model or by estimating the coefficients of an econometric model, but by introducing, explaining, and applying a number of economic concepts, principles, and understandings drawn from several economic subfields: Austrian economics, behavioral economics, constitutional political economy, new institutional economics, and public-choice economics. The analysis is fairly elementary and does not require any previous training in any of these areas. Thus, any intelligent readers should be able to absorb the book's contents fully.

Early in the book, Coyne presents a preview of the main lessons he intends to convey:

1. "Although policymakers and social scientists know what factors constitute a successful reconstruction, they know much less about how to bring about this end" (p. 20).
2. "Uncontrollable variables serve as a constraint on controllable variables" (p. 22).
3. "Reconstruction efforts suffer from a nirvana fallacy" (p. 24).
4. "Sustainable social change toward liberal democracy requires a shift in underlying preferences and opportunities" (p. 27).

Although many social scientists may view these lessons as more or less obvious and already well established, the lessons have nonetheless been honored more in the breech than in the observance by the practitioners of reconstruction. If we assume that these practitioners are sincere about what they say they are trying to accomplish, then they stand to learn important lessons from Coyne's book. Coyne himself follows in the footsteps of such great Austrian economists as Ludwig von Mises and F. A. Hayek by giving the policymakers the benefit of the doubt. Rather than calling their projects into question as smokescreens for other, more genuine objectives, he proceeds as if the policymakers actually intend to carry out reconstruction along the lines they themselves stipulate.

• • •

In Coyne's scheme, successful reconstruction requires changing both preferences and opportunities so that members of the society will not "defect" but choose the "cooperate" option in a metagame of social interaction with their fellows. Individuals, families, tribes, firms, and other organizations must act as though they expect others to play cooperatively along the lines typical of a liberal democracy. "Reconstruction efforts seek to foster preferences for freedom, democracy, the rule of law, markets, and tolerance. Likewise, these efforts seek to create a new set of opportunities that were not feasible prior to the occupation" (p. 28). Successful reconstruction turns on incentive compatibility; it "entails finding and establishing a set of incentives that make people prefer continuing within a liberal democratic order as compared to any available alternatives" (p. 9).

After presenting the prisoner's dilemma game, to capture "the fundamental importance of incentives for cooperation with institutional change" (p. 34), Coyne moves to the Folk Theorem, which "suggests that a repeated prisoner's dilemma game can have a cooperative solution, provided that time horizons are sufficiently long. . . . If individuals hold the appropriate conjectures and expectations, cooperation will be a dominant strategy" (p. 35). The crux, then, is whether they hold such conjectures and expectations or not, and if they do not, whether the occupiers can bring them to do so. Thus, "a key part of understanding reconstruction is identifying the factors and mechanisms influencing the initial coordination around good or bad conjectures" (p. 37).

Although these game-theoretic perspectives provide insight into the reconstruction process (or its miscarriage), in reality people are playing a number of overlapping games simultaneously with various sets of other players, and the actions chosen in each of these games add up to the people's way of playing the overall, or metalevel, game, which determines the success or failure of the reconstruction effort. A specific individual normally chooses the cooperative option in some of the nested games and the defection option in other nested games. Hence, the game-theoretic perspective provides not a definitive solution to the reconstruction puzzle, but more a way for the analyst to organize his thinking about what is going on. Coyne astutely observes that "the nested games may be so complicated that the meta-game cannot be easily characterized let alone solved by occupying forces" (p. 59). Moreover, the occupiers' presence in the country creates a variety of new games nested among all those already being played there, complicating the situation even further.

Coyne asserts that the suggested framework of analysis comports with several stylized facts about actual reconstructions:

1. "Very rapid reconstruction is, in principle, possible" (p. 40).
2. "Some countries seem never to reconstruct or even turn the corner" (p. 40).
3. "Reconstructions will work either very well or not at all" (p. 40).
4. "Coordination is a necessary but not a sufficient condition for a successful reconstruction" (p. 41).

Most of the book contains detailed descriptions of specific cases of attempted reconstruction, which illustrate the foregoing stylized facts and the lessons listed earlier.

These empirical materials indicate why in most cases "the predicted outcome of the Coase Theorem fails and conflict persists" (p. 44). Not surprisingly, we are shown that ill-defined property rights and high transaction costs have impeded bargaining to the efficient Coasian outcome. When, for example, groups in the society being reconstructed have histories of enmity or conflict and therefore do not trust one another to keep promises, they may refuse to bargain in good faith or even to bargain at all, and hence no Coasian deals can be struck. Sunni Arabs, Shia Arabs, and Kurds in Iraq illustrate this difficulty currently. In Coyne's phrase, borrowed from Alexis de Tocqueville, they have not mastered the "art of association" with one another. Their inability to strike bargains works against credible commitment and thus precludes successful cooperative play of the metagame along liberal democratic lines.

Coyne also discusses a number of further complications related to, among other things, the limitations of the occupiers' knowledge and administrative capability and the possible perversity of the occupied people's expectations. In light of all the difficulties he brings to light, one might well be astonished that an attempted reconstruction has ever succeeded. Infighting among individuals and agencies engaged in the reconstruction, an oft-observed aspect of the process, further diminishes the odds of its success. Coyne's discussion of the process in the light of public-choice principles comes close to a revelation that reconstruction is little more than an attractive cover beneath which various special interests and their allies in the executive and legislative branches of government strive to achieve their own objectives, regardless of what happens in the occupied nation ostensibly being reconstructed. This discussion (pp. 85–103) may be the most analytically compelling and persuasive part of the book, although the other parts are by no means to be taken lightly.

In wrapping up the first, mostly analytical part of the book, Coyne concludes sensibly that "in reality policymakers face incomplete knowledge, imperfect information, and a non-neutral political system," and therefore one may make "a very strong argument for refraining from foreign interventions aimed at exporting democracy" (p. 117). It is difficult to understand how any disinterested person can seriously contest this conclusion.

• • •

The second, somewhat shorter part of the book consists for the most part of three chapters, each of which considers in detail two countries about which analysts may conduct instructive case studies, balanced against Coyne's initial empirical survey in chapter 1, which deals more generally with twenty-five cases of U.S. reconstruction. From the Polity Score data he uses to evaluate these cases, he concludes that "efforts to export liberal democracy at gunpoint are more likely to fail than succeed" (p. 16), by a substantial margin. (For a similar evaluation of how infrequently U.S. and British reconstructions have succeeded, see James L. Payne, "Does Nation Building Work?" *The Independent Review* 9, no. 4 [Spring 2005]: 563–72.) One might note further that even the apparent successes may be spurious, inasmuch as a country that became a liberal democracy sometime after undergoing reconstruction by U.S. forces might have become a liberal democracy even without this outside intervention.

In chapter 5, Coyne takes up the U.S. reconstructions of West Germany and Japan after World War II. These cases have tremendous importance because they are the ones to which most advocates of reconstruction point when they argue that the United States can succeed in such endeavors. Coyne's detailed analysis, however, more or less demolishes this oft-advanced argument, showing it to be in large part a *post hoc ergo propter hoc* fallacy writ large. In fact, when one proceeds systematically, applying the economic concepts and principles Coyne develops in the first part of the book, one finds that the successful reconstructions of these defeated powers owed little to U.S.

intervention and much to the subjugated people's own prior and contemporary actions.

"[M]any of the preexisting Japanese political, economic, and social institutions 'passed through' from the pre-war to postwar period" (p. 121). Although the occupiers "clearly had an impact of many fronts, including the new constitution, the court system, education, the structure of business and land ownership, and the purging of some members of the previous regime," they "were able to work within a preexisting institutional framework that generated a sustainable solution to the larger Japanese meta-game" (p. 122). The Americans employed existing Japanese institutions, such as the emperor's national leadership and the national legislature (the Diet), to signal credible commitment to carry through the reforms. General Douglas MacArthur, the effective dictator of Japan during the reconstruction period, astutely permitted considerable flexibility and widespread Japanese involvement in the day-to-day implementation of reform details.

Similarly, "the German meta-game was solved prior to the reconstruction effort" (p. 127). Here also the occupiers worked with established political institutions, which "had a long history of legitimacy among the German populace and served as the foundation for reconstructed institutions at the meta-level" (p. 128). Exhausted by years of war and economic deprivation, the defeated Germans "expected change and were willing to accept forced demilitarization and denazification in exchange" (p. 129). Ultimately, however, the reconstruction succeeded "not because of the occupation but despite it" (p. 130), when, among other things, Ludwig Erhard evaded the occupation authorities and removed price controls, enabling the market process to bring much-needed goods and services to the populace. Coyne concludes that "the policies of the occupiers were only effectively implemented to the extent that they aligned with the desires and wants of the German citizens. . . . [The] occupiers were largely unable to effectively govern the German population during the occupation let alone centrally design and implement sustainable liberal institutions. . . . [T]he German reconstruction should be seen less as an exercise in imposing liberal institutions and more as an exercise in overseeing emergent indigenous institutions of self-government" (p. 131). Coyne might have strengthened his case by citing the extensive evidence that U.S. reconstruction of Germany, especially during the first few years, was never even intended to implant liberal democracy, but for the most part to punish the German people for having gone to war and to ensure that they would not do so again (see James L. Payne, "Did the United States Create Democracy in Germany?" *The Independent Review* 11, no. 2 [Fall 2006]: 209–21).

Coyne turns next to a chapter on the attempted reconstructions of Somalia and Haiti. The former began as a United Nations operation to relieve starvation and suffering in the wake of revolutionary turmoil during the early 1990s. Everything that could go wrong went wrong, and the United Nations, despite heavy U.S. involvement, "was not able to effectively end conflict and generate sustaining political, social, and economic change" (p. 138). Despite the absence of an effective central government during the past seventeen years, however, Somalia has not done so badly, especially in comparison with many other sub-Saharan African countries, because in many parts of the country people have employed long-established traditional institutions to govern themselves and to regulate their economic and social affairs reasonably well. No doubt to the great astonishment of Hobbesians, "many individuals can enjoy an environment of peace, lawfulness, and security in the absence of a central government. . . . [A]ttempts by foreign governments since 1991 to revitalize a central Somali state have only served to increase the level of armed conflict" (p. 142) because the Somali people, correctly identifying a national state as potentially the chief predator in their society, have fought either to gain control of it or to prevent its establishment, and when a makeshift state has been launched, most Somalis have resisted its authority.

In Haiti, which suffers the distinction of having endured a failed state from its independence two centuries ago to the present time, reconstruction efforts proved equally unavailing. Unfortunately, the Haitians, unlike the Somalis, did not enjoy the luxury of well-established traditional institutions on which they could fall back in the absence of an effective central state. Haiti seems always to have been and to remain today a semichaotic thugocracy and hence a society in which economic activity never rises much above the subsistence level for want of secure private-property rights and a reliable rule of law. "Haitians have come to expect institutions characterized by further coercion and predation," and the best advice one might give a young Haitian is, "Get the hell out." Coyne aptly concludes that "policymakers lack the knowledge of how to establish credibility and legitimacy where it does not exist" (p. 151). He might have added that the U.S. intervention in the 1990s occurred only because of domestic political pressures on the Clinton administration, and it represented little more than a costly and futile display of good intentions inasmuch as no one had any sound reason to expect that the occupation could turn Haiti into a liberal democracy, not even a badly functioning one. Haiti comes as close to being a hopeless case as one can find anywhere on earth.

In chapter 7, Coyne considers Afghanistan and Iraq in detail. Because these cases have been constantly in the news for the past ten years, many readers will be fairly familiar with the information he presents. Thus, not many will be surprised to read: "Ethnic, linguistic, and sectarian differences have created an array of nested games in Afghanistan that must be solved before any meaningful solution to the larger meta-game can be achieved" (p. 164). The situation in Iraq presents similar difficulties, which are greatly aggravated by ill-advised actions by the occupiers during the past eight years. Notwithstanding these cases' familiarity, Coyne summarizes them nicely and shows how the grave difficulties of reconstructing these countries can be understood better with reference to the economic concepts and principles he brings to bear in his analysis.

• • •

In the final chapter, Coyne summarizes his empirical surveys by observing that "reconstruction efforts are least likely to work precisely where they are needed most" (p. 173). Dismissing both brute force, such as outright colonization, and military peacekeeping approaches as also deeply flawed, he turns to a consideration of alternative, noncoercive means of achieving the objective—nonintervention and free trade. These approaches, he argues, "will be the most effective in spreading liberal democracy around the world" because they avoid "many of the pitfalls to which the other strategies for liberal democratic nation building are prone" (p. 181). He supports the unilateral opening of U.S. markets in preference to bilateral trade liberalizations or the formation of free-trade blocs. Free trade will promote not only economic progress on both sides of the exchange, but also cultural accommodation and melding. Moreover, "free trade can be viewed as a means of potentially establishing the complementary institutions that are required for formal Western-style institutions to operate effectively" (p. 185). As evidence of this effect, Coyne points to the mellowing of autocracies in Mexico, South Korea, and Taiwan in the wake of these countries' more active engagement in international trade.

Other benefits include, for Americans, shedding the image of the Yankee imperialist or "hypocritical hegemon" (p. 193) that U.S. reconstruction efforts have fostered in the past. As open traders, Americans would lead by example, not by pointing guns at people and dictating that they fall in line according to an American blueprint for their societies. This free-trade approach promises to diminish the hatred and blowback that have attended so many previous U.S. interventions abroad, no matter how humanitarian or liberally inclined they might have been. The West, Coyne concludes, "must move away from the belief that Western values are universally desired and relevant and therefore can be exported at the point of a gun" (p. 194). In essence, he is calling for a return to the traditional U.S. policy of offshore noninterventionism and open commerce as the default option for American engagement with the rest of the world. (For a compilation of recent studies that point in the same direction, see Robert Higgs and Carl P. Close, eds., *Opposing the Crusader State: Alternatives to Global Interventionism* [Oakland, Calif.: The Independent Institute, 2007].)

• • •

To sum up. In *After War,* Coyne demonstrates convincingly that national reconstruction seldom succeeds, and he presents the essential economic concepts and principles that allow us to understand why it usually fails, especially in the countries that seem most in need of it. The book is clearly written in precise, straightforward prose. The tone is scholarly, disinterested, and devoid of polemics. Although economists will find all the economic ideas arrayed in the analysis to be familiar ones, the book should make a significant contribution to the understanding of the specialists in international relations, political science, history, journalism, and other areas, who are the ones usually engaged in the planning and evaluation of reconstruction efforts. Economists will gain enlightenment from Coyne's compact, well-documented presentation of a great variety of relevant facts about some of the leading cases of national reconstruction in which the U.S. government has engaged during the past century. Although the analysis as a whole is eclectic rather than strictly Austrian, it makes apt use of key Austrian ideas—Hayekian knowledge problems, unintended consequences, and the Misesian dynamics of intervention. It does so unobtrusively, however, without needlessly provoking non-Austrians, and thus it exemplifies nicely how Austrians may engage in mutually beneficial intellectual exchange with other economists.

29

Review of

Magic and Mayhem:
The Delusions of American Foreign
Policy from Korea to Afghanistan

by Derek Leebaert

DEREK LEEBAERT IS an interesting and unusual man who combines active involvement in the world of business and government with an intellectual bent and a wide-ranging mind. He describes himself as a management consultant, currently a partner in the Swiss management consulting firm MAP AG. The holder of a D.Phil. degree from Oxford University, Leebaert spent seven years as a postdoctoral fellow at Harvard's Center for Science and International Affairs, where he became the founding editor of the journal *International Security.* Since 1996, he has taught foreign affairs at Georgetown University while continuing his consulting activities.

Of Leebaert's books, several deal with information technology and several with foreign and defense policies and events. In 2002, his book *The Fifty-Year Wound: How America's Cold War Victory Shapes Our World* (Boston: Little, Brown) was published. This 700-page tome is, if not the best comprehensive history of the Cold War, certainly one of the better ones. Packed with carefully documented information, it is critical of U.S. policies and actions in many respects, yet it remains well within the bounds of respectable scholarship in establishment circles, as does everything Leebaert writes. He is not a radical.

His most recent book, *Magic and Mayhem: The Delusions of American Foreign Policy from Korea to Afghanistan* (New York: Simon and Schuster, 2010), is a less meaty but even more critical book. By saying that it is less meaty, I do not intend to suggest that it lacks a great deal of factual evidence or careful documentation, but that it jumps about more, relying more on anecdotes and portraits of key actors and less on a sustained analytical narrative. Nevertheless, it is a worthwhile book, especially for those who retain their faith that U.S.

foreign and defense policymakers actually want to serve the general public interest better if only they knew how to do so—a view I do not share.

Leebaert focuses on several dimensions of what he calls the foreign-policy makers' reliance on "magic"—a collection of assumptions and convictions about what the United States government can and should do in its dealings with the rest of the world. He calls it "magic," he explains on page 1, because "shrewd, levelheaded people are so frequently bewitched into substituting passion, sloganeering, and haste for reflection, homework, and reasonable objectives." As Leebaert illustrates with a great variety of cases, decision makers forgo careful study, detailed and factual evaluation, and judicious evaluation of alternatives (including the alternative of doing nothing) and instead opt for plunging almost blindly into efforts that almost any serious, informed thinker could have told them were doomed to fail. They are supremely self-confident, notwithstanding their all-too-frequent lack of any real basis for such confidence.

Such decision making almost always represents the work of what Leebaert calls "emergency men": "the clever, energetic, self-assured, well-schooled people who take advantage of the opportunities intrinsic to the American political system to trifle with enormous risk" (p. 5). "Many people," he notes, "are ready to play with dynamite" (p. 38). Emergency men may be found in the upper reaches of the government hierarchy—examples include such heavyweights as McGeorge Bundy, John F. Kennedy, Henry Kissinger, and Paul Wolfowitz—but they are also represented by a large number of political appointees at slightly lower levels and by many advisers and consultants, including putative experts on leave from academia or think tanks. All of these people may be distinguished from the officials who occupy permanent places in the bureaucracy in the State Department, the Defense Department, the armed forces, and the CIA. Such long-term functionaries receive relatively generous treatment in Leebaert's assessment, being credited with greater knowledge of what they are doing and less eagerness to take the next big plunge.

Emergency men do not sit idly by, waiting for an emergency to arise. They look for one, and should they fail to find one, they may try to create one or the impression of one. Thus, Richard Nixon noted that Kissinger "would be ready to spark a crisis over Ecuador did Vietnam not exist" (p. 126). This search is scarcely a modest contribution to the promotion of national security. As Leebaert writes, "[T]he same policy expert who detects a 'crisis' will make darn sure that he or she is part of the effort to solve it. . . . Emergency men identify a calamity . . . then sound the tocsin, offer quick verdicts, and jump forth with action-oriented remedies" (p. 126).

To make matters worse, "emergency men, so often synonymous with war hawks, tend to prevail in policy arguments." They exploit the "'action bias' in decision making. Individuals feel compelled to 'do something,' anything, when confronting a challenge," even though "leaving a 'crisis' alone can be a better means of handling a problem" (p. 159). All serious students of history are familiar with this pattern. It is the story, for example, of Theodore Roosevelt's rise to power and of nearly everything Franklin D. Roosevelt and his lieutenants did during the early New Deal. Rare is the government official who goes down in history as a great man because he had the mature judgment and sage willingness to recognize that "doing something" would only make matters worse. Until recently, for example, hardly anyone had credited Warren G. Harding's hands-off approach to the depression of 1920–21 for helping to bring about a quick, full recovery from this sharp economic contraction.

Emergency men tend to make a hash of matters for a variety of reasons, and Leebaert devotes the heart of his book to an elaboration of a half-dozen chronic problems along these lines. He identifies these categories in the introduction:

1. A sensation of urgency and of "crisis" that accompanies the belief that most [*sic*] any resolute action is superior to restraint . . . joined by the emergency man's eagerness to be his country's revealer of dangers, real and imaginary.
2. The faith that American-style business management . . . can fix any global problem given enough time, resources, and appropriately "can-do," businesslike zeal.
3. A distinctively American desire to fall in behind celebrities, stars, and peddlers of some newly distilled expertise who, in foreign affairs especially, seem to glow with wizardry.
4. An expectation of wondrous returns on investment, even when this [expectation] is based on intellectual shortcuts.
5. Conjuring powerful, but simplified images from the depths of "history" to rationalize huge and amorphously expanding objectives.

6. The repeated belief that America can shape the destiny of other countries overnight and that the hearts and minds of distant people are throbbing to be transformed into something akin to the way we see ourselves. (pp. 7–8)

Leebaert finds the origin of this syndrome in the U.S. response to the Korean crisis of the early 1950s, "the moment when magical thinking began regularly to insinuate itself with decisions of 'national security'" (p. 28). As I have suggested, however, such modes of thought in policymaking surely have earlier roots, although perhaps only from Korea onward were they so deeply embedded in defense and foreign-policy making as opposed to domestic-policy making. Any activist U.S. government will probably tend toward this sort of "magical" syndrome because of the syndrome's affinities with important strains in American politics and culture.

Leebaert's book contains a number of finely etched cameos of emergency men such as Bundy, Robert McNamara, Kissinger, Douglas Feith, Dick Cheney, Donald Rumsfeld, Richard Perle, and Wolfowitz. For the latter five—prime examples of the neocon emergency men who played leading roles in bringing about the disastrous Iraq War and the subsequent ill-fated U.S. occupation—Leebaert has scarcely a kind word. He subjects to scathing criticism even Cheney and Rumsfeld, the two who at one time seemed to have had genuine talents and accomplishments. Given that Leebaert seems to be fairly evenhanded—indeed, almost uninterested—in regard to ideology and political party affiliation, his disdain for the neocons is especially striking. In his view, their chief shortcoming was not their ideology as such, but the fact that with their less-than-half-baked ideas about cakewalk victories, Iraqi oil paying for the war, and democratic dominoes falling across the Middle East, among other things, they were simply disconnected from reality.

In view of the stupidity that goes into so many U.S. defense and foreign policies, Leebaert considers why the smart, well-educated people in decision-making circles who see through the stupidity do so little to object to or obstruct the disastrous policies as they are being formulated. Part of the answer has already been given: emergency men who are eager to "do something" tend to carry the day by dismissing those who prefer to go more slowly as obstructionists, defeatists, and saboteurs. Being on the receiving end of such internecine attacks does not generally promote one's career. Of course, political leaders tend to surround themselves with cowardly yes men in the first place, so keeping one's negative views to oneself often seems the obvious thing for such flunkies to do. Moreover, people who take a longer view of their careers must take care not to become known as a troublemaker, a pessimist, or a foot dragger. One needs to remain a player. "To be a player entails consulting off and on for government, maybe getting confirmed by the Senate for a job or a sinecure on a presidential commission, participating on panels at the Council on Foreign Relations along with grandees from previous administrations, identifying yourself as an 'owl' rather than as a hawk or a dove, and writing books that with any luck can get blurbed by Dr. Kissinger. This opulently carved door opens but narrowly, if at all; it can close completely on those who ask awkward questions or bring up troublesome facts" (pp. 174–75). In short, go along to get along, even if going along means keeping silent or voicing agreement when the emergency men are barking for precipitous, ill-considered, and potentially disastrous policies and actions.

Besides, if things do go wrong, one can always deflect the blame onto others. After the catastrophe of the U.S. war and subsequent occupation in Iraq, for example, all of the leading neocon warmongers have had the gall to publicly blame those who, they allege, poorly *implemented* the policies they formulated, even while they have continued to find nothing wrong with the policies themselves. Political actors rarely admit to having made mistakes, but this blatantly twisted, self-serving interpretation leaves one aghast.

I wonder, however, whether Leebaert himself, notwithstanding all of his astute critical observations about policies and policymakers, also might have fallen victim to the temptation to express himself in a way that allows him to remain a player. As I noted at the beginning of this review, he is clearly a man of some consequence in the establishment. He has all of the right credentials, experience, and connections. His footnotes sometimes document a point as something a general, a diplomat, or another significant decision maker told him in person. Although he levels criticism at some people and some policies, he readily supports others, such as the Gulf War and the U.S. war on Serbia, that in some eyes (including mine) seem to exemplify all of the foolishness he finds so obvious in other foreign engagements. Had his book ventured beyond the bounds of polite foreign-policy debate, it would not have received, as it has, dust-jacket endorsements by a former secretary of the U.S. Navy, a former vice chief of staff of the U.S. Army, and a former secretary of the U.S. Air Force and member of the Defense Science Board.

Leebaert's approach to criticizing U.S. defense and foreign policies bears an interesting similarity to the criticisms Ludwig von Mises and F. A. Hayek leveled against socialism. These famous Austrian economists never criticized the socialists as bad people or as people who sought to act in a way that would harm the general public. They invariably gave their socialist ideological opponents the benefit of the doubt with regard to their good intentions. Although this approach has a certain theoretical justification in the development of economic theory, it flies in the face of historical reality. Many leading socialists, especially but by no means exclusively in the USSR, were little short of fiendish. It strains credulity to suppose that they were simply misguided men of good will.

Likewise, much of what seems merely foolish to Leebaert strikes me as the result not of faulty thinking about policies and their likely consequences, but of the desire for political power and personal aggrandizement and of ideological and political motives that will not bear scrutiny. About such possibilities Leebaert has little—shockingly little, really—to say. In his view, it appears that the emergency men have been good men who allowed themselves to be seduced by "magical" thinking when they should have gone about their business in a more rational, deliberate, and evidence-based manner. He therefore thinks that a book such as his might well serve to educate policymakers and lead them to abandon magic and to adopt a sounder approach to making their decisions. In this regard, I believe he has slipped into wishful thinking as much as did many of the foreign-policy makers he so aptly criticizes.

Whenever we try to understand why policymakers act as they do, we must answer the question: Are they fools or charlatans? Leebaert concludes, in effect, that in the defense and foreign-policy realm, they are often fools. I am inclined to the conclusion that they are both. Indeed, they are even worse: all too often they are fools, bunglers, charlatans, liars, and murderers. Such persons' playing with dynamite poses a grave danger to the rest of us. By now, we ought to have seen through them and their schemes a great deal more clearly than most of us have.

Index

About the Author

ROBERT HIGGS IS Senior Fellow in Political Economy for The Independent Institute, Editor of the Institute's quarterly journal *The Independent Review*, and Profesor Honorario at the Universidad Francisco Marroquín in Guatemala. He received his Ph.D. in economics from Johns Hopkins University, and he has taught at the University of Washington, Lafayette College, Seattle University, and the University of Economics, Prague. He has been a visiting scholar at Oxford University and Stanford University, and a fellow for the Hoover Institution and the National Science Foundation.

He is the recipient of numerous awards, including the Alexis de Tocqueville Award, Gary Schlarbaum Award for Lifetime Defense of Liberty, Thomas Szasz Award for Outstanding Contributions to the Cause of Civil Liberties, Lysander Spooner Award for Advancing the Literature of Liberty, Friedrich von Wieser Memorial Prize for Excellence in Economic Education, and Templeton Honor Rolls Award on Education in a Free Society.

Dr. Higgs is the editor of The Independent Institute books *Opposing the Crusader State*, *The Challenge of Liberty*, *Re-Thinking Green*, *Hazardous to Our Health?* and *Arms, Politics, and the Economy*, plus the volume *Emergence of the Modern Political Economy*.

He is also the author of *Depression, War, and Cold War*; *Neither Liberty Nor Safety*; *Politická ekonomie strachu* (*The Political Economy of Fear*, in Czech); *Resurgence of the Warfare State*; *Against Leviathan*; *The Transformation of the American Economy 1865–1914*; *Competition and Coercion*; and *Crisis and Leviathan*. A contributor to numerous scholarly volumes, he is the author of more than 100 articles and reviews in academic journals.

His popular articles have appeared in *The Wall Street Journal*, *Los Angeles Times*, *Providence Journal*, *Chicago Tribune*, *San Francisco Examiner*, *San Francisco Chronicle*, *Society*, *Reason*, *AlterNet*, and many other publications, and he has appeared on Fox News, NPR, NBC, ABC, C-SPAN, CBN, CNBC, America's Talking Television, Radio America Network, Radio Free Europe, Talk Radio Network, Voice of America, Newstalk TV, the Organization of American Historians' public radio program, and scores of local radio and television stations. He has also been interviewed for articles in the *New York Times*, *Washington Post*, *Terra Libera*, *Investor's Business Daily*, *UPI*, *Orlando Sentinel*, *Seattle Times*, *Chicago Tribune*, *National Journal*, *Reason*, *Washington Times*, *Al-Ahram Weekly*, *Creators Syndicate*, and elsewhere.

Dr. Higgs has spoken at more than 100 colleges and universities and at the meetings of such professional organizations as the Economic History Association, Western Economic Association, Population Association of America, Southern Economic Association, International Economic History Congress, Public Choice Society, International Studies Association, Cliometric Society, Allied Social Sciences Association, American Political Science Association, American Historical Association, and others.

Independent Studies in Political Economy